READING BODY LANGUAGE & PERSUASION TECHNIQUES

THE ULTIMATE GUIDE TO ANALYZE PEOPLE, HOW TO INFLUENCE HUMAN BEHAVIOR WITH SUBLIMINAL MANIPULATION, COVERT NLP, DARK PSYCHOLOGY SECRETS & MIND CONTROL

Darren Brown

© Copyright 2020 - All rights reserved.

The content contained within this book may not be reproduced, duplicated or transmitted without direct written permission from the author or the publisher.

Under no circumstances will any blame or legal responsibility be held against the publisher, or author, for any damages, reparation, or monetary loss due to the information contained within this book. Either directly or indirectly.

Legal Notice:

This book is copyright protected. This book is only for personal use. You cannot amend, distribute, sell, use, quote or paraphrase any part, or the content within this book, without the consent of the author or publisher.

Disclaimer Notice:

Please note the information contained within this document is for educational and entertainment purposes only. All effort has been executed to present accurate, up to date, and reliable, complete information. No warranties of any kind are declared or implied. Readers acknowledge that the author is not engaging in the rendering of legal, financial, medical or professional advice. The content within this book has been derived from various sources. Please consult a licensed professional before attempting any techniques outlined in this book.

By reading this document, the reader agrees that under no circumstances is the author responsible for any losses, direct or indirect, which are incurred as a result of the use of information contained within this document, including, but not limited to, — errors, omissions, or inaccuracies.

Table of Contents

Part 1 Reading Body Language 6

Introduction 8

Chapter 1: What Is Body Language 12

Chapter 2: Interpreting Body Language 18

Chapter 3: Nonverbal Communication 22

Chapter 4: Personality Types 28

Chapter 5: Deception And Lies 36

Chapter 6: "How To Analyze" Concept 42

Chapter 7: Speed Reading People 48

Chapter 8: Manipulation And Psychology 52

Chapter 9: Understanding How Our Bodies Communicate ... 58

Chapter 10: Reading Body Parts 64

Chapter 11: Reading The Eyes 70

Chapter 12: Body Language Proposals To Improve Your Negotiation Skills. 78

Chapter 13: How To Show Dominance Through Body Language 82

Chapter 14: Undetected Mind Control 90

Chapter 15: Spotting Romantic Interest 96

Chapter 16: How To Analyze Body Language (Facial Expressions And General Body Language) 102

Chapter 17: Matching Body Language 108

Chapter 18: Nlp Secrets And Reading Body Language 112

Chapter 19: Finding The Pressure Button And Using It To Your Advantage 120

Chapter 20: Influence And Leading Without Authority 126

Chapter 21: Kinesics 132

Chapter 22: Differences Between Men And Women When Using Body Language 138

Chapter 23: Understanding People's Outward Personality ... 144

Chapter 24: How To Read A Lady's Sexual Language 150

Chapter 25: How The Brain Controls Body Language 156

Chapter 26: Guilt Body Language 162

Chapter 27: The Power Of Body Language Over The Spoken Word 166

Chapter 28: How To Take Control And Manipulate Your Body Language .. 172

Conclusion 178

Part 2   Persuasion Techniques 180

Introduction 182

Chapter 29: What Is Persuasion? 184

Chapter 30: Human Behavior 190

Chapter 31: What We Can Get From The Power Of Persuasion 196

Chapter 32: Advanced Persuasion Techniques 202

Chapter 33: How To Resist Persuasion 208

Chapter 34: Mind Control And Dark Psychology 214

Chapter 35: Speed Reading People 220

Chapter 36: Influencing People 224

Chapter 37: Hypnosis 230

Chapter 38: Types Of Persuasion 236

Chapter 39: Self-Persuasion 240

Chapter 40: Techniques To Influence Human Behavior 244

Chapter 41: Honing Your Persuasion Skills 248

Chapter 42: Methods Of Persuasion 254

Chapter 43: What Is Dark Persuasion And How Is It Different From Regular Persuasion? 260

Chapter 44: Elements Of Persuasion 264

Chapter 45: Fundamental Persuasion Techniques 270

Chapter 46: Difference Between Persuasion And Manipulation 274

Chapter 47: Principles Of Persuasion 280

Chapter 48: Persuasion At Work: How To Create A Better Workplace 286

Chapter 49: How To Analyze And Manipulate People 292

Chapter 50: Secrets Of Persuasive People, How To Stop And Spot Manipulation 298

Chapter 51: Power Is Influence: Strength Is Persuasion 302

Chapter 52: Subliminal Persuasion 306

Chapter 53: The Basics Of Deception 312

Chapter 54: Brainwashing 316

Chapter 55: How To Defend Yourself From Persuasion And Manipulation 322

Chapter 56: Dark Persuasion And Covert Manipulation 328

Chapter 57: How To Turn A No Into A Yes 334

Chapter 58: Traps Of Persuasion 340

Chapter 59: How Persuaders Sell You Anything 346

Conclusion 350

PART 1

READING BODY LANGUAGE

Introduction

Body language is incredibly powerful. When you make use of body language, you are looking at controlling the vast majority of the communication that happens between people. What many people do not realize is that, for the most part, communication is nonverbal. We spend most of our communication trying to engage with people nonverbally. You can see this clearly when you are looking at how people respond to you. The way that you approach someone else is incredibly telling—when you run at someone with a scowl, you are naturally going to see them react first in fear and then possibly in anger if they decide to fight back. Your body language and the way that you hold and present yourself can greatly change the way in which the other person that you are interacting with sees you. You can take advantage of this regularly—you can ensure that you are better able to control the others. You can see that you are much more likely to be able to control them just by making sure that you present yourself the right way. The way that you move will naturally trigger the other person's unconscious mind. Their unconscious mind will register what you are doing and create feelings. Those feelings will then directly influence the way that the other person interacts with you. You can make someone feel like a child with the way that you look at them, or you can make them feel at ease. You can scare someone, dominate someone, or even attract someone, all by the way that you present yourself. Learning to control your body language may be difficult at first, but if you can master it, you can constantly be controlling the ways that you influence those around you. You can determine how you present yourself so you can then ensure that the other person reacts the way that you want them to. It is not always guaranteed, but you can usually create these reactions.

The body language of leaders is typically that of confidence. If you want to lead a group or be considered a competent leader, the best way to make this happen is to ensure that you are able to better be deemed as a confident person. Confidence and leadership go hand in hand, and people will almost always engage more with the people that they consider to be more confident just due to the fact that confidence is typically seen as being something that is trustworthy. When you want to make sure that you change your body language to that of a leader, then you want to try to make use of the following changes:

Eye Contact

To engage with people with decent eye contact will help you to be seen as confident. However, the catch here is that your eye contact with the other person should not be seen as dominant or overbearing. You are not trying to intimidate someone here—you are trying to find a way that you can better relate to them. You are trying to show that you are listening and therefore that you are paying attention, but also that you are not afraid to make that eye contact in the first place. When you make use of this, you can usually ensure that the other person does not worry about what you are trying to present to them.

Standing Tall

To be confident is to keep your own body language tall. You are looking to stand in a way that will be seen as confident. When you are tall and confident, you must keep your head level. Straighten out your spine, but do not tilt your head back to look down your nose. Rather, you should always be looking straight at people.

Release Tension

Tension screams nervousness, and if you want to be assertively calm, you will want to make sure that you can release that tension just enough that you will be able to control what you are doing. You want to be able to show that, at the end of the day, you are not nervous, but rather, you are in complete and utter control.

Open Body Language

You should keep your body language open to be deemed as confident. This means no crossed arms and no crossing your legs, either. Do not hide behind any items and be able to remove any barriers between yourself and those around you.

Talk with Your Hands

When you talk with your hands, you keep them busy, but you also prevent yourself from falling into the trap of being too nervous or fidgeting with your hands. When your hands are unnaturally still, or you try to hide them in your pockets or somewhere else, you tell the other person that you are hiding something.

Dominant body language is another type of body language to consider as well. You can use this to essentially intimidate those around you. You use it to try to show the other person that you are in control and at the top of the pecking order. Dominant body language is particularly useful to use if you are trying to prove that, at the end of the day, you are in control of everything going on. It is your way of showing that you get to be the one in control rather than anyone else. To dominate people, whether at home or in the workplace or anywhere else, there are some very simple body language rules that you should follow to ensure that, at the end of the day, you are the one that gets to control what is going on. A lot of dominant body language is about going as open as possible. When you are dominating space, you are taking it all up. You are essentially asserting that you are the one in control. You tell everyone around you that you matter more than others and that you will get what you want, how you want it.

Chapter 1: What is Body Language

Body language is the mechanism by which humans use conscious or subconscious motions, body movements, or facial expressions to convey information.

The body language seems to have three extensive uses: as a deliberate replacement for speech, to reinforce statement, and as a mirror or attitude betrayer. Nonverbal equivalents of spoken phrases typically involve silent messages of direct involvement (for instance, winking), insults, and thumbs-up approvals. Speakers very often use hand gestures subconsciously to reinforce the points they are vocally making. The signals also reflect their desire to have their listeners accept what they say. Many nonverbal cues, like a happy smile or an angry scowl, are often created intentionally and are easily spotted and understood. Others—for example, pupils with body-points and dilated eyes are not conscious signals with conscious moods. They seem to reveal an inner feeling or disposition that they don't recognize or want to hide from the individual who signals them. When seen in their social context or as part of a' gesture pattern' affecting certain parts of the body, these gestures may often be ignored or misidentified.

History of Body Language

Body language is as ancient as our culture, but scientific understanding of it stems largely from the last few decades when social psychologists and anthropologists mainly based in the United States started to study its components in depth. However, there were a few who did studies before the 20th century. Body language analysis is a relatively modern discipline-indeed, you only have to look back to the latter part of the twentieth century to find when interest in the subject both academically and among the general public-really started to grow.

Nevertheless, there are pioneers in the study of body language whose curiosity in the subject can be traced back to much earlier.

Francis Bacon was a British author, physicist, and politician. Writing in The Proficiency and Advancement of Knowledge, Divine, and Human-first written in 1605-Bacon had the following to say about the body's movements while discussing the concept of self-knowledge. Who is called the King of body language? Francis Bacon may not only be the first one to analyze body language from an analytical standpoint, but he also recognized the world's first authority on body language-King James the First.

Kinesics and Proxemics

The basis for the modern study of nonverbal communication is kinesics and proxemics.

Kinesics

The word kinesics emerges from the root term kinesis, meaning "movement," and refers to the study of the movements of the hand, arm, face, and body. Furthermore, the use of movements, rotation of the head and body, eye contact, and facial expressions for non-verbal communication. Kinesics, in other words, is the science of coordination used by body movements as people speak to each other.

Gestures

Gestures are movements of the hand, arm, body, head, or face that express a thought, opinion, or emotion.

Emblems: These are gestures that have a particular meaning agreed upon. These still differ from the signs used by people with hearing impairments or others who communicate using American Sign Language (ASL). Although they have a generally agreed definition, they are not part of a standardized signage program such as ASL that is specifically communicated to a group of people. The raised thumb of one hitchhiker, the "OK" sign with thumb and index finger connected to the other three fingers in a circle, and the raised middle finger are all examples of emblems that have a defined meaning or meaning in a culture. The emblems can be in motion or still. Emblems are gestures that have a particular meaning.

Illustrators: These are the most popular type of gesture and are used to demonstrate their corresponding verbal message. You could use hand gestures, for example, to signify the size or shape of an object.

Proxemics

Proxemics is the study of how people use the space around them to convey information nonverbally. Proxemics is a fascinating concept that people engage in every day. Most people may not have heard of the term ' proxemics' and are amazed to learn that it plays an important role in our regular communication. The concept proxemics relates to researching the manner in which humans use physical space to relay messages. It is the individuals in space when interacting in different situations, keep between themselves and others. A person usually uses a subconscious type of behavior to assess the gap that should occur between him/herself and the person he/she communicates with. Proxemics is particularly interesting because it is something people engage in on a daily basis but may not be fully aware of it.

What is the Significance of Proxemics?

There are several explanations for why knowing proxemics is relevant, some of which might include:

- It affects the communication process significantly

- It affects people's views of others

- It provides non-verbal indications that influence how people perceive a message

Types of Proxemics

There are four types of "distance" in the United States, which people use to interact face-to-face.

- Intimate distance (0-2 ft.)

- Personal distance (2-4 ft.)

- Social distance (4-12 ft.)

- Public distance (> 12 ft.)

Intimate distance is that which is used to connect very confidentially. This zone of the distance between two individuals is characterized by 0 to 2 feet of space. The indication of emotional space is that two individuals embrace, hold hands, or stand side by side. Intimate-distance people share a unique level of comfort with each other. Those who are not relaxed in the intimacy zone with someone approaching them can feel a great deal of social anxiety or awkwardness. Personal distance is used to communicate with family members and close friends. Although it allows an individual somewhat more room than intimate distance, it is still very similar to that of intimacy and may require contact. The individual distance can vary between 2 and 4 feet. Unlike interpersonal space, if someone in the personal zone is confronted by a stranger, he or she will probably feel awkward in such close proximity to the stranger. Social distance is used throughout business transactions, relational space is used to meet new people and communicate between groups of people. Virtual distance has a wide range within the gap it can embed. Social distance between students, co-workers, or acquaintances may be used. Individuals within the social space usually do not participate in physical contact with each other. Individuals may be very particular about how much social space they want. Many individuals may need a far greater physical distance than others. Most times, if a person gets too close to another human, the individual will probably back up and give himself the amount of space he feels more comfortable in.

How Does Culture Affect Proxemics?

Culture is "information acquired, used to perceive experience and produce behavior." This is defined from an anthropological point of view on how people will react not only to their surroundings but also to those around them. Because culture is used to perceive interactions and create behavior, the amount of space individuals like to hold inside themselves plays a very significant role. Let's describe culture first. Then we'll look at how that influences the behavior of people and the use of proxemics. For example, anthropologist Edward T. Hall observed in Western societies that people retain more room around themselves than do other ethnic groups. According to Hall, "people from different cultures live in different sensory environments. Not only do they arrange areas differently because they feel it differently because the sensorium is' programmed' differently." We perceive things differently because of the way people's beliefs are formed in a particular society. As they are' programmed' or conditioned to act by their cultural values, they do not see eye-to-eye how to distance themselves from others. Hall has stated that "in one society, physical contact between two individuals can be perfectly correct, and in another, totally taboos." Hall's research has shown that the fact that proxemics can have extremely different views, and one's culture is of significant influence. Throughout Western cultures, for example, it is completely acceptable for a man and a woman to be together in public. They can engage in close contact with each other, as is acceptable in their culture. However, in India, women cannot interact with men so freely, or there could be severe consequences. Consequently, the use of proxemics varies significantly between people of different cultures. Let us look at an example of how differences in culture influence individuals to react differently to the very same situation. People who might be strangers in Latin America can participate in very close contact. Often, they greet each other by kissing on their cheeks. On the other side, North American people prefer to shake hands. Although they have made physical contact with the shake of the head, they also hold some physical space between the other individual.

Problems can arise as people from different cultures get in contact with each other.

As you can see, cultures have different expectations of what is socially acceptable with proxemics. North Americans love a more social distance, while Latin Americans love more close contact with each other when interacting. People of different cultures have specific beliefs about which spatial areas in a given situation are acceptable. Awareness of such differences is critical for successful intercultural communication.

Chapter 2: Interpreting Body Language

The four body groups or types used in body language are: the head, posture, facial expressions, and hands and legs. This means that we can analyze each body group in terms of its uses, what these mean, and how people may react to them. The art of persuasion comes in when we become adept at using all these body groups in unison so that we present a whole unified picture that can manipulate the people we interact with. This may sound devious and utterly deceptive, but it is a skill that salespeople use all the time, and it should be in your arsenal of communication if you want to be effective in your dealings with people. The head is a complex system all in itself, but as a basic body part, we can consider which way we turn it, nod it, shake it, and move it. But it also contains all of our facial expressions because it is the canvas for our eyes, eyebrows, nose, mouth, and even our ears. It's a busy place, which is why it is the part that people look at first.

The facial features all speak for themselves, no pun intended.

Genetically, we are predisposed to finding some features as being honest or dishonest. Being shifty-eyed can already put you on the back foot when it comes to body language, but that just means that you need to work harder to overcome that challenge, much like someone with a lisp has to work harder to be understood.

The direction of our gaze, what we do with our eyebrows while we talk, and obviously rolling eyes, all add context to our words, whether we mean to or not. We are usually not even aware that we are doing something with our faces, despite the proliferation of selfies.

Facial expressions, or the absence thereof, can become a conversation all in itself. Often you will hear people say that someone gave them a look. It may be something which can't even be put into words, but rather a combination of the face's activities which leave a bad impression on the viewer.

As an interesting experiment, video yourself talking to your friends and focus on your face. For most people, the face is not a dead zone, and there is a wealth of activity happening there. Watching that video, are you amazed or surprised by the things that your face is doing? Did you mean to suck your lips while you wait for a turn to contribute to the conversation? Do you know that you have a habit of raising one eyebrow when you turn to someone and wait for them to answer a question? Being aware of the things we do with our expressions is the first step toward using them more effectively and avoiding confusion.

Posture is also something that says a lot during our human interactions. Being too much of something can be very damaging, such as being too upright or too slouched. Sitting as stiff as a board most certainly conveys a feeling of discomfort and tension, while slouching indicates disrespect and inattentiveness.

The fourth group is made up of the actions and positioning of the hands, fingers, and legs. The obvious example here is someone who points a finger at you. The intent is quite clear and unpleasant in most cases. This is probably why we are taught that it is rude to point fingers at people. There are a multitude of other hand signals, each with their own meaning, but the way in which we use our hands can express a wealth of meanings. Even how we shake someone's hand can tell them about us. Squeeze too hard, and you appear competitive, too soft, and you may seem weak and unreliable. Even the temperature of your hands can create an impression. No one enjoys shaking a cold and clammy hand; it certainly indicates nervousness on the shaker's part.

There is also a fifth factor to consider in body language, which is our interaction with the world around us. The world contains people, objects, and events that we have a relationship with or to. For a fine-tuned viewer of body language, even acts such as setting down a cup of tea or opening a door can leave an impression. The space that someone leaves between themselves and other people can also be indicative of their emotional state. Standing too close could be a sign of dominance or neediness. Standing too far may seem aloof or disinterested.

It should be mentioned here that most of this interaction, these subtle signs and actions happens in the blinking of an eye. This is what makes effective use and reading of body language so challenging. It is also why it is such an incredible tool for persuasion. These interactions happen so swiftly that they don't leave a tangible memory on the uninitiated; however, they do leave a feeling that is so powerful that it's akin to brainwashing! People may afterward say that they can't quite put their finger on it, but so and so had a lasting impression on them.

So how do you decipher the plethora of body language interactions? Is there anything remotely resembling a dictionary or guide to study and prepare from? Not a dictionary as such, but a set of common combinations of body language indicators does exist.

Chapter 3: Nonverbal Communication

When we think of communication, typically the first thing we think of is speaking. Speaking is definitely an important way for us to communicate, but most of the communication is going on around the words being said. The words actually account for very little. Communication is the act of sending or receiving information between two or more individuals, and this is not always spoken. By communicating, we're able to share knowledge, lessons, and skills. This information is shared in two major ways: verbally and nonverbally. Nonverbal communication, then, is quite simply all the kinds of communication we conduct without words. This includes actions that are both happening at a conscious and an unconscious or subconscious level. This might be the clothes worn by the communicator or the posture with which he or she stands. It might be facial expressions and gestures. There's even nonverbal communication present within verbal communication, such as unspoken communications like the speaker's tone, pitch, cadence, volume, timbre, register, or even their silence. Every little piece of information which is not directly said is nonverbal communication.

Where you might be able to control and even stop yourself from what you say, most nonverbal behaviors are largely involuntary and thus quite revealing. It is only when we study the art of deliberate communication that we begin to gain control over those largely involuntary behaviors. It's critical to understand that most of a person's opinion of you is derived from the nonverbal communications you broadcast. The words you speak have very little to do with what someone thinks of you. If you've been rehearsing a speech over and over in order not to mix up your words, you should consider how much more beneficial that practice time would be to make adjustments and controls to the nonverbal cues you're sending.

When an individual says one thing, but their body says another, the audience picks up on this, either consciously or subconsciously. Impressions, opinions, and decisions are made based on this information. If the visual or physical doesn't seem to match the verbal, we instinctively recognize that something is amiss.

In various studies, scholars agree that the very words you use in your speaking make up only about 5% of someone's opinion of you. The nonverbal voice cues you're sending will make up for about 45% of an opinion of you, while a whopping 50% of the opinion consists of your nonverbal body language communication.

Keep in mind that this is an approximate measurement for face-to-face interaction. Written communication operates a bit differently, and while writing, communication does incorporate many of the same nonverbal elements; it must be observed and measured separately.

With so much of an opinion being formed on communications other than our words, it doesn't seem so strange to spend more time practicing the nonverbal parts of your speech than the words themselves.

Types of Nonverbal Communication

With so much information packed into nonverbal communication, it's probably not a surprise that there are many forms of it. These very common behaviors below fall into three main groups.

The face communicates very often through:

- Eye contact

- Eyebrow movement

- Smiling

- Fake smiles

- Lips

- wrinkling the nose

- Facial expressions

Facial expression is the main way we communicate emotions without the use of any words or noises. Facial expressions are universal in nearly every case. No matter where you go, you'll see the same facial expressions to convey emotions of surprise, fear, disgust, anger, sadness, and happiness. You may notice that facial expressions are very often used in conjunction with other verbal speech and nonverbal behaviors in order to make as clear a display of emotion as possible. This is evident in the dramatic example of theatre actors and the like using exaggerated expressions, body language, and gesticulation, in order to make it clear to the audience what the character is feeling - and better yet, what the character wants other characters to think he feels.

The body communicates very often, though:

- Hand gestures

- Posture

- Body orientation

- Body language

- Space and distance, or proximity

- Touch

- Personal Appearance

- First impressions

The perceptions others have about you are largely drawn from how you hold and carry yourself. Body language and body movement give others ideas about you, whether they are conscious or unconscious of decoding this information. This could be the posture you keep when you walk in the room, when you stand to speak, when you cross the street, and when you meet someone for the first time. Consider your clothing and appearance and the extension of body language. Surveys indicate that most people judge an individual based on their appearance in less than 3 seconds. Among the most popular elements judged first are the shoes someone wears, the hairstyle (including facial hairstyle) someone chooses, the clothing they wear, and the hands, including nails.

Paralinguistic communication very often consists of:

- Humor
- Silence
- Symbolism
- Sarcasm
- Tone
- Volume
- Pitch

Paralinguistic are bits of information communicated with sound, and with the vocal cords in particular, without actually being words. This could be a gasp of fear, a sigh of relaxation and contentment, or a groan when a terrible smell is encountered. This also can include using elements of conversation subtly, such as humor and sarcasm. This could also be the myriad ways an individual uses the voice while communicating words. When a speaker changes pitch and tone, there is a recognizable change in the decoding of that information. When a speaker speaks loudly and then whispers, it elicits a different response from the audience in each case.

Shaking Hands

Another component of body language, which is often overlooked, but truly deserves its own attention, is the handshake. Unlike facial expressions, the etiquette and expectations of a handshake can vary from region to region. Some handshakes are fast, and some are slow. Some are aggressive, and others are soft. Some deliberately impose a subconscious signal to assert dominance, and others seek to show compassion and ultimate respect. Some handshakes should not be made unless the two individuals are of the same gender. In still other cases, the handshake can be seen as cold and callous, where a closer greeting, such as hugging or kissing, might be more appropriate.

But all of these examples, under analysis, are revealing critical information to you. Whether for personal reasons or socially imposed ones, some information can be derived that hints to whether the person feels confident or shy, entitled, or unworthy.

Handshakes as a social behavior seem to go back at least to the 5th century BC and have been depicted as communication of greeting, congratulations, and particularly, agreement. In almost every case, the handshake is taking on the whole to symbolize honesty and respect between the two individuals. We see this in sports, politics, business, and in customs like shaking the hand of a newly married groom.

In some parts of the world:

- Men are more likely to shake hands than women

- It's appropriate to shake a woman's hand before a man's

- Children shake hands when meeting

- A firm shake is rude

- A kiss is part of the shake

- Both hands are used

- A soft shake is a sign of respect

- The handshake is held during the entire conversation

All over the world, in communities where handshakes are expected, there are individuals who do not want to shake hands, and furthermore, are afraid to shake hands. In some respects, this makes sense, as the fear comes from that of contamination and not necessarily connecting via touch. Some individuals, though, do not physically like the way it feels to touch others. For whatever reason someone has, they may not want to shake hands. In many cultures, this has been taken as a sign of disrespect, and certainly there are still many regions that observe it as such, but in the modern world, and especially in cultures where business and commerce takes precedence, we become more accepting of skipping the shake and bonding and building rapport in new ways. Sometimes we might see this as the elbow bump (and similar shared gestures like it), which seems to be an acceptable compromise somewhere between making contact and not making skin contact.

Another part of the handshake that is often overlooked is the eye contact that goes with it. In most cases, you should make appropriate eye contact with the individual when you shake their hand. A handshake that includes eye contact conveys honesty and truth. Likewise, a handshake that includes one or both individuals avoiding eye contact is a sign of mistrust and deception. Keep in mind that both the handshake and eye contact could be getting encoded deliberately, then pay attention to signs of deception and lying.

Chapter 4: Personality Types

Your personality will remain predominantly stable over time. The traits you display as a child may change a little as you grow older, but it generally predicts the kind of behavior you're likely to demonstrate as an adult. Humans are an adaptable species, and we can alter and change our personality based on need and necessity.

Examples of positive personality traits include responsibility, adaptability, honesty, compatibility, determination, compassion, loyalty, courage, and understanding. Negative personality traits, on the other hand, include selfish, rigid, unyielding, lazy, disloyal, backstabbing, and lying. The latter is the one you want to learn to analyze and watch out for.

Interpreting Personality Types

The assessments that we make about someone's personality are informal, often based on the way they behave and why they behave the way that they do. Psychologists, on the other hand, have a more theoretical approach to describing personality types.

The word personality has Latin origins to it, derived from the root word persona, which refers to the theatrical mask that performers usually wear to disguise their identities or play or project different roles. To put in more succinct terms, personality involves the characteristic patterns of feelings, thoughts, and behaviors, making each person unique. These traits from within and will remain fairly consistent throughout their lives unless there is a deliberate attempt to change it.

Our personalities are what make us the unique individuals we are. It is a pattern that involves an individual's permanent traits, in addition to their distinctive characteristics. These traits give consistency and individuality, which contribute to our unique thoughts and behavior.

Personality theorists have a myriad of ways to describe what the term "personality" encompasses. In their study of personality traits and types, on the patterns of behaviors and characteristics that can help explain and predict the way someone behaves. There are several factors which could influence the expression and development of our personalities, among them:

- Genetics.

- Culture.

- External environment that shifts and changes through the different stages of life.

- Parenting.

- Societal expectations.

- Cultural norms.

Consistency, when here is a recognizable regularity and order to the behavior seen. People generally act or behave in the same ways, no matter what the situation. Personality also has an immense effect on what causes us to act, behave, move, and respond in certain ways. The way human personality develops and changes over a person's lifetime is an extremely exciting element of life that one can study. This study and the results gained serves as an important insight into understanding the practical applications of the real- world, why people act and behave a certain way, and what motivates the behaviors and thoughts.

Tests are conducted to assess the different personality types. A quick search on Google will reveal plenty of online personality tests you can do on your own to help you understand and learn more about your strengths, weaknesses, and even character, although not all these tests may be entirely reliable to accurate. Psychologists carry out their own tests in their profession to interpret and understand the different personality types, which are more definitive than the generic tests you do online.

Personality assessments can be conducted in a range of areas. Some assessments may focus on how some people rank in terms of conscientiousness, extroversion as well as openness. Some assessments focus on specific aspects of changes in personality over the course of time, whereas other assessments are used to help people determine the kinds of careers that go well with their existing personality and how they can perform certain job tasks.

Competing Personality Views

Two competing views exist on personality, which is the idiographic view and the nomothetic view.

The idiographic view sees personalities as being unique to an individual. No two people can be compared with one another because their psychological components are integrated as an entirety and not as a sequence of comparable characteristics. Originating from the Greek word "idios," which means "private" or "own," psychologists pursuing this approach focus on experiences to discover what makes each individual unique. The idiographic view is all about free will and what it means to be uniquely human. Studying this view involves data based on qualitative research and investigation into an individual's personality in a detailed manner. Methods of study could include unstructured interviews, case studies, and personal documents, self-reports, and even autobiographies. One strength of this approach is that it focuses entirely on the individual. Gordon Allport, who founded more than 18,000 terms to describe personality characteristics, argued that only when you get to know a person as a person will you be able to predict what they might do in any given situation. The nomothetic view is that personality traits can be compared among individuals, and each person has a scale of that trait. This unique personality is seen by mapping their position along with these traits. Stemming from the Greek word "nomos," which means law, psychologists who follow the nomothetic school of thought focus on studying the personality similarities between individuals. Therefore, this approach centralizes around establishing generalizations or laws which can be applied to everyone. The strengths of the nomothetic approach lie in its scientific and precise measurements. This approach has helped the scientific approach to psychology through the development of theories and laws, all of which can be empirically tested. However, the limitation to this approach is that predictions can be made about the various groups of individuals, but these predictions may not apply to all the individuals concerned.

Two examples of this approach are Raymond Cattell's 16PF (Personality Factors) theories of personality traits and Hans Eysenck's personality type. Cattell narrowed down the major personality traits into 16 different terms, which are:

- Abstractedness
- Apprehension
- Dominance
- Emotional stability
- Liveliness
- Openness to change
- Perfectionism
- Privacy
- Reasoning
- Rule conscious
- Self-reliance
- Sensitive
- Social confidence
- Tension
- Vigilance

- Warmth

Eysenck believed that personalities were divided into two dimensions. The first was introversion-extroversion, and the second was emotional stability-emotional instability (neurotic).

Understanding Personality Types

Personality types are described as psychological classifications that are given to individuals with specific behavioral patterns and tendencies. Businesses and organizations have started incorporating personality tests to designate individuals to certain job functions or roles within the organization based on the outcome of their test results.

Myers-Briggs Personality Type Indicator

This is one of the most commonly used tests to figure out what everyone's personality is. Per the Myers-Briggs indicator, there are 16 various types of personalities. The very fact that there are 16 types in the Myers-Briggs Indicator goes to show how complex people are and how their emotions and behaviors are all different at varying degrees.

For the purpose of analyzing body language and learning how to recognize the warning signs of lies and deception through nonverbal communication, there are four main personality categories you need to focus on:

Peaceful Personalities - They are patient, diplomatic, and easy-going and prefer to avoid confrontations with people. This group prefers having order and peace and thrives best in this sort of environment. They are known to be very down to earth people and are quite stable emotionally. They bring balance to companies that are fast-paced and have strengths to build a working team. Because of their nature, it's generally easier to spot the telltale signs of a lie when it's happening, since peaceful personalities are often uncomfortable being deceitful. They encourage respect, value, and harmony between people in the workplace.

Playful Personalities - These individuals are easy enough to recognize. They're funny, energetic, enthusiastic, and loud and are generally considered extroverts, and they love socializing with people. They've got plenty of ideas, are innovative, creative, and work fast, but the downside is that sometimes these creative types tend to be disorganized. Not all playful personalities will be your friend, though, and if someone is being too friendly in certain situations like work (especially if you've only just met them), be on guard because they might not be trustworthy. Playful personalities prefer fondness, approval, and attention.

Powerful Personalities - These confident, in-control individuals are generally both authoritative and productive. Most people classified under this personality are known to not give up easily. They like to take control and face any situation head-on. They have great inner strength, and they usually stop at nothing until their goals have been accomplished. This competitive streak, though, tends to bring out some less than pleasant qualities, depending on the individual in question. Some may have no qualms about having to resort to lies and deception if it means they can get on step ahead. These personality types are attracted to credit, loyalty, and appreciation.

Precise Personalities - Precise personalities are perfectionists. They value order, as well as structure and compliance. They're organized, but their work before play or social life and only stop working until they are done with their tasks. Typically, these personality types prefer space for them to work solo, choosing quiet and sensitivity over chaos and disorganization.

Before you can begin analyzing someone else's personality type based on their body language, you need to understand your personality first. From the friends you choose to the work you do, the passions that you have, and even the candidates you vote for, all of these boils down to your personality. Your personality affects almost all major areas of your life and the decisions that you make. By understanding your personality, you gain better insight into what your strengths and weaknesses are. It helps you develop insight into how the people around you perceive you. The way that you interact with others is inevitably going to affect their body language to a certain degree as well.

Psychologists have classified personality types into five major categories, known as The Five-Factor Model. They believe that each of us has some degree of these characteristics within our own personalities.

Openness - Having a broad range of interests as well as a vivid imagination could mean you've got high levels of openness in your personality. People with this personality trait are creative and curious, preferring variety over rigidness. Open individuals pursue self-actualization through euphoric and intense experiences, like living abroad, for example, or going on self-discovery missions. Sometimes, they can be seen as unpredictable and unfocused.

Conscientiousness - Usually known to be dependable, efficient, well-organized as well as self-sufficient, these personality types prefer to plan their day and their tasks in advance and are always aiming to achieve better. That is if you have a high level of conscientiousness in your personality. On the other end of the spectrum, those with low levels of conscientiousness are usually seen as obsessive and stubborn.

Extraversion - Those with high levels of extraversion in their personality thrive in social activity. You might even say they're social butterflies. They are outgoing, talkative, and have no trouble being in the spotlight. Sometimes, this can be seen as attention-seeking and domineering.

Agreeableness - Being agreeable in nature makes you kind, trustworthy, and affectionate towards people. Those with agreeable personalities are known for their prosocial behavior, and they are committed to altruistic activities and volunteer work. Some people might perceive this personality trait as being naive and overly passive.

Neuroticism - High levels of neuroticism in your personality could mean you're regarded as being "emotionally unstable." Tendencies of this personality trait include being reactive and excitable, but that also means they have a higher capacity for unpleasant emotions like irritability, insecurity, and anxiety.

Chapter 5: Deception and Lies

We need to pause a moment to look at what deception really is. Deception is deceit. Deceit is misrepresentation. This is the truth not being presented, and something else put in its place to occupy an individual. Fake news comes to mind. This is a recently coined term. What is it really? When we start to look at fake news and see what is actually under it, we begin to see conspiracies and concealment. We could write a complete manuscript on fake news.

The point made is that we trust the news to report the truth. Like the individual we choose to trust, when the news lies to us and deceives us and conceals the truth, we become injured. Being the complex beings that we are, we are also intrigued that the news lies to us and get an odd sense of satisfaction when the concealment is revealed, and the truth comes out.

It is on this reveal that the dark can also play. The lie is one thing. The reveal is another. Think about it. What happens to us when we are lied to? We do not know, honestly, what is going on until we begin to uncover the truth. And what kind of state is the human in when it is lied to? Calm, reassured, and mostly unaware of what is actually going on. This is a state of bliss. We all like to be told everything is going to be okay. Especially when there is truth to back it up.

However, we are talking about the reveal. What happens to us when the reveal happens? We pause. Stare in disbelief. Our jaws drop, and our minds go into overdrive.

This is a supremely vulnerable moment for the mind. A vicious individual can do some serious damage here.

Watch what the news is actually doing when they call fake. When the reveal comes, take a look at how everyone reacts. You will be surprised at how much more manipulation can come from the reveal than the actual lie itself.

As they say, the bad press is the press nonetheless.

A lie is a creative thing. It is an invention from the situation and facts at hand. The lie does not exist until someone dreams it up. This invention is a powerful one, and it gives a false sense of power to the one creating the lie.

When we are talking about power, we are talking about control. No one can successfully sustain a lie to control. Eventually, the truth prevails. Well, mostly.

This invention is a creative artistic process. The mind creates all the time. One can even go so far as to say dreams are a lie. A pure fabrication of what is not true. Some deny dreams in their life for just this reason. Dreams are not true, therefore they are a lie, therefore not real. However, they are a creative thing. One has to give a little credit to the master liar. They are creative and inventive. So, what makes the difference between a piece of fiction and a lie? Intention comes into play here. When we know it is a piece of fiction, we have the opportunity to give it a wide latitude. At this point, we can choose to believe the lie. The more pretty the fiction, the more attracted to it we are. Some can spin fiction to such an extent that it becomes pure. This pure fiction is the master liar at the canvas creating the masterpiece. Knowing that the other party knows its fiction, the liar creates and spins a web of lies that entices and almost controls an individual. We are creatures moved by art. Art, being a seriously creative process, includes fabrication and fiction. We are drawn to the false of life. This is due to something inside us that reminds us that life breaks free. That we are not perfect or even close to perfection. This fiction can be a source of escape because it touches upon our artistic side and draws us out of ourselves and into someone or somewhere else.

Fiction spreads across art. Art spreads to represent us. We have incorporated the lie.

Let's get off of fiction for a moment and get back to what is false and what is true. Falsification is the act of taking something that is true and making it false. This can be anything from a theory to a proof. When we falsify things, we take value away from them. There are various ways to falsify information. Some more innocent than others.

The fairy tale is something we read to children when they are going to sleep. The tales we tell ourselves are representations of what we are and, hopefully, what we will be. This is, of course, a falsity. However, we can look at it in a more innocent light. We are not creatures of pure truth. We need a parable or two to get the message across. The fairy tale does just that. So, is a fairy tale dark? It can be. Read the original Grimm's fairy tales and make a determination. We, however, know what a fairy tale is, so we can give it a wide berth concerning truth and lie.

When we start looking at falsification, we begin to take more and more deception into account. The cock and bull story is the following in line when it comes to the severity of lie. This phrase originates from two establishments competing against one another for the best fabrication.

The point we want to address here is that a lie can perpetuate another lie. And those can stack on top of one another. The cock and bull story is an example of this. The stacking of fabrication, one upon the other, and we take this lightly. It is very serious, yet we treat it is as a jovial thing. We are intrigued by the cock and bull story sometimes more than the lies and the reveal of those lies.

The one lie that really gets us and hits us square in the face is the barefaced lie.

A barefaced lie is a lie-flat out. There are no hidden complexities. It is an untruth plain and simple. This is not the tool of the dark. There is no power and control in the barefaced lie. It just is. The reveal of it is where it becomes a barefaced thing. It is when the fabrication of truth is almost completely opposite. This is the barefaced lie.

So, we can see that there is an immense amount of complexity when it comes to lying. How lying applies to dark psychology is in how the issuer of the lie uses that lie and the intentions behind that lie. Lying can do everything from shutting down a situation to the flaring of a situation to an uncontrollable fire. We lie to conceal what we consider personal and precious. We just have to be careful not to lie to deceive. This is the difference between a dark and a white lie.

Lies

The position of us physically when we are not on our feet is to lie. When we are on our backs, we are vulnerable and exposed. This is the physical aspect of a lie.

We are going to talk about the mind of the lie. A lie in its mental form is the opposite of the truth. It is the opposite of fact. Maybe not in the exact opposite, but in contradiction and subterfuge.

Concealment of truth is the deflection within the practice of dark psychology. It is untruth. The untrue can be a powerful tool to distract from what is actually happening.

We are creatures of curiosity, and we can sense when something is not true. It is a feeling as well as a logical thing. It engages us both mentally and emotionally in a way that strikes something deep within us when we sleuth it out.

We get a buzz when we catch someone in a lie. From the most powerful individuals in society to the child and brushing teeth, uncovering the lie sparks us. There is a gray area here where the dark works. To perpetuate the lie and keep it going, or possibly come up with a better lie to justify the first one, keeps an intended victim distracted while the dark run their agenda.

This is the complexity of the double spy. Or the double lie. A lie put into place to hide the actual lie taking place. And they can be stacked over and over again to throw an individual into a flurry of trying to figure out what the actual truth is.

Falsehood is what we are talking about when we really look at what lying is. What is true and what is false makes sense to us. We are about what is on or what is off. What is dead or what is alive is the most basic of truths. The lie takes one and turns it into another with language action and the impression of the mind.

There are various degrees of the lie. Some of the smaller ones that we as a society dismiss are fibs. A fib is an unimportant lie. What determines importance is up to all parties involved?

Once what is important is separated from what is not important, a fib can be spotted for what it is.

There is a fundamental flaw in looking at untruth this way. This fabrication of truth can be wiggle room for bigger and more serious ways to deceive. A fib can lead to a fabrication. That fabrication can deceive in a way that can cause serious damage. Yes, a lie can damage. It damages trust and honor and light. A fib can be the original conceptual spark.

Fabrication often leads to deception. There is where we can make a true determination of what a lie really is. When one party is deceived, this is where the lie is defined.

We, humans, keep things to ourselves. We are social with a personal area within us that is only shared with the most intimate. What is the difference between being introverted and keeping things to yourself and a lie?

Chapter 6: "How to Analyze" Concept

Analyzing people is a natural action every one of us carries out when we are relating to other people. Primarily, it borders around the confines of using what they say and do to make an assumption of the way they reason.

As intelligent people, we should be able to find out that people really are by being able to analyze what they say and do. Using their verbal and nonverbal information will give us the necessary information on which people really are, beyond what they look like on the outside.

In analyzing people, you must primarily understand that people show different behaviors, and these behaviors can just be a simple display of manners, for example, clearing of the throat, head-scratching, tilting of the head, a crossing of arms and legs, pouting, and jiggling of feet. These behaviors can be so normal that we might not even notice them in others, and even if we notice them, we pay little or no attention to it.

Although these behaviors in some people can be just their natural way of acting, for other people, these same behaviors can carry unspoken words of deception, anger, anxiety, nervousness, etc. So, you must be able to draw the line between the normal behavior of people and when those behaviors are to communicate a detail. When you have done this, then note when there is a difference in the actions and gestures of the person. Basically, know the way the person behaves.

You must give in to very important forms of information that will lead you into properly interpreting the vital hints that people normally give through unspoken words that are seen in their actions. If you must hear those unspoken words, you must stay objective in your analysis, neutral, and not twist any information the person is giving you. This means you will have to put away preconceived notions, any feeling of anger or displeasure you have toward the person, especially if the person has wronged you before, any contemplations you are holding in mind toward that person who you are trying to analyze, and you must avoid allowing your ego get in the way. One single behavior may carry no message, and you have to put together numerous activities and watch the behavioral trend, find out if the behavior is specifically toward you or if the person relates that same way with others. So, it doesn't matter who you are trying to analyze; your spouse, superior at work, your colleague. The rule remains the same, stay unbiased and bring down your ego defense walls. Well trained human analysts are those who are able to hear the unspoken and see the invisible. They put into full use their well-trained intellect to go beyond where every other person will put their attention, and this helps them reach out to mind-blowing deductions. They are able to pay attention to these places where others do not pay attention to because of their ability to freely drop of earlier emotional baggage they have about others, especially the people they are trying to analyze.

Basically, there are three methods one can employ in the art of analyzing people;

Pay Attention to Hints from Body Language

Firstly, do not put all your attention on forcing yourself to notice the hints the person gives through his/her body language. Just observe in a relaxing manner. No pressure and discomfort also stay flexible. Paying attention to body language is a very important and primary method in the art of analyzing people because research has proven that body language accounts for 55 percent of how we communicate. Words account for just 7 percent, and the tone of our voice accounts for about 38 percent.

Things to observe as you pay attention to body language hints:

1. Appearance

Note that most times, a classic suit and well-polished shoes show a drive for success and business-minded, a casual outfit like a shirt on Jean shows being comfortable with being casual, and an overly body fitted top with cleavage on display shows seduction.

An ornament that has a cross pendant shows the person has spiritual values.

2. Notice Posture

In reading posture, hints like head position, steps, chest posture should be observed.

If the person's head is held high, it is a sign of confidence and healthy self-esteem. As they walk, do they work in a disorderly manner? If they do, it is a sign of low self-esteem. Is the person always walking with their chest out and heaved? It is a sign of a big ego.

3. Physical Movements

In analyzing physical movements, pay to observe the hints like leaning and distance, a crossing of limbs, Hand movement and position, biting of either the lower lips, upper lips, or both, and picking of cuticles.

Normally, people tend to lean towards those that they have an emotional connection with and away from those they share no emotional connection with. The crossing of limbs is generally a sign of anger and self-defense. A person who crosses his/her legs will have his/her toes, pointing to the person or persons he/she is comfortable with. Hand movements like placing of hands on the laps or putting them back or hiding them could suggest that there is something the person is hiding. Most times, when people are under pressure or in circumstances where they feel awkward, they bite their lips or pick their cuticles.

4. Facial Expression

Often times, the looks on our faces are expressions of how we feel. Hence, in analyzing people, you must pay attention to the looks on their faces. Most likely, when a person is overthinking or is worried, the look on the face is usually a deep frown. Angry people show pursed lips. The same applies to people who are bitter. People under tension will clench their jaws and grind their teeth.

Pay Attention to Your Intuition

Intuition is the feeling that comes from your gut. It is not what your head says, so it might not be logical sometimes. This feeling is an unspoken detail that comes to you through images, and it is not via logic. Who a person is, is the most important detail you need to really understand someone. The outer appearance may matter but doesn't really count. What this feeling from your inside will do for you is to give you further insight beyond the obvious.

Checklist of Intuitive Hints

1. Honor Your Gut Feelings

It is often said that the first impression matters a lot, so when meeting someone for the first time, pay attention to that feeling from your within. This most times will precede logic. That feeling will tell you if you feel comfortable with the person or not. These feelings are the voices of truth from within you, and they tell you if you can commit to people.

2. Feel the Goosebumps

Often times, when you have a Deja-vu experience, it will send a cold shiver down your spine and produce on you Goosebumps. These feelings are components of those inner voices that tell us about the person we are relating with, even though we might just be meeting them for the first time. Often times, as they begin to speak, what they say will resonate with these feelings we have been having inside us.

3. Pay Attention to Details That Come in Flashes

As you converse with people, be vigilant, you may get a quick flash of information. Try not to miss them, and they carry very important details that will help you in critical analysis of the individual. Do not be in a hurry to go to the following detail, and this will cost you these flashes, and once lost, you may not get them again.

4. Be Vigilant for Empathy from Your Intuition

As you talk with people, they sometimes communicate how they feel with you, and your intuition will communicate this to you. It is like a transfer of their feeling. So, when reading people, find out if the feelings you are having were there before meeting the person. If it started at the course of the meeting or after, it is your intuition communicating those unspoken words to you. This can even go down to physical symptoms like pain.

Feel Emotional Energy

Our energy is usually given hands and limbs via our emotions. The emotion is the vibe we send when we are with people. This energy transferred via emotions alter the mood, behavior, and even emotions of the people we are around. So, do well to acknowledge these emotions. Did you notice that there are some people you will come around, and you will feel good? These people, through their emotional energy, heighten your mood and activeness. Also, there are some people you will be around, and your vitality and vibe will die off. In fact, they drain you of your own emotional energy. You just want to leave their space. This energy is cunning and can be felt from a distance, they are not visible, but they can be felt.

How to Analyze Emotional Energy

1. Since People's Presence

When we say presence, this is the vibe individuals send or the energy they emit. They are not necessarily expressed in words or deeds.

This energy cannot be touched, but it is being felt. The energy effect on the atmosphere has an impact on the environment. It is contagious. As you study people, note the energy their presence gives off; does the presence attract or repel you?

2. Pay attention to Eye Signals

The qualities of a person can be seen in the eyes, from the eyes you can tell if the person is caring, happy, concerned, surprised, scared, pissed, scary, shy, at peace, paying attention, or indifferent. The eye can give off energy that extends beyond the body.

Also, by looking into the eyes you can tell if the person is hiding something or telling the truth.

3. Note the Energy in the Handshake, Touch, and Hug

Emotional energy can be transferred through physical contact, and it is like electricity. Find out if you felt warmth with the hug and/or handshake. Did it boost your confidence? Did it ease the pressure for you? Cold hands often show anxiety and fear. A firm handshake shows confidence.

4. Listen for Tone of Voice

Emotions can clearly be seen in voice tone and volume. The voice of your tone affects others, when studying people, notice how the tone of their voice affects you. Vibrations are created by sound frequencies, and these vibrations carry energy with them. Is their voice tone soothing? Does it scare you? Is it abrasive? Is it manipulative and subtle?

Knowing how to analyze people will influence to a very great extent, your dealings and relationship with them. The signs are all there, the signals are always there, finding out what is going on in people's mind doesn't necessarily require that you become a top-notch interrogator, just know what to look out for and pay attention to the signs bad signals the person presents to you. No matter who you are dealing with, you can have firsthand knowledge of how to relate with them. Understanding how someone feels will help you choose a perfect style of communication so that your message can be understood, passed across effectively, and received well.

Learning to analyze people accurately takes time, but continuous practice will make us better in doing this. Although there are exceptions to the rule, the principles must be kept in mind as you continue your journey to being a pro in learning to analyze people accurately.

Chapter 7: Speed Reading People

There are typically three methods you can use to effectively read people, and those are:

1. Facial Profiling

2. Body Language

3. Human Psychology

Each method has its own ways of applying information and learning appropriately in a given situation. Additionally, there are different levels of approximations for each type. For example, for racial profiling, you can read and analyze people based on their facial expressions. To understand body language cues, you need to spend more time with the person who you are trying to analyze. For human psychology methods, you need to spend even longer durations of time to read and analyze any person and his or her personality. We will define one of the three in this chapter.

Facial Profiling

Our face is the most obvious and visible reflection of our personality. Faces don't just help in remembering an old long-lost friend or keep us different from each other. They also help in understanding the underlying personality traits and characteristics of people. The study of personality through the person's face has been in existence since ancient times in Greece. This science-based art form is called physiognomy, which roughly translates to 'to judge nature' in the Greek language.

Physiognomy was very popular in ancient Greece, and during the Middle Ages, travelers relied on it to categorize and understand various new tribes and peoples that came in contact with during their travel. Johann Kaspar, the famous pastor of St. Peter's Church in Zurich, studied and revived this art in the modern time. He believed and preached that the body and mind interact with each other, which influences facial features and facial expressions, which can be used to study and understand the individual's personality and thought process.

Today, there are multiple studies, which prove a deep connection between personality and facial features. Most experts accept that there are five types of faces, including:

1. Convex

2. Concave

3. Plane

4. Convex-Concave

5. Concave-convex

Each type tells you a lot about the person. Let us look at them in a bit of detail:

Convex Type Face

People with a convex type of face usually have a sloped forehead with a hooked nose. Their jawlines will look weak too. People with this type of face are known to be fairly stubborn and demanding with little patience for anything. Many times, people with the convex type of face have a very sharp mind and are great to have as business partners because of their affinity towards business skills.

Concave Type Face

People with this type of face are characterized by a strong chin and a protruding (or bulging) forehead. Their noses are usually small in structure. People with this type of face are usually known to be kind, compassionate, patient, and thoughtful about everything they say or do. Moreover, these people spread their kindness and compassion for the goodness of society and usually do not reserve it for one specific person.

Plane Type Face

People with the plane type of face have neither an underdeveloped nor overdeveloped part. There is a profile of balance across their faces. People of this type are usually known to be stable and calm and are great to have as partners both in personal and professional aspects.

Combining the first two types, face experts have been able to discern two more hybrid types of faces, which are the 4th and the 5th in the above list.

Convex-Concave Type Face

These people have their forehead and nose in the convex shape, and the chin is concave. The personality traits of such people are usually associated with dominance and egotism. They are highly confident individuals and nearly always are a valuable member of the society they live in.

Concave-Convex Type Face

This is the opposite of the above type and is characterized by a strong forehead combined with a weak chin. They are usually associated with moral weakness and emotional instability. However, these people are capable of understanding and empathizing with the emotional status of the people around them. Face types of women are difficult to discern because their features are not very distinctive and normally have a seamless appearance. But, the typical face type can be discerned, and then these women reflect a very strong tendency towards the respective face type characteristics.

On the other hand, it is very easy to discern the face type of men as their features are more distinctive.

Facial profiling or face reading techniques are very useful to read and understand a person's nature and character. With sustained practice and patience, you can learn to notice the facial structure and more or less come to a reasonably correct conclusion about a person's character. There is a lot of history and literature covering the subject of racial profiling. It has been around since ancient Greece times with

Aristotle doing a lot of work. While the initial face reading techniques were restricted to the descriptions of the faces concerned, during the Middle Ages the techniques moved to astrological and predictive aspects. By the 19th century, facial profiling was being used to sort and detect criminal types. We humans are always curious to know more about our neighbor's personality and what is his mind thinks. The ancient Chinese had a face reading method based on the belief that the face is a reflection of our thoughts and inner spirit. Another way of categorizing faces is one that is based on the shape.

Shapes of Faces

Round

People with round faces are also referred to as water-shaped. They have a fleshy and plump profile. Round-faced people are known to be an emotional set and very caring and sensitive too. They are believed to have very powerful sexual fantasies. Round-faced people are best suited for you if you are looking for a long-term stable relationship.

Oblong

The thin, long face is also called wood-shaped. These people tend to have an athletic and/or muscular physique. Oblong-faced people are usually very methodical and practical, resulting in, more often than not, being overworked. They can be quite narcissistic, and their relationships are quite problematic.

Square

All referred to as metal-shaped faces, people with square-shaped faces are believed to be highly analytical and intelligent with a decisive mind. They can be quite dominating and aggressive by nature.

Triangular

Triangular faces are usually combined with thin bodies and highly intellectual thinking skills. They are usually of a fiery temperament and can be very creative too, as per Chinese face reading techniques.

Chapter 8: Manipulation and Psychology

Dark Psychology is the art and science of manipulation and mind control. Psychology, in general, seeks to study and understand human behavior. It is focused on our thoughts, actions, and the way we interact with each other. Dark psychology, however, just focuses on the kinds of thoughts and actions that are predatory in nature. Dark psychology examines the tactics used by malicious people to motivate, persuade, manipulate, or coerce others into acting in ways that are beneficial to themselves and potentially detrimental to the other person.

The point of dark psychology, as a subject, is to try to understand those thoughts, feelings, and perceptions that cause people to behave in predatory ways towards each other. Experts in dark psychology work under the assumption that the vast majority of human predatory actions are purposeful. In other words, most of the people who prey on others (99.99%) do it for specific reasons, while the remaining people (0.01%) do it for no reason at all.

The assumption is that when people do evil things, they have specific motivations, some of which may even be completely rational from their point of view. People do bad things with specific goals in mind and specific rationales for their actions, and only a tiny fraction of the population brutally victimizes others without a purpose that can be reasonably explained by either evolutionary science or some form of religious dogma.

You have heard many times that everyone has a dark side. All cultures and belief systems acknowledge this dark side to some extent. Our society refers to it as "evil," while some cultures and religions have gone so far as to create mythical beings to which they attribute that evil (the devil, Satan, demons, etc.). Experts in dark psychology posit that there as some among us who commit the worst kinds of evil for purposes that are unknown. While most people may do evil things to gain power, money, retribution, or for sexual purposes, there are those who do evil things because that's just who they are. They commit acts of horror for absolutely no reason. In other words, their ends don't justify their means; they cause harm for its own sake.

Dark psychology is rooted in 4 dark personality traits. These traits are; narcissism, Machiavellianism, psychopathy, and sadism. People with such traits tend to act in ways that are pointlessly harmful to others.

Let's look at examples of how dark psychological aspects are manifested in the real world:

"I-Predators" are people or groups of people who use modern technology to prey on others, either directly or indirectly. As we have mentioned, everyone has a dark side, and the anonymity that the internet offers has a way of bringing out that dark side in many of us. The result is that there is an ever-increasing number of people who are looking to exploit, coerce, stalk, and victimize others online and through the use of other technological tools.

These predators seem to be driven by deviant fantasies, which they feel free to play out because the internet makes it possible for them to lurk in the shadows. In other words, they are not restricted by the usual social norms that keep people from revealing their dark side because no one online knows their real identities. These people tend to have all sorts of prejudices and preconceptions, which they go to great lengths to impose on others.

I-Predators come in different shapes and sizes; there are stalkers, harassers, criminals, perverts, terrorists, bullies, conmen, and even trolls. No matter what kind of predators they are, they all tend to have a self-awareness of the fact that they are harming others. They also tend to go out of their way to cover their tracks, which means they don't want the people who know them in real life to discover that they have a dark side.

Arson is also a different manifestation of dark psychology. Arsonists are people who tend to be obsessively preoccupied with setting fires. Some of them become serial arsonists; they set fires regularly and in a manner that is highly ritualistic.

Necrophilia's are people who are sexually interested in the dead, while serial killers are people who murder three or more people over a prolonged period of time. These are some of the most extreme manifestations of dark psychology, and although they are rare (as a function of the overall population), they are still worth discussing if you want to understand dark psychology. Experts in the field of criminal psychology believe that serial killers and other evildoers are motivated by the pursuit of psychological gratification, which they can only achieve by performing those brutal acts. To the people who perform the worst kinds of evil acts, those acts are like drugs to them; they are addictive in a way. For instance, when a serial killer gets some form of gratification from murdering someone, he may feel the urge to do it again in order to experience the same gratification.

How to Protect Oneself from Dark Psychology and NPL

1. Being Extremely Wary Of People Copying Your Body Language

People who tend to practice NPL tend to mirror their targets. They can take the same seating style as their targets, copy how their arm is positioned, or the inclination of the head. A person is supposed to test such a person by changing a few of these things. If a person's copy of the adjustments is made, one is supposed to be very worried and avoid such a person.

2. Moving of the Eye Randomly and in Unpredictable Patterns

An NPL user is prone to looking keenly at an individual's eyes during the early stages of establishing a good rapport with his or her target. One is likely to mistake these people for them being interested in what you are saying to them. However, that is not the case since they care more about one's thoughts. They can access how much information an individual has in his or her head by reading a person's eye. Therefore, they can know when a person is telling a lie of the truth through the look of the eye. The best trick to avoid this trick by an NPL person is by being able to dart the eye several times while concealing important information or when generally talking.

3. Not Letting Anyone Touch You

This form might sound obvious to an individual. People who have good knowledge of NPL tend to have a conversation that has high emotional states. The emotional state can either involve intense levels of laughter or tightened angry moments. These moments are mostly accompanied by several forms of touches when an individual is in these states. They can tap a person to ask them what happened to reposition them to their earlier states.

4. Being Wary of Vague Language

It is one of the primary tricks that were learned from Mr. Milton Erickson, who used language, which is vague to induce a hypnotic trance. He was able to discover that a more vague language was able to lead a person to become more into a trance. This is because the vague language used was able to make a person disagree less or react to it. On the other hand, the use of a language that is not vague has the potential of making a person or people get out of the trance. A good depiction will be the use of words such as positive change.

5. Trusting of One's Intuition

There are moments a person's instincts can detect if something is off or a miss. People who practice NPL with dark agendas always seem to look off or be doggy. A person is supposed to follow his or her instincts during moments with such people.

6. Reading Between the Lines

People who practice NPL with hidden agendas tend to use language with hidden meanings. These layered meanings can be able to be accessed by keen people. During court prosecutions, this is a common phenomenon. Lawyers with evil agendas can be able to twist words to either incriminate an innocent person or to release a guilty party in courts of law. People are always caught off guard during such moments because NPL users are always subtle with the usage of this technique.

7. Being Wary of Permissive Language

Good NPL users can use good language to lure a person. This was also a discovery by Mr. Erickson, who was able to make people do something. It is possible because an individual will have been lured into the trance. It is very funny because a person gives the NPL user permission by following his or her guide willingly. These people have the edge of fines with their words, and it will be hard finding them using commanding language.

8. Watching of One's Attention

A person is supposed to be keen about zoning out or losing his or her concentration when holding a conversation with an NPL user. It is because this helps to invite him or her into the unconscious cue. Through the vulnerability of the mind during these states, they can unearth the subconscious part of the brain and access the information they need.

9. Not Agreeing to Anything

When a person finds out that he or she is being led to making quick decisions, he or she is supposed to loop out from the situation. A person is not supposed to be swept away into making an emotional decision within a fraction of a second. People who use NPL are prone to making people undergo such with a good example being impulse buying.

Chapter 9: Understanding How Our Bodies Communicate

There are a number of individuals in the world who seem genuinely kind, compassionate, and caring about the needs of others. Some of these people are actually that way, and there are just as many people who have ulterior motives behind the things they do and say. So how might you recognize when somebody seems kind and caring, but under the surface is manipulative? It is not a very simple case.

When you see someone wearing a badge and a gun on their belt, you know they are a police officer. If a person is wearing a blue button-up with their name embroidered on the breast, you can assume they are some sort of mechanic. Manipulators don't wear uniforms. You will sometimes not know whether someone is genuine or trying to persuade you. Individuals don't come with preliminary rules. If they did, we probably wouldn't listen to them anyway. It is easy to wind up blinded to somebody's actual nature since it's a natural part of our relationship to need something from them.

For example, sociopaths can be the most enchanting individuals on the planet. They have a method for making you believe their motives rather than your own. You might not realize just how charming a narcissist can be until you look back on the relationship after discovering their true colors. These individuals are great at charming their victims in a few seconds while making a 180-degree turn for the worse in the following few seconds. So, it is imperative to keep an eye out for these individuals without having to bump heads with them first.

It very well may be hard to detect the contrast between somebody who is captivating because he is genuine and somebody who is an expert manipulator. Thus, here is a guideline for reading manipulative body language when deciding whether you are dealing with such a person or not.

Signals and Responses

The first thing that many manipulators will do is mimic your body language in whatever way possible. They might start by sitting in the same position as you and then even move their arms or legs in the same way that you are. They do this because they want you to feel more open and vulnerable around them. Your mind picks up on these similarities and is aware of a sort of mirroring effect. This makes it think that it can trust this person more because you better understand who that person is. Rather than sensing that it could be a manipulation tactic, our minds believe that since this person is like us, they must be someone whom we can trust. What ends up happening is that we get lost in their words and don't become aware of the actual tricks they might be doing to try and persuade us.

You might wonder then if we need to be aware of everyone who sits the same way as us. It is true that this is a manipulation tactic, but that doesn't mean that every person who does this is trying to persuade us. The best way to decipher whether or not this is someone trying to manipulate us is to look at the nature of the conversation.

Sometimes, we subconsciously mirror the other person when we are feeling anxious. It is a way for our bodies to try and connect to the other person more, so we don't feel as uncomfortable sitting. If you have noticed that someone was mirroring the way that you sit, try looking at the nature of the conversation. If the other person is trying to get you to believe something or you were talking about a matter related to change, then there is a chance they were trying to get you on their side. If it was more of a casual conversation or one in which you were doing most of the talking, then it was likely a coincidence or a sign that the other person was feeling anxious.

Another sign that someone might be trying to persuade you is that they are standing as tall as possible, potentially with their arms on their hips. This can be the other person trying to make sure that they look as big as possible. In extreme cases, it is an intimidation factor. Most of the time, it is simply the person's attempt at showing authority and a sense of strength amongst others.

Remember that, again, this can also be a sign of anxiety. If a person is feeling like they are being overlooked or that someone is not listening to them, then this tactic can be a way to boost that energy. It is still important to be aware of all people's body language so we can get the actual context of the situation rather than what is happening on the surface level. Don't be fearful of everyone who stands tall like a superhero, but remember to not let yourself fall under the influence of someone who was simply trying to make their body look bigger.

One of the biggest body language signals that the conversation might not be the most positive is that the other person is closed off, keeping their arms crossed or even their hand over their mouth. It can yet again be a sign of not wanting to open up or feeling scared and defenseless. If a person is being confronted about something negative or being told some terrible news, they might have body language like this. If the situation is one where you are more openly discussing yourself and the other person is sitting like this, they might be trying to gather personal information against you that they can use. If the situation should be one where both of you are opening up, and they are sitting like this, make sure to hold back on some of your juicy secrets until they are ready to open up just as much.

Similarly, they might be more manipulative than this and even open up their body language so that they can be more persuasive. They might open their arms and put their arm around you even if the relationship isn't personal and sit with a broad chest to show that they are welcoming of you. This is healthy to do in many conversations, but don't let yourself fall for this tactic if they are simply trying to get more personal information out of you.

What Others See in Your Body Language

When someone might be trying to persuade us, they are also going to take into consideration our body language. It is important to be aware of the things that might give them the signal that we are feeling weak, scared, or anxious around them. If they are able to sense these kinds of emotions, then many people can find that it is easy to take advantage of others.

Let's first start with the top of our bodies and then work our way down. When you are wrinkling your forehead is a sign that you might be stressed. This can lead others to think that you are feeling anxious and might take advantage of that vulnerability. They can start talking about things that stress you out even more, which can lead to confusion. This can enable them to take advantage of what you are thinking. They can also use your confusion to plant more ideas in your head and get you thinking about them. If they are good ideas, this can be especially persuasive because you will be more interested in listening to positive things to distract you from what it was that was causing stress. Manipulators can look at your eyes to see what you are thinking. Squinted eyes can show focus, and others can exploit this much like they would a wrinkled forehead. Eyes that are wide and open can show focus and that you are an open person to new ideas. Others can see this and might assume your good nature, looking to take advantage and exploit your empathy levels. The same thing goes for wide and open smiles. Happy people can sometimes seem to be easier to manipulate because they are less defensive and more open to persuasion.

They will also look at the way you are holding your arms. Closed arms mean that you might be a little more skeptical of what they have to say. They can see this and think that they might need to work a little harder to persuade you. A more open demeanor can show them that they have the opportunity to persuade you.

When you are showing any forms of anxiety, this can also be a signal that you are feeling nervous and vulnerable around them. If you are fidgeting with your hands, twisting your hair, picking nails, shaking legs, or looking around a lot, they know that you might be nervous around them. This can help them get the idea that it will be easier to take advantage of and sway you a certain way.

You don't have to feel anxious all the time about how you are sitting or holding yourself because not everyone is going to meticulously study your body language. When you are in a position where others are seemingly trying to persuade or influence you at all costs, then it is important to make sure that you are protecting yourself. Stand tall and confident, maintain the right level of eye contact, and stay focused on the context clues of the situation rather than simply what the words are that are coming out of their mouth.

We are going to go over the other ways that manipulators are taking advantage of you through their actual language and the actions they take to try and keep you under their spell. Then we are going to give you the tools needed to find positivity from this and become a persuasive person yourself.

Chapter 10: Reading Body Parts

There is no part of the human body that is redundant when it comes to conveying unspoken intentions. From the crown of our heads down to the tips of our toes, every part of the body plays some role in communication. Even our skin can reveal a lot about how we feel; it can become flushed and can also instantly generate Goosebumps to communicate how we are feeling in a particular moment. Although "talking" with our body parts may not be audible, others around us can pick up the messages loud and clear, especially if they are versed in the art of reading people. Keep in mind that people, adults especially, usually are good at hiding their feelings and intentions from showing up on their faces, so they may want to cover up their body language with polite facial expressions and words. However, if you are observant enough, you can pick up discrepancies between their words and other parts of the body that are a bit difficult to consciously manipulate.

Here are some of the cues from different parts of the body and the likely intention that they signify.

The Head

Head movements can be quite easy to read if you know how to. Unfortunately, not everyone knows how to do this, which is why even the most obvious head movements go unnoticed by the ignorant and inexperienced person.

Let us assume you are a salesperson delivering your well-practiced sales pitch to a prospective client. The potential buyer appears engrossed in the sales pitch, but at a point, he tilts his head slightly back. If you do not understand this subtle head movement, you will carry on with your sales pitch without pausing to ask if the potential buyer or client wants something you said clarified. Your sales pitch is important, but it will be ineffective if you cannot quickly identify silent objection signals.

Let us take a look at the most common head movements alongside what they may be possibly indicating.

- Let's start with a nod. In most parts of the world, a nod indicates encouragement. However, not all nods are made equally. When a person nods slowly, especially if they are doing it unconsciously, it connotes a deep level of interest or rapt attention. Another head movement that indicates interest is when the person tilts their head sideways. So, if you are making some form of presentation in class or at a meeting and you notice these two head movements, it is very likely that your points are well expressed and understood.

- Hurried nods or frequent nods during a presentation could signal disinterest like in the second example above. If you notice this during your presentation or discussion, change your tactics or presentation style. Alternatively, pause the presentation and ask for input from the other person or people.

- In the case where a person tilts their head back while you are talking with them, it is a possible sign of disbelief, doubt, or suspicion. Whether it is a one-on-one conversation or a formal presentation in front of a board of directors, take a moment to clarify what you were talking about before you noticed that head movement. If you are unsure, ask them if there is something they would like you to make clearer. You could say, "I'm getting the feeling that you may need some further clarifications. Would you like me to clarify my last point or something I've said earlier?"

The Face

The face conveys messages that are very obvious to notice. Expressions such as frowns, smiles (grin or smirk), grimaces, dropped jaw, squinting, raised eyebrows, yawns, and so on can be read by almost everyone. Since it is not difficult to decode the emotional intent (anger, excitement, surprise, fear, confusion, disgust, and so on) by simply looking at the face, most of us have learned how to effectively hide these indicators so that we can appear polite. That notwithstanding, a careful study of a person's face can still reveal true intentions.

The following are some of the facial expressions and what they signify.

- A smile is one body language cue that has a universal meaning. Even infants can read this non-verbal cue. It strongly indicates acceptance, agreement, and comfortableness. When a smile spreads to cover the entire face, it is genuine.

- When a smile doesn't reach the eyes of the giver – when there are no crinkles at the corners of their eyes – it shows that it is a forced or fake smile. There are several reasons a person would want to wear a fake smile. They may want to be polite, they may want to be deceitful, or they simply want to seek approval from another person, especially from someone superior.

- A slight smile accompanied by a slightly raised eyebrow is one facial expression that indicates confidence and friendliness. When you are talking with someone and notice this expression on the person's face, it indicates that they believe what you are saying. If you are the one wearing this expression, you are conveying to the other person that you are trustworthy.

- The lips are used for smiling and also for telling truth or falsehood. When someone touches their lips repeatedly while telling you something supposedly confidential, there is a high chance that they are withholding some of the information from you.

The Eyes

There are a whole lot of messages that can be passed using the eyes.

- When someone keeps their eyes looking downward, it is an indication that they are feeling guilt, shame, or they are simply shy. For example, a child who has done wrong and feels guilty will probably keep their eyes down when their parents speak to them about what they've done. Also, a shy person is very likely to look down in the presence of someone they are not used to. When someone feels another person is very superior to them, they will look downward not as a sign of shame, guilt, or shyness, but as an indication of submissiveness. A very junior worker in a company, for example, is most likely to keep their gaze on the floor when they are in the presence of the company's CEO.

- When the person you are conversing with keeps stealing a look at the exit, it is a strong indication that they want to get away from that conversation to something else. It could also indicate that they are nervous, anxious, or apprehensive about something which their words are not saying, but their body is communicating very clearly.

The Shoulders

Shrugging is usually considered as a sign of ignorance or cluelessness. However, it can indicate other things, such as an unconscious need to protect our necks (vulnerable part) from danger. For example, notice how people generally react with they hear a sudden loud bang of a gun or even a seemingly harmless thing like a balloon bursting. The first reaction for most people is to raise their shoulders to hide their neck. You can also observe this when people walk in front of a crowd that is focused on something, like a movie in a cinema. The person walking in front of the crowd tends to shrug so that their necks are hidden inside their shoulders in an unconscious attempt to protect themselves in case of an attack from the angry crowd. Even children speak this unconscious protective body language when they hide their necks by raising their shoulders if their parents attempt to hit them.

Hand Movements and Gestures

- Keep your hands out of your pocket if you want to communicate openness and honesty.

- Someone holding an object between you and them is unconsciously trying to put a barrier between you and them. Their body language is indicating that they are looking for any excuse to block you out. For example, if a salesperson is trying to sell a product to a prospective customer, and the customer keeps fidgeting with a volume, a paper bag, or just about anything, it will serve the salesperson well to first turn his or her attention to enlisting their trust before attempting to sell them anything.

- When someone habitually points to another person while talking in a group or in a meeting, it is a strong indication that they have many things in common, or they have some type of affinity. Here's a great way you can use that to your advantage, especially in a situation where you are canvassing for support: seek the support of one of the pair, and you are most likely to get the support of the other.

The Arms

- When someone has their arms crossed along their chest while beaming with a warm smile, it signifies self-confidence.

- However, the same body pose without the smile is likely to indicate aggression, disagreement, or defensiveness.

- Placing the hands on the hips suggests dominance, power, or authority. This can also take the form of placing the hands firmly on a table while standing behind the table. For example, a boss or superior in an office can take this pose to add emphasis to the point they are making.

The Feet

One of the most ignored body parts when it comes to body language is the feet. Yet, the feet reveal a lot more than people realize. So, while people work so hard to hide their emotional intent from their faces, their feet may be all you need to observe in order to understand what is truly going on inside of them. Here's what to look out for:

- When someone's feet are pointing towards the door when you are talking with them, they are probably thinking about leaving or ending that line of discussion. Take the cue and summarize what you are saying or change the topic completely.

- When the other person's feet are pointing towards you, it signifies that they are interested in you or whatever it is you are saying. It may also indicate that they like you. If you are presenting an idea to a person and notice this signal, cash in on this opportunity to hit hard on your strong points in order to win them over quickly before they get bored, and their feet turn towards the door!

- When someone is nervous or feeling apprehensive, they are likely to have their ankles locked. The locked ankles are usually unconsciously used during an uncomfortable discussion. For example, when a friend is talking with you about a not-so-pleasant event in an environment that is not private, they may lock their ankles to signify that they are worried about another friend walking in during the discussion. The ankle lock can also indicate that a person is nervous about some news. For example, a patient waiting for a doctor's report may unconsciously lock their ankles in nervous anticipation of the report. If you notice this body language with someone you are talking with, you can take the cue and try to calm them down if the situation makes it appropriate for you to do that.

Chapter 11: Reading the Eyes

If you are meeting someone for the first time, where do you look? Obviously, the eyes! This tells how important the eye is in communication. There is a whole lot of information that can be conveyed with the eye.

Think of it—you probably can tell when someone is happy, sad, dejected, furious, excited, in love, and so forth, all by looking at the eyes. I guess this explains why people came up with the saying that "the eyes are the window to the soul."

Apart from the common and obvious emotions listed above, the best thing about the eyes is that there are a whole lot of other subtle emotions that you can deduce from them. It takes a deep understanding of the eyes and their behavior to detect such cues and pass the associated meaning.

You can deduce if someone has a crush on you, if someone has a hidden agenda and many more all by studying the eyes. There are many nonverbal cues that can be revealed from the eyes. Think of FBI agents, gangsters, and those in the Secret Service. Part of why they go around in dark spectacles is to appear mysterious to people so that no one will be able to read their eyes.

It is important to note that reading the eye starts at a very early age. Babies from seven months old, for instance, can interpret some emotions from the eyes that set the foundation for bonding. That is why they respond to laughing, giggling, and smiling.

Baselining the Eyes

It is vital to explore the meaning and importance of baselining before delving. For all the various eye clues to make sense, you need to establish a baseline. This is often used as the first step in figuring out if someone is lying.

This is how someone behaves in normal conditions when they are not stressed. The easiest way to establish a baseline is to have a simple, non-stressful conversation with the person about casual topics. During the process, it is important to note how they act, respond, and most importantly, react with the eyes.

This will help understand what the person's normal eye behavior is. Having established a baseline, you can detect and interpret gestures people make with their eyes. With this, we can go further into establishing various nonverbal clues from the eyes.

Eye-Related Nonverbal Clues from Eye Movement

Looking Up

It is common for people to look up when they are thinking. This is the indication of someone making mental pictures in their head, an indication of deep thinking. In an interview or an oral exam, a person, in a bid to recall a piece of information, could look up.

People typically do look up and to the left in trying to recall a piece of information. Someone making a mental picture, on the other hand, would look up and to the right. This might be reversed for a lot of people. This is why baselining is pretty vital if you will use this to detect a liar. You can establish a baseline by asking the person to recall a fact.

People also look up when bored. They are trying to look for something interesting to catch their attention in the environment.

Looking Down

Since this removes direct eye contact from someone, it points out to quite a number of things. In some cultures, it could also be a sign of submission.

Someone might also look down when they feel guilty or when hiding information. It could also indicate discomfort with the interaction.

When some look down to the left, check if they are talking to themselves. All you have to look for is a sign of movement of their lips. Looking down to the right, on the other hand, could be someone addressing their inner emotions.

Looking Sideways

Someone looking sideways is likely distracted and trying to find the source of distraction since the field of vision of humans is on the horizontal plane. A quick, sideways glance is an effort to check out the source of distraction, whether it is a threat or an interest. It could also be used to point out dissatisfaction or displeasure—for instance, if they hear a comment that is not cool.

Lateral Eye Movement

Moving the eyes from side to side might point out to someone lying. This can be interpreted as a person looking for an escape route should they be caught or a person trying to read the expression of people to see whether they bought the lie or not. A person looking toward the door is likely bored and wants to leave.

Other Cues from the Eyes

Eye Blocking

When people do not like what they see, they are likely to block or shield the eyes. It is not about sight alone. People often do this also when they hear what makes them uncomfortable. This gesture often relates to an unpleasant or uncomfortable situation.

Eye blocking is not only about covering the eyes. It can also be expressed by excessive blinking or rubbing the eyes. Besides, when people disagree with someone, they are also likely to rub their eyes.

Pupil Size

There are other subtle messages that can be passed from the size of one's pupil. In low light, for instance, or in the presence of something exciting, the pupils dilate. This happens mostly when we like our environment. Hence, in a bid to have more of it, the pupils enlarge. It is common for people in a romantic relationship to have their pupils dilated. In an effort to make products appealing to would-be customers, advertisers make the pupils of the model dilate. This is to create an appealing effect on the customer.

On the other hand, when sighting something unpleasant, the pupils constrict. This is an effort to block out the offensive sight or image.

Squinting

This also works like eye blocking. It is an eye gesture common when people are faced with something they do not like. People do this to avoid what they do not like. Be sure to take note of the eyes of the people you are interacting with. Take this as a cue to clarify your point should you see someone make this gesture.

Eye Cues and Romantic Relationship

The eyes convey a lot of information. This explains why people in romantic relationships derive pleasure in looking at each other's eyes. Here are subtle ways people use their eyes to communicate in a romantic gesture. Ladies who try to look helpless and defenseless pluck their eyebrows. Men receive this as a cue to defend the lady as this action releases some hormones in a man. People could gaze and stare at others in a bid to make attraction known to the person. Women, in particular, use this move as a flirting tactic. A sideways glance over a raised shoulder sends a subtle signal of attraction to the man. This is a clever move to see the smoothness of a lady's face and the vulnerability of her neck.

Gazing

An interest in someone is usually matched by a continuous focus on that thing. This makes people unable to take their eyes away from their object of interest. Many people could also follow the direction of your eye to check out the object of interest. Gazing at something, at times, signifies someone who is carried away without a specific interest in what they are looking at.

When someone looks at someone, and the person returns the gaze, it signifies interest or love. If a person looks down on another person's body, it signifies lust. It does depend, though, on the part of the body that the eyes are fixed on. Gazing at the breast, for instance, does signify a sexual intent.

Looking at someone from head to toe carries several meanings. This could indicate sizing another person up. It could also signify sexual interest or assessing a threat. A lingering gaze does tell the true intention of someone. Prolonged gaze, however, could be quite insulting and domineering. It is used to communicate authority.

Someone gazing at another person's forehead could be a sign of being distracted and lost in thoughts. You can also use your gaze to force your will on someone. Just give the person a short and intense gaze. This is called a power gaze.

Concealing a gaze is not easy as people can simply find out the direction of the eyes. The presence of large eye whites helps in nonverbal communication.

The best salesperson knows that the product that attracts someone will often catch their gaze. They could use this to hype the product and make the sale. The customer already has an interest; all he has to do is to build on the interest.

People will often glance through a store when shopping for goods to find what they want to purchase. No matter the size of the store, a person's gaze will often return to the object that catches their interest.

Glancing

Glancing also indicates a desire for something. For example, glancing at the time reflects a desire to leave a place. This is why glancing at a person, even in the midst of people, could signify an interest in having a discussion with them. When a hurtful or embarrassing comment about someone is made, people tend to glance at the victim as a sign of concern.

When glancing is done with a raised eyebrow, it means disapproval.

Important Things to Note About Eye Contact

When it comes to eye contact, you should put some things in mind. For instance, eye contact could lead to more, although we cannot rule out the possibility that some people might not welcome eye contact.

In initiating eye contact as well, bear in mind that the other person might look away at first. Keep the gaze. If after locking eyes the second or third time they do not return the gaze, let them be.

Do Not Be Creepy

The right eye contact can help pass the right message. However, not everyone will welcome or feel comfortable with your eye contact. As a result of this, do not force it if the person does not welcome it. Bear in mind that people can sense your gaze even without looking at you.

Rotate Your Gaze

Your focus might be on a single eye for a moment while you switch to the other eye after a while. Look between the ridges of the eyes as well if the gaze is starting to get intense. Be careful, however, not to turn this into a dart.

Do Not Be Too Obvious

Locking gaze for the entire conversation period is creepy. It is okay to look away for a bit while having a conversation. In breaking eye contact as well, do not look down. It sends the wrong message. Rather, look sideways.

Breaking Eye Contact

You do not have to lock eyes for the entire period of the conversation. Apart from trying to be polite, there are many reasons people do break a gaze.

Someone uncomfortable with a conversation or interaction might break a gaze or avoid eye contact altogether. When an insulting or disturbing statement is made, for instance, the gaze will break.

People also do break eye contact as a result of discomfort not relating to the interaction.

Long Eye Contact

There are several meanings and reasons for extensive eye contact.

In a meeting or other active-listening sessions, for instance, long eye contact is justified. This is common, especially when we are interested in the conversation. People who construct mental images, however, might not make long eye contact as they try to make a mental picture of the subject of discussion.

Chapter 12: Body Language Proposals to Improve Your Negotiation Skills

Strong negotiation skills are all tremendously beneficial throughout One's lifetime, from the boardroom into the pub. These abilities mostly rest on your capacity to back up your voice with bodily actions, which exude willingness, honesty, and assurance. This raises the want to respond and achieve an arrangement of the party and promotes confidence. Based on a study from speech and psychologists specialists, Gengo, body language, and also nonverbal communications have a larger effect in a conversation than the real words that you state. More than 55 percent of messages conveyed via nonverbal Cues such as posture and gestures, and various studies have proven body language is a more accurate indicator of somebody's true attitudes and goals compared to their tone of voice or phrases. Various studies have demonstrated that individuals are 80 percent more likely to keep information that has connected to both vocally and visually. Gain the advantage in discussions and your rate of success to raise and remain far ahead of the match.

1. Show Up On Time

As it is put by Woody Allen throughout his rocketing to stardom with the launch of Annie Hall in 1977, "Eighty percent of success is showing up," And it is true. The very first impression, which you will create on a new customer, prospective manager, or business adversary, happens before you step in the area or say a phrase. Lateness damages the negotiation procedure in two manners: Primarily, it has been seen as discourteous (or perhaps insulting) and suggests incompetence and lack of ethics on the part of the latecomer, which makes another party irritated and not as inclined to want to achieve an agreement. Second, the anxiety you will no doubt encounter at being overdue will shatter the calm, focused, and positive demeanor you'll want to summon if you are to be prosperous at the dialogue itself. Give yourself a chance and show up on time.

2. The Perfect Handshake

You've arrived on time! What is subsequent? The dreaded handshake Attesting to an old-fashioned's forces Handshake, mythical Hollywood talent agent and dealmaker Irving Paul "Swiftly" Lazar formerly said, "That I don't have any contract with my clientele. Only a handshake is sufficient." A Fantastic deal has been written Through the Years on the artwork of the handshake; however, you can overlook it all. The most and the only significant thing about your handshake is you have one at all. Researchers at the University of Chicago published a set of research concluding a handshake (any handshake, the floppy one by the man down the hallway) makes people feel comfortable, promotes guilt, and also raises the combined behaviors that result in deal-making.

3. Negotiate with the Ideal People

Tony Hsieh, CEO of Zappos, explains his plan for achievement in the poker table for a parallel to company: "I discovered that the most significant decision I could make was that table to sit. This comprised understanding when to alter tables" Just as a lot of your capability to set a tone for a

Successful discussion rests on maintaining control of your body language, which does your instinct in reacting to the entire body language and also non-verbal cues of your prospective competitors before opting to engage together. As Mr. Hsieh mentioned and some other poker player will say, the results of a match are usually more than half determined when they choose to sit down.

4. Maintain Friendly Eye Contact

Shakespeare talked as much for politicians, businessmen, and poker players wrote that "the eyes are the windows of the soul" Eye contact is one of the most influential Communication tools between two individuals, as it communicates confidence, sincerity, and openness. A rapport is kept by eye contact at a negotiation from growing. It gives the person the impression that you are being dishonest or evasive, each of which makes negotiating hard. On the other hand, eye contact is so strong that it may be viewed as intimidating or aggressive and threatening. You should maintain constant eye contact but keep in mind that it's natural to look off the processing or when thinking.

5. Be Conscious of Your Facial Expressions

You do not need to become a business tycoon to know about the unwelcome impacts your expressions, which are casual, may have on the result of a discussion. Anybody who has ever been in a relationship has likely undergone the feeling of utter frustration when their spouse stops short during dialogue and says, "What exactly does this look mean?!" Like it or not, at a discussion the expressions are going to be under the exact microscope try to be certain they improve the cues that are favorable that you are giving. Be careful not to moisturize or wrinkle your brow worryingly and have the chance to grin when 22 and nod in agreement. Keep your chin up, evoking your eye's degree, along with positivity. Bear in mind, the person will probably look to find your gestures reflect your words to keep them positive and receptive.

6. Maintain Personal Space: Proxemics

The science of space known as "proxemics" targets the space between individuals as they socialize. Ever felt pressured or uncomfortable while talking with you every time co-worker, acquaintance, or a stranger endured a bit too close? To the point, you're shuffling your feet and prepared them by paying attention? As you can imagine, a scenario disrupts the Negotiation procedure. It is important for every party to feel they're not being intimidated, and their private space has been respected. Examine the individual to judge their comfort level and a safe guideline is to stand or sit at least four feet off.

7. Keep Your Limbs Calm and Open

Much like you want the words which you are saying to exude Strength, confidence, and serene in a discussion in case your physique. If you are always tapping your hands or toes, entwining your palms, or crossing and uncrossing your legs, then it is going to indicate that you're in a stressed, instead of a thoughtful, condition. Keep your legs and hands moving together calmly. Non-verbal stations are 12.5 times stronger than Communicating feelings and attitudes. Any amount of hands or limbs are Going shut off and interpreted as being negative, which will not enable you to elicit confidence. Nobody wants to speak to somebody who appears to have made their mind up! Uncross thighs and your arms and maintain some space between your palms to seem prepared and amenable to follow others' points of view.

8. Hands Down

Talking of hands they may add and are expressive A great deal to your communication. The guideline is to keep your hands away from the face after negotiating. Head or face is viewed as a symptom of stress, and it really is. Similarly, having your palms you might be in the practice of lying or concealing. By keeping your hands away from the head, Look confident and honest, unclenched, and start.

9. Slow Down and Keep Quiet

Regardless of the Circumstance, everyone desires to feel good before making a countermove, to listen, to admire, and to believe. On the other hand, the strain of this dialogue, together with your enthusiasm and desire to get your point across, can make you jumpy and overenthusiastic, hurrying your words or perhaps speaking within another individual. Listen closely to another individual, pause for some time to show you're considering what they started, and maintain your answer calm and slow. This conveys esteem but confidence in your position. People remember only 20 percent of the information that's offered to these and orally visually. 80% of the information that's presented to an individual aesthetically and orally is kept, meaning that the body language is as essential as being outspoken. Moreover, do not be afraid to be quiet for a while, assessing the individual's insecurities. You could surprise. Since Lance Murrow advised, "Never overlook the power of silence, that hugely disconcerting pause that goes on and off and might, in the beginning, induce competition to babble and backtrack nervously."

Chapter 13: How to Show Dominance through Body Language

People who want to imply being in charge usually use dominant nonverbal cues. These people may not be aware these body language signals may not even be aware that they are doing so and may just be a factor in their dominant personality.

Used properly, showing dominance through body language can help you gain respect and popularity, a method usually employed by politicians during the campaign period. Here are some actions that express dominance.

Appearing Larger

Appearing larger and more powerful is an important factor in showing dominance, and this can be traced back to man's prehistoric roots. This action is also very evident in animals, where in fights for dominance are often settled by size comparison, saving the parties involved from altercations.

This behavioral bias was inherited by modern humans and can be seen practiced when competing with others. Using the same size and body language signal, they try to show their superiority by appearing to be threatening and should be avoided. Here are examples of these size signals:

Make Your Body Appear Bigger

A bigger person is often seen as more dominant and more threatening. If you have the height advantage, then good for you because you are already large, and this effect comes naturally to you.

It's one of the main reasons why taller people tend to be more successful than others, not only in sports but also in the corporate world. For the smaller ones, here are some gestures, postures, and body language tricks to appear bigger.

- **Place your hand on your hips**. This will make you appear wider than you usually are, thus adding to your size.

- **Stand upright**. Straightening your back can add inches to your height.

- **Sit or stand with your legs apart**. This is applicable to men, and like placing your hands on your hips, it also adds to your 'width.'

- **Hold your head and chin up**. Another technique you can use to add to your height.

Stand Higher

When you are standing higher than the other person, you are in a more dominant position giving you a natural advantage. You can do this by:

- Stand while the other party sits. This instantly gives you the height advantage.

- Stand on a platform or step to give you extra height when compared with the other party

- Stand tall and straight. Tiptoe if you must.

- Wear a large hat or wear high heel shoes.

- Style your hair to make you look taller. This is a common practice with women.

Remember, people who make themselves appear larger or bigger aim to be more dominant, threatening, or powerful.

Claiming Territory

Humans are quite territorial, thanks to our ancestral origins and heritage. People shot a lot of territorial signals, and you can use these to predict behavior. When trying to be more dominant, you can do the following nonverbal signals to claim territory:

- Claim a particular area in a conference room, exhibition center, meeting room, or office room and expect other people to comply with the rules you set for that area.

- Invade the personal space of the other person to imply dominance. You can even emphasize the act with a touch like lightly holding the arm or patting the person's back, which indicates ownership. A study showed that a show of affection may not always be the reason when a man touches a woman. Instead, it can be a show of dominance or ownership.

- Invade an area currently owned by the other person. You can sit at the edge of that person's table or on their chair, which is a common gesture of dominance. This move is often used by power-tripping managers or bosses who invade other people's territory to show them who is in charge.

- Touch or hold the other person's possessions. When this gesture is made with a relaxed composure, this implies that you own what they own, which is another indication of domination. You may pick the other person's favorite pen or phone or rearrange their desk. It's like saying, 'what's yours is also mine, and you can't do anything to stop me.'

- Walk in the center of the corridor so that other people stay out of your way. This is a claim to common territory, which implies authority and dominance over others. The same can be observed from some drivers during heavy traffic wherein they don't let other drivers merge into their lane.

- When the meeting room has a long table, sit at one end. This position is usually reserved for someone with a superior role or power. Sitting here emphasizes your dominance over others.

- When talking with a group, position yourself at the center, which forces others to pay attention to what you're discussing. Since your back will be vulnerable, ensure that persons you trust are behind you.

Signaling Superiority

There are various direct or indirect power cues that you can show if you want to appear dominant, particularly in social contexts. You can either plan these signals or improvise when the need arises. These power signals can be a combination of verbal and nonverbal languages. Here are some of the techniques that you can use:

Show of Dominance Through Wealth

- Wear expensive clothes, watch, jewelry, accessories, and makeup. Doing so makes you appear rich, powerful, and well-connected.

- Show off your possessions indirectly. This can be done by paying hefty bills in a relaxed manner, flashing the latest flagship mobile phone, or driving an expensive car.

Show of Dominance Through Control

- Order a staff or team member to bring you something in front of another person. This implies that you are in charge of the area. For example, you can tell someone to bring you a cup of coffee, print a certain report immediately, or have them call another person and bring that person into the meeting room.

- Controlling and giving orders can also be combined with a display of wealth to emphasize importance. For example, call your secretary while in the presence of others and have her book you a business class flight, a five-star hotel with all the bells and whistles, and a chauffeured luxury car. Showing that you can get whatever you want indicates power and dominance, and this is a move usually exhibited by top corporate executives to impress their customers.

Controlling Time

No, you don't need a time machine for this technique. Similar to dominating other people's space, you can control their time as well by setting a pace for them to follow. You can use nonverbal cues to exert time pressure on other people. Here are some verbal and nonverbal techniques you can use:

Interrupt

- Interrupt a discussion by leaving early or arriving late

Hurry Other People

- Set a fast pace for other people to follow

- Walk using wide strides. This implies you're determined a certain goal quickly and that you are confident with your actions. When you're walking with another person, walk a bit faster to set your own pace. This shows who's in charge, and the slower person will be forced to also walk fast in order to keep up.

- Talk faster than usual. This forces others to also talk fast and give you control of their time.

Slow Down Other People

- When talking with another person, interrupt him by asking for a concise and brief talk. This implies you value your time more than his. You can also use this technique when breaking a pace set by another person so you can change the discussion's focus. This may also be effective in counteracting the hurried pace of a dominant person.

Facial Expressions

To show dominance, it's important to extensively use facial expressions to show power and control. Here are some examples.

Avoid Eye Contact

To suggest that someone is not important to you, you can simply avoid looking at them.

Make Prolonged Eye Contact

When you gaze at the other person intensely while proving a point, it implies that you stand by your word, and you're not budging an inch. It also shows dominance, being uncooperative and unwilling, and being strong-minded.

Make a Neutral Face

This can be very useful during negotiations because making this facial expression can be interpreted by the other person that you are unimpressed. When you hold this facial expression while another person is pitching his product or case enthusiastically, it can cause him to buckle or be unnerved. This is often exhibited during academic debates when a domain or subject expert, such as a professor, wants to show dominance by showing that he's not interested in the other person's ideas.

Smile Sparingly

People who want to show dominance smile less often than the submissive ones. Although there's a chance that some people might dislike you, smiling less often shows you mean business and you are in control.

Display Your Crotch (Applies Only to Men)

Of course, you need to have your pants on when you do this move or risk spending the night inside the jail. Stand with your feet shoulder-width apart with both feet firmly planted on the ground. This is called standing crotch display and is a very masculine way of highlighting your genitals to show dominance or superiority. You can emphasize this move by 'adjusting' or lightly 'touching' the crotch area. You can also do this technique sitting down by opening your legs and knees.

It's very uncommon for women to show this gesture because it can be interpreted as an invitation to sexual intimacy, although some may do so as a show of strength and equality with men.

Counteract Dominance

But what if another person in the room is showing dominance using the techniques mentioned above? You can derail their actions by utilizing these nonverbal strategies:

Return the Gaze

If the other person looks you in the eye longer than what you consider normal, look back, and return the gaze. Doing so might get you distracted by their piercing eyes, but there's a way around that. Instead of looking directly into their eyes, imagine a triangle formed by the eyes and forehead and then look at the center of that triangle.

Initiate the First Touch

Just before that person is about to touch you, touch him first. Or retaliate with your own touch when he touched you. This shows that you're not one to mess with or dominate.

Take it Slow

When the dominant person is trying to rush you, breathe slowly, remain calm, and slow down the pace. This can imply that there's no need to hurry. Show that the slower pace you're trying to set is more ideal and be persistent about it. This applies to both walking and talking

Use Humor

A dominant person always aims to take over conversations. Break that dominance by telling a joke and take back control of the conversation. You can get a laugh by telling a joke or using nonverbal funny actions. You can use this break to shift the discussion back to your preferred topic.

Body language can be used to show dominance and influence the action of others. You can also use it to counteract dominance being imposed by others.

Chapter 14: Undetected Mind Control

An innate need for mankind is to feel that we are in total control of our self, believing that we have a safe space inside our mind where we can have private thoughts that are inaccessible to the outside world. Our mind is our sanctuary! Consider the fact that when you are dreaming, you are never in control of what happens. When you are trying to get through that assignment, are you able to control your mind from wandering? Our minds are extremely powerful and able to process completely distinct thoughts in the same moment at an unparalleled speed, but at the same time our thoughts can easily be influenced by external factors.

As is consistent with the dark pattern of predatory behavior of people with active Dark Psychology, the undetected mind controllers also exhibit the desire to influence the prey for their own benefits. Undetected mind controllers are highly logical and are likely to act only after carefully assessing the situation and the state of their victim. However, unlike other manipulators, they tend to be more cowardly. The art of mind control is no easy endeavor to begin with, but trying to keep your motive hidden through the process is like climbing the Himalayas on a cold breezy night. The undetected mind controller has to be patient and cunning and carefully study their target and use all that knowledge about the victim to their own detriment. They are as afraid of being caught in their action as a deer drinking water at the ravine is afraid of being pounced by the tiger lurking in the bushes.

In reference to undetected mind control, we are talking about situations where the victim fails to recognize and acknowledge that their thoughts and feelings are being influenced by the external stimuli presented by the manipulator. This unawareness prevents the victim from defending themselves verbally, physically, and mentally. The victim is unable to exercise control in the situation or even bring his "fight or flight" reflex into action, leaving them highly vulnerable. To be able to put our defenses up in time, our mind needs to be able to detect the threat.

At a very high level, undetected mind control techniques can be categorized into two: interpersonal interactions and the use of mass media. Some research studies have suggested that a handful of dominant institutions are exerting power to affect how you think, act or feel, without us even noticing it. The conventional media mind control tactics were reserved for large companies, but with the advent of modern electronic gadgets and readily accessible internet, media mind control tactics are increasingly used by the dark manipulators.

For those of you who have watched the famous TV show, "Mad Men," you are probably familiar with the 1960's world of advertising on Madison Avenue and, of course, the genius workings of the top ad man, "Don Draper." What if I told you there actually was a "Don Draper" in the real world? In the early 19th century, Edward Betrays, nephew of Sigmund Freud, was deemed as "the father of public relations." Betrays successfully applied the insights he received from his uncle on the subconscious human mind to develop his own methods of mind control, creating the modern day American consumer. Betrays was quick to realize that public opinion, thoughts, attitude, and behaviors could be studied and highly malleable. For example, with the turn of the century and the industrial revolution, cigars could be made by machines. The traditional cigar smoker sought pride in his authentic hand-rolled cigars. So to promote a brand of cigar that was made by machine, Betrays campaigned against the adverse health effects of someone else's spit and distributed 30,000 anti-spit warnings. He changed the focus of the cigar smokers from the authenticity of the cigar to how it was being produced, creating the environment where his product seemed like the natural choice.

Another example of Bernay's genius of controlling the public mind set to benefit his product is the American luggage industry. In the 1920s, the massive decline in luggage sales and increasing preference for small luggage was rather alarming to the luggage industry, so they turned to Bernays to pull them out of the deep end. In response, Bernays sent articles to popular women magazines highlighting the need for women to travel with a versatile wardrobe and appropriate clothing for various activities. He encouraged store owners to display luggage in their windows to establish a link between new clothes and new luggage styles. He even created the "Luggage Information Service" and lobbied to increase the free weight allowance on airplanes. Sounds a lot like the cunning of "Don Dapper," right? In 1934, green became the color of the chic fashion statement. How? Thanks to the ad campaign run by Bernays for the cigarette company called "The Lucky Strikes." Ding, ding, ding…your "Mad Men" recollection is spot on! When George Washington Hill, owner of "Lucky Strikes" refused to change the appearance of the box of his cigarettes from "big red bull's eye on green backdrop" to more neutral colors, that Bernays had suggested would coordinate more with people's clothing, Bernays decided to make the color green fashionable. Few of the tactics he used in his campaign are: encouraging artists and psychologists to discuss the color green; organized a "Color Fashion Bureau"; sent 1500 letters to interior decorators, club women, and home furniture buyers on green letter-headed paper; convinced the President of "Onondaga Silk Company" to have green menus for his lunch event for magazine editors, and to serve green food.

The use of mass media in promoting desires and status symbols plays a pivotal role in our capitalist ecosystem. The human mind has evolved to process visual signals far more powerful than the signals received by any of our other 4 senses. When we remember someone, we quickly visualize their picture rather than associating any other sensory input with them. As they say, "A picture is worth a thousand words." Traditionally, the usage of mass media was confined in the hands of institutions or companies to ethically sway public opinion. However, what has changed is the use of the burgeoning technology of social media by the new generation of mind controllers to penetrate the minds of innocent people, even deeper than what our forebears could deem possible. The contemporary interfaces of our new daily routines are the sound of a new text message on our smartphones and the number of "likes" and "thumbs-up" emoji on our posts or pictures telling us how popular we are. Our mind subconsciously turns on behavioral loops in the presence of these external stimuli, known as "hot triggers." These sources of instant gratification turn us into the rats on a wheel, always wanting to go back for more. Think about it, started in a dorm room, "Facebook" has grown into a multibillion-dollar company with over 1.5 billion active users worldwide.

It's growing public knowledge that the Internet has an underground "Dark Web" where individuals with Dark Psychological Traits are watching the world in search of their prey. The fact that Facebook has been involved in numerous controversies from the 2016 Presidential Election of America, concerning the spread of biased and false rhetoric undermining American democracy is alarming. As a matter of fact, Facebook conducted a research on its mass penetration and influence on the American people by sending a "Go Out & Vote" notifications to over 60 million users on the 2010 Presidential election day. They reported a positive outcome from over 340k who were unlikely to vote without the Facebook reminder. Now, if Facebook selectively sent the notifications to the supporter of a particular party, they could potentially flip the election results without coming under the radar. Another controversial experiment carried out by Facebook was the manipulation of the emotional state of over 600k users by sending them excessive positive or negative words on their new feeds.

The undetected mind control is not restricted to just social media platforms. Most people assume that when they use online search engines like Google, Yahoo or Bing, they are carefully conducting research on a particular topic, but the reality is that 90% of our views are on the top ten links presented to us by the search engine. Sure, Google produces thousands of web pages containing our search phrase, but its underlying algorithm also prioritizes the results for us and influences what most of us will learn about our topic. Psychologist Robert Epstein called this phenomenon the "Search Engine Manipulation Effect." Epstein conducted an experiment to assess whether the "Search Engine Manipulation Effect" could impact how people cast their votes in an election. He asked three groups of Americans to research candidates for an Australian election, using his own mock search engine, served up the same search results to each group but changed the order in which the results were presented. He created a bias for each group to favor one candidate over the other. The results showed a 48% increase in each group for the search engine's "favored" candidate, confirming the validity of the "Search Engine Manipulation Effect." Unethical hackers with dark psychological traits can easily use these web technologies to exert mind control on their prey and never get caught.

An experiment conducted on subliminal influence studies two sets of people, one set was thirsty, and the other was not. Both sets were shown a film with a hidden image of an iced tea. They were then allowed to purchase a drink from the wide selection of beverages. The people from the thirsty set purchased iced tea in greater numbers than statistically expected. This goes to show that when a person's mind is desperate for something, it is more open to suggestions. If a dark mind controller finds a victim yearning for some deep emotional need, the manipulator will have greater ease at controlling their mind. For example, an individual who recently suffered a breakup and is craving company encounters a mind controller, they will easily influence the victim into thinking that they are the victim's savior when, in reality, they are the predator. Some real-life vulnerabilities that dark mind controllers seek in their victims are: their need for financial stability, their need for belonging, and their need for love. The dark mind controller may seek to sexually or financially abuse their victim, gain their allegiance to some form of cult, or simply play with the victim for their own sadistic pleasure. If you ask people if they are familiar with mind control, they will probably tell you that they are indeed familiar with "Brainwashing." In the 1950s, American journalist Edward Hunter had first used the term brainwashing in his report on the treatment of American troops in Chinese prison camps during the "Korean War." More people are aware of brainwashing than mind control, and they mistake their vague familiarity with the concept of brainwashing for accurate understanding. Psychologist Steve Hassan made a key distinction between mind control and brainwashing, stating "In brainwashing, the victim knows that the aggressor is an enemy." For example, prisoners of war often choose to change their belief system, even when they are aware that the brainwashing is behind done by the enemy, as a resort to stay alive. However, when the prisoners are able to escape the enemy, the effects of the brainwashing disappear. Unlike brainwashing, mind control is subtle, and often the manipulator is considered a friend, so the victim never even tries to defend themselves and acts as a "willing" participant. A majority of the Dark Psychology techniques are like sniper bullets and directed at one particular person at a time, whereas brainwashing is like an atomic bomb, capable of causing mass destruction in a second.

Chapter 15: Spotting Romantic Interest

We are going to be taking a look at how to spot romantic interest through the analysis of body language, facial expressions, and other non-verbal clues. Also, we will be making gender-specific analyses as romantic interest varies greatly based on a person's gender.

Spotting romantic interest is one of the most popular topics of all time. Consistently, both men and women are interested in learning more about how they can determine if a person is genuinely attracted to them.

This topic is part science and part art. There is plenty of scientific evidence that backs up the reasoning behind attraction while there is an instinctive component, which cannot be adequately measured or quantified through scientific methods. What this implies is that if you are looking to gauge someone's level of attraction, then you need to have both a scientific approach and reliance on gut feelings.

To start things off, it should be noted that attraction works differently in men than it does in women. While the underlying biochemistry is essentially the same, the physical manifestations are different. In addition, cultural norms may govern romantic interactions to a varying degree.

In that regard, it is worth mentioning that while many of the non-verbal clues are the same, women tend to be a lot more subtle than men are. In contrast, most men tend to be very open about their feelings toward the object of their attraction. While this shouldn't be taken as a blanket statement, it is a general rule of thumb. After all, there are plenty of shy men out there who have trouble making their interest known, while there are plenty of women who are quite overt about their feelings for the object of their interest.

One other note with regard to attraction is that romantic interactions are generally perceived to be between men and women.

That being said, I intend to have this discussion cover the entire spectrum of male and female interaction within a romantic context. That way, the information presented herein will provide you with the insights you need in order to improve your ability to pick up on the non-verbal clues indicating potential romantic interest and attraction.

Now, the first to keep in mind is that attraction is somewhat hard to define. The reason for this is that men and women seek different things in a potential mate. We are operating under the assumption that there is a genuine attraction among those involved and not some hidden agenda spurring interest. In that regard, the attraction is based on the qualities of an individual that meet or exceed the needs of the other. Hence, women tend to focus on different qualities in their potential romantic partner, whereas men tend to focus on a different set of qualities.

For instance, women tend to seek security and stability in a romantic partner. This is due to an instinctive need for survival and preservation of the species. In order to fully comprehend this, we would need to go all the way back to the day of primitive humans in which there was no guarantee that offspring would make it past their first year of life. As such, women, designated as a caregiver from the start, needed to secure the means and resources needed to ensure the survival of their offspring. On the other hand, the males were in charge of playing the role of provider. In the early days of humankind, males were mainly hunter-gatherers. This means that they needed to go into the fray to find food. Whether food came from hunting or foraging, males were expected to provide the sustenance needed to ensure the survival of their offspring.

In contrast, males needed to find healthy females who had the physical qualities that would ensure their fertility and ability to bear children. I know that this sounds very primitive, but it is important to underscore this point as humans we are hardwired under this context. Consequently, thousands of years of evolution and biology are just now being challenged by the new social paradigm in which we find ourselves.

Over the last two hundred years or so, the dating paradigm has shifted dramatically.

Traditionally, most marriages were arranged. As such, it was not so much about love and romance, but about the position and financial stability. This paradigm lasted for a few centuries. Since the outset of the Industrial Revolution, the attitudes of society changed in such a way that men and women were free to choose who they wanted to marry. This opened the door for a number of circumstances.

So, men went from courting women to dating them. This meant that men needed to ensure that a woman would be willing to reciprocate his intentions and feelings. In contrast, women played a more passive role, and they were conditioned to wait for men to make the first move. However, they could drop subtle hints regarding their interest. That way, the man would be certain that he had a chance with a given woman.

In modern times, we are faced with a very liberal dating scene. While some countries have far more cultural and religious restrictions, most countries are fairly open about the manner in which they can pursue the object of their desire.

Consequently, it is imperative that both men and women gain deeper insight as to how attraction is expressed by either gender.

So, let us start off with men.

Men are a lot easier to read, as they tend to be far more overt about their interest in someone. They will generally seek the object of their interest and engage them in some manner. Typically, men will try to engage the other party by displays of strength, wealth, or status. These are signs that they are providers or protectors. In short, men try to position themselves as the best possible mate their object of interest can find. Some general guidelines include direct eye contact, tilting their body toward the person they are attracted to, and seeking constant physical contact. The latter generally tends to make most women uncomfortable, as unsolicited physical contact can get rather awkward quickly.

Other not so subtle hints that men drop are following the object of their affection around, placing their hands or arms as a sign of possession, and frequent fidgeting. In fact, fidgeting is a dead giveaway as it is a sign that a man is nervous in the presence of whom they are attracted to.

In addition, some men might go silent (remember the freeze response?) and even fail to react in the presence of the object of the attraction. This reaction is partially due to the freeze response, but it also due to the fact that some men freeze up when they don't know what to do or how to react.

This is why you see most dating advice that is oriented to men focus on what to do and what to say in various situations. What this does is that it eliminates a man's reliance on his wits by providing him with a set of tools. These tools are certainly useful even if they may not be universally applicable.

One common method used by men is to approach and pull back. This method consists of approaching someone they are attracted to and then pulling away. Then, they will engage and withdraw until they are able to make progress, say, go on a first date. The logic beneath this approach is that men tend to come on very strong when they are attracted to someone. As such, this approach allows them to find a balance between displaying their intentions and giving the object of their attraction some space.

As you can see, men are far more open about their attraction toward someone based on the permissiveness that society has afforded men throughout history. However, women have been traditionally tagged with a more submissive role. Therefore, women are not always able to express their intentions overtly in the same way that men do.

Some not so subtle signs of attraction in women are eye contact, hair pulling, and trailing off in conversation.

When a woman is attracted to a person, she will seek eye contact. This eye contact tends to be rather brief as women are not interested in winning a staring contest. They just want to signal to the object of their interest that they are willing to be engaged.

Another telltale sign of attraction in a woman is related to her hair. If you see a woman playing or pulling on her hair when speaking to someone they like, you can be pretty sure that she is indicating a willingness to be engaged.

Also, women who are interested in a person will allow for closer physical contact. Any time a woman keeps people at arms' length, it is a clear indication that they have no interest in them. By the same token, any time a woman avoids eye contact and tilts their body away from the person she is interacting with, it is safe to assume they are not interested in being engaged.

Women are generally focused on faces. What this means is that when a woman is attracted to someone, they will not only focus on their eyes but also their mouth. They generally tend to watch the other party's lips when they speak. This is an instinctive reaction based on their desire to find a strong and healthy mate. Consequently, healthy-looking eyes, teeth, lips, and skin are clear indicators that a person is in good physical condition.

Women also drop many hints with their arms and hands. A woman who is uninterested will almost always cross her arms and/or legs at some point. If you find that a woman is sitting in the manner on a date, then the other party has a tough time ahead for them.

Conversely, if a woman is actually interested in the other person, she will sit, or stand, in a very "open" position, that is, hands at her sides (or folded on a table) and legs uncrossed. Also, leaning forward while listening to the interlocutor is a good indication that they are interested in what the other person has to say. If they make direct eye contact on various occasions, then the combination of clues is virtually a declaration of intent.

Some women refrain from eye contact when they are genuinely attracted to someone. They may cross gazes but quickly look away or perhaps look down. In some cultures, this is the norm, as it is a sign of submission. Western cultures don't normally have such customs, although women may still prefer to avoid eye contact in order to prevent themselves from being too obvious.

Additionally, women will allow some type of physical contact as a sign of attraction. For instance, they may lightly brush their hand up against another person's, or they may even give the object of their attraction a gentle tap on the shoulder or arm.

While this is, by no means, an invitation for further physical contact, it is a sign that a woman is comfortable and ready to take the interaction to a more personal level. This type of light touching can be reciprocated by similar touching.

Finally, a woman's voice says a lot about the way she feels. Women tend to speak with a higher pitch when they are in the presence of someone they are attracted to. Also, they may raise the tone of their voice in order to be "noticed" by the person they are attracted to. In one on one interactions, don't be surprised if you see a woman speaking somewhat faster. However, if she begins to slow down, then that might very well be a signal that she has lost interest.

Chapter 16: How to Analyze Body Language (Facial Expressions and General Body Language)

Whether at the workplace or out with companions, non-verbal communication techniques of the general population around you say a lot. It has been said that non-verbal communication comprises in excess of sixty percent of what we impart, so figuring out how to peruse nonverbal signals that individuals send is important expertise. From eye behavior to the course in which an individual focuses his or her feet, non-verbal communication uncovers what an individual is truly thinking. The following are important hints to enable you to figure out how to peruse non-verbal communication and better comprehend the people you associate with.

Take a look at the other individual's feet. A piece of the body where individuals frequently 'release' significant nonverbal prompts is the feet. The reason individuals unexpectedly convey nonverbal messages through their feet is that they are typically so centered around controlling their outward appearances and chest area, situating significant pieces of information, which can also be uncovered by means of watching the movement of the feet. When standing or sitting, an individual will point their feet toward the path they want to go. So if you see that somebody's feet are pointed toward you, this can be a decent sign that they have ideal regard for you. This applies to the one-on-one connection and gathering association. Truth be told, you can tell a great deal about a person just by considering the way people communicate non-verbally, especially watching the direction that their feet are pointing. What's more, if somebody gives off an impression of being occupied with discussion with you, but their feet are pointing toward another person, it is presumable that the individual in question would prefer to converse with that individual (if the signs on the chest area recommend something else).

Watch hand signals. Like the feet, the hands release significant nonverbal signals when looking for non-verbal signs. This is a significant hint when perusing non-verbal communication signals, so give close consideration to this. Search for specific hand signals, for example, the other individual putting their hands in their pockets or hand on the head. This can demonstrate anything from anxiety to a goal to mislead. Oblivious pointing used as hand signals can likewise say a lot. When making hand signals, an individual will point in the general direction of the individual whom they like (look for this nonverbal prompt during gatherings and when communicating in gatherings). Supporting the head with the hand by laying an elbow on the table can show that the individual is tuning in and is keeping the head still so as to center. Supporting the head with the two elbows on the table, you can demonstrate again the fatigue At the point when an individual holds an article between the person in question and the individual they are communicating with, this fills in as an obstruction that is intended to shut out the other individual. For instance, if two individuals are talking, and one individual holds a stack of paper before the person in question, this is viewed as a blocking demonstration in nonverbal correspondence.

Look at the face and the movement of the mouth. In spite of the fact that individuals are bound to control their outward appearance, you can now get significant nonverbal prompts if you give close consideration. Give specific consideration to the mouth when attempting to disentangle nonverbal behavior. A straightforward smile as a type of non-verbal communication fascination method can be an amazing motion. Grinning is a significant nonverbal prompt to look for as well. There are various sorts of smiles, including certified smiles and phony smiles. A veritable smile draws in the entire face, while a phony smile just uses the mouth. An authentic smile proposes that the individual is glad. A phony smile, then again, is intended to pass on joy or endorsement, yet proposes that the person smiling is really feeling something different. A 'half-smile' is another normal facial behavior that just draws in a single side of the mouth and demonstrates mockery or vulnerability. You may likewise see a slight frown prior to smiling. This ordinarily proposes that the individual is concealing his or her disappointment behind a phony smile. Tight, pressed lips additionally demonstrate disappointment, while a casual mouth shows a casual disposition and positive mindset. Covering the mouth or contacting the lips with the hands or fingers when talking might be a sign of lying.

Focus on proximity. Proximity is the space between you and the other individual. Focus on how close somebody stands or sits by you to decide whether they see you positively or not. Standing or sitting in closeness to somebody is perhaps the best sign of compatibility. Then again, if somebody backs up or moves away when you move in nearer, this could be an indication that the association isn't common. You can tell a ton about the sort of relationship that two individuals have simply by watching the proximity between them. Remember that a few people incline toward less or more separation during association, so proximity isn't generally a good signal of approval or disapproval.

Check the movement of the eyes. Eye behavior can also be telling. When speaking with somebody, focus on whether the person looks or turns away. Powerlessness in the eyes can show weariness, lack of engagement, or even duplicity, particularly when somebody turns away. In the event that an individual looks down, it usually shows apprehension or accommodation. Likewise, check for enlarged pupils to decide whether somebody is reacting positively toward you. Pupils become large when subjective exertion increments, so if somebody is centered on a person or something they like, their pupils will naturally expand. Pupil expansion can be hard to distinguish, but under the correct conditions, you ought to have the opportunity to spot it. An individual's flickering rate can likewise say a lot about what is happening inside.

The rate by which the eyes open and close increases when individuals are thinking more or are pushed to think fast. Now and again, expanded 'flickering' rate shows lying, particularly when joined by contacting the face (especially the mouth and eyes). Looking at something can propose a longing for that thing. For instance, in the event that somebody looks at the door, this may demonstrate a longing to leave. Looking at an individual can demonstrate a craving to converse with the person in question. With regard to eye behavior, it is additionally proposed that looking upward and to one side during a discussion demonstrates that a lie has been told while looking upward and to one side shows that the individual is telling the truth. The purpose behind this is that the individual turn upward and to one side when utilizing their creative mind to come up with a story, and they gaze upward and to one side when they are rereading a genuine memory.

Check if the other individual is copying you. Reflecting includes mirroring the other individual's non-verbal signs. When cooperating with somebody, check whether the individual mirrors your behavior or not. For instance, if you are sitting at a table with somebody and you lay an elbow on the table, wait up 10 seconds to check whether the other individual does likewise. Another basic reflecting signal includes sipping the beverage simultaneously. If somebody imitates your non-verbal communication, this is a generally excellent sign that the person is attempting to set up an affinity with you. Take a stab at changing your body stance, and check whether the other individual changes theirs likewise.

Look at the position of the arms. If an individual folds their arms while cooperating with you, it is normally observed as a cautious, blocking signal. Crossed arms can likewise show uneasiness, defenselessness, or a closed mind. Whenever crossed arms are joined by a certifiable smile and loosened up stance, at that point, it can demonstrate a certain, casual frame of mind. When somebody puts their hands on their hips, it is ordinarily used to apply dominance and is utilized by men more regularly than women. These tips can give you knowledge into the genuine intentions behind an individual's behavior; however, it is not exactly idiot-proof. When dissecting non-verbal communication, remember that these methods will not work for all individuals constantly. Certain elements, for example, culture and an individual's general non-verbal communication propensities, must be mulled over to precisely interpret nonverbal signals.

Watch the movement of the head. The speed at which an individual gestures their head when you are talking demonstrates their understanding—or absence thereof. Moderate gesturing shows that the individual is keen on what you are stating and needs you to keep talking. Quick gesturing shows the individual has heard enough and needs you to get done with talking or give that person a chance to talk.

Tilting the head sideways during a discussion can be an indication of enthusiasm for what the other individual is saying. Tilting the head in reverse can be an indication of doubt or vulnerability. Individuals, likewise, point with the head or face at individuals they are keen to share a bond with. In gatherings, for instance, you can tell who is a person of charm or power. Perhaps it depends on how regularly individuals take a glance at them. Then again, the less noteworthy individuals do not receive glances as frequently as the others.

Chapter 17: Matching Body Language

It is not uncommon for us to match the same body language as those that we might be talking to. Sometimes it happens naturally without even thinking about it. How often have you found that you picked up on the smaller habits that other people have? Maybe they have a certain catchphrase or laugh in a specific way. Sometimes we just do this naturally, but look out for people who do this quickly or in a way that makes you feel a little suspicious. If someone is already saying your catchphrases after just a few hours of hanging out, then they might be intentionally trying to match your body language or behavior.

A manipulator is going to use this tactic, and they are going to take it way over the top. If you turn your head to the side while talking, they might turn theirs as well. If you take a sip of your water, so might they. If you get up and move around, they might as well.

It will be natural for others to want to turn themselves toward you so they can better hear the things you have to say. However, if their body language is constantly mimicking yours, then be careful about whether or not they're trying to manipulate you.

This is because they want you to feel more open with them. They want to make you feel as though the two of you can share everything together. This is an attempt to be more relatable. If you really want to see whether or not they are being vindictive or doing it intentionally, start to change your body language. If they are matching and mimicking everything that you do, then it will be easier to notice this tactic in others.

Frequent Staring

Those that aren't fully listening to you will try to overly stare. Rather than actually engaging with what you're saying and staring at you to get a better comprehension of what you're saying, some manipulators will instead try to convince you that they're listening. They might be planning what they are going to say, especially if you are in the middle of an argument. Then, rather than actually taking in what you are saying, they will think to themselves, "Keep eye contact to let them know you're engaged."

Sometimes this staring is even a way to intimidate you. They might use their glare to make sure that you know that they're watching you. They might overly emphasize that they are looking at you and actually turn their entire body in order to direct it right at you. This is a method that they can then use in order to make you feel like they have more power over you.

They might make a face with their eyes but then tell you that you are crazy if you call them out for it. Manipulators are really good at keeping their brow straight in order to give you a direct glare. They will squint their eyes or make a grimacing face. If you ask something like, "What's wrong? Why are you making that face," they will reply with something like, "This is just my face." They will find a way to act as though they aren't giving you a weird look in order to make it seem as though you are misinterpreting the scenario and thinking too deeply about something that isn't true.

They will often be thinking about what to say rather than actually listening to the things that you are sharing. All of these methods are easily picked up on if you start to really look at the way that they are looking at you. Either too much or not enough eye contact could be a sign that they're not fully engaged. Some people really have trouble making eye contact, and others will be anxiously thinking in their head, so they might try harder to make eye contact. Just look out for shady eyes and shifty patterns that might indicate they are attempting to gain control over you.

Quick Talking and Hand Movements

Manipulators will make sure that they talk with their hands and as fast as they can. These are two methods that you will frequently notice if someone is trying to convince you to do something. This is an especially common tactic if they want to convince you of something that will clearly be harder to push you over the edge on. They will want to urge you to agree because they know if you're given too long to decide, you will easily spot the weak points in the plan.

They'll talk fast so that you will not even be able to pick up on all the little things they might be saying. They might want to slip something in that you don't notice, but they still state it so that you can't say that they didn't warn you afterward. Think of the last commercial that you watched for a medication. They'll start saying all of the amazing benefits that their products provide, but then they will also slip in the warnings and side effects at the end of the commercial. The beginning will include dramatizations or "customer" interviews selling the medicine for you with pretty pictures and grand promises. After they've done this, the commercial ends with a speed talker stating scary things like, "This medicine may cause internal bleeding, bone loss, skin lesions, random hair growth, and could make your current side effects even worse." Make sure to always listen to all the fast talk you hear because you never know what scary warnings might be hidden within them. Manipulators will also try to overstate their point by using hand movements. This is something that you will see with a lot of salespeople or those who are at least trying to be persuasive in minor negative ways. They will really talk up their point and try to prove what they're stating using grand gestures and wide or rapid hand movements. It's almost like they are the conductor of an orchestra trying to make sure that everyone is following their lead. This isn't as bad of a tactic because some people will just be more vivid storytellers who overdo the hand gestures. Just be cautious of this method, especially when in a position where someone is trying to sell you a product or service.

Chapter 18: NLP Secrets and Reading Body Language

NLP stands for neuro-linguistic programming. While many have heard of it, they cannot explain just what it is. The good news is that there is always a time to know—and that time is now. Read on below as we let you in on what NLP is and the connection to body language. We will also let you know how you can read body language to help you understand what an individual does think.

What Is Neuro-Linguistic Programming Therapy?

NLP is used as an approach to personal development, psychotherapy, and even communication. The concept is the brainchild of two people; John Grinder and Richard Bandler in the 1970s. John Grinder was a linguist, and Bandler was a mathematician and information scientist. Other people who contributed to the concept were Leslie Cameron Bandler, Judith DeLozier, David Gordon, and Robert Dilts. The name neurolinguistic means that as the creators of the concept believe there is a connection between neurological processes, language, and behavior patterns that are learned through experience. They believe that programming can be changed to achieve some goals in life. Grinder and Bandler say that the NLP technique can model the behavior and skills of an exceptional person. This technique may also appeal to you if you have phobias, tic disorders, depression, allergy, near-sightedness, learning disorders, and psychosomatic illnesses. There was a growing interest in this approach towards the end of the 70s because the two authors started marketing it as a tool that could help individuals achieve success. It is no wonder that NLP has been adopted by hypnotherapists and companies that use leadership training as a tool for improving business and government agencies. To this end, it is used in fields including but not limited to medicine, law, counseling, business, sports, performing arts, military, and education. As such, this concept incorporates sensory and language-based interventions together with behavior modification techniques to help improve the communication skills, confidence, and self-awareness of an individual. The belief is that one individual, usually the therapist, can understand the way another accomplishes a task and so help them copy and communicate this information to others so that they can accomplish a given task as well. The goals of NLP are, therefore, to help the client understand their views of the world and how it affects how they operate and lets them know that it is necessary to change behavior patterns and thoughts for better outcomes. The concept is meant to help change patterns that have proven not beneficial in the past.

Core Concepts and Components of the NLP Technique

In NLP, there are three main components and central components crucial for its understanding. They include:

Subjectivity

Grinder and Bandler suppose that the world is experienced subjectively by us, therefore, it follows that humans create a subjective representation for each experience that they have. The experiences are constituted in the five senses that we have and in language. Our conscious experience is, therefore, in terms of smell, touch, sight, taste, and hearing when we think about an activity that we will carry out in the future, we anticipate what it will feel like and the tastes, sounds, and flavors that we will experience. The theory further claims that these subjective representations come in a discernible pattern/structure. As such, euro-linguistic programming is usually described as the study of subjective experience's structure. The behavior of a person can be understood and described based on these sense-based subjective representations. Behavior can either be verbal or nonverbal, adaptive or maladaptive, competent or incompetent, and skillful or ineffective. Your behavior and that of others can be modified. Consciousness Neuro-linguistic programming is founded on the knowledge that consciousness as a component is divided into the conscious and unconscious. Sometimes, subjective representations occur outside of the individual's awareness and comprise what we refer to as the unconscious mind.

Learning

Neuro-linguistic programming utilizes modeling, which is an imitative learning method. Modeling is the method through which a person's experiences can be codified and reproduced in any domain of activity. An essential part of the coding process is describing the sequence of the linguistic and sensory representations of the subjective experience of the example during execution.

When Is the Neuro-Linguistic Programming Therapy Used, and What Should You Expect?

Neuro-linguistic therapy has been used to treat adverse psychological issues, as outlined above. It is used as a tool against most of these issues as they tend to reduce the overall quality of life. If you are reading this far, then it is only fair to know what to expect when neuro-linguistic programming comes into play. Below we outline some of the techniques used in NLP therapy:

Visualization: forming a mental image of something through the help of the therapist

Visual kinesthetic dissociation: being guided by the therapist so that the client can revisit the past traumatic events so that the victim can live out the experience from afar, in an imaginative out-of-body manner.

Using these techniques, the therapist can tap into his patient's past and correct faulty language that results in faulty communication and negative thinking. These techniques can be employed both in the short and long-term, depending on the extent of the problem being solved and who the victim is. The assumption here is that all human action is positive. As such, if a plan does not go through, and when the unexpected happens, there is no good or bad side. However, this experience can be a source of useful information that can be used to understand life. Through the use of neuro-linguistic programming techniques, the therapist helps the client understand his own minds and how they came to the present state in which they operate-how they communicate, think, and behave.

Sets of Practices in Neuro-Linguistic Programming

An interaction in the neuro-linguistic programming can be understood as a series of stages that include establishment of a rapport, gleaning of information about a problem, the mental state and the goals desired by the person, then using specific techniques and tools to make interventions, and finally, integrating these proposed solutions into the life of a client. This entire process is usually guided by the client's non-verbal responses.

Establishing and maintaining rapport is done through activities such as pacing and leading the verbal, for instance, through keywords and sensory predicates ad through non-verbal behavior, for example, matching the non-verbal behavior and responding to the client's eye movements.

The gathering of information happens after rapport is established. At this stage, the practitioner gathers information from the client through the use of meta-model questions. These questions are meant to reveal much about the client's desired goal during the interaction, which comes right after the description of his current state.

Particular attention is paid to the responses of the client's verbal and non-verbal cues when he/she defines their present and desired states and the resources that they may need to bridge the gap. During this time, the practitioner encourages them to consider what the consequences of the desired outcome would be and how these consequences may be of effect to his relationships, personal or professional life. They take an ecological check of any problems that may arise. An ecological check is virtually positive intentions that arise from a problem.

The fourth stage involves the practitioner assisting the client to achieve the outcomes they desire by using some tools and techniques that will change internal representations of the stimuli they find in the real world into their lives. At this stage, the practitioner may, for instance, require that the client steps into the future and describe or represent through the senses what they feel like after achieving the desired outcome.

How the Technique Works

The key elements in neuro-linguistic programming include modeling, action, and effective communication. To the believers in the model, everyone has a personal map of what they would consider reality. As such, a person that practices NLP analyses their own perspective together with the perspectives of others to create what is considered a systematic overview of just one situation. By understanding different perspectives, a user of the neuro-linguistic programming technique gains information. It is believed that the senses play a vital role in information processing as well. Hence, the body and mind have an influence on each other. This approach is experiential. So if a person wants to understand an action, he must engage in it so that it transforms into an experience that they can learn from. According to NLP adherents, there are hierarchies of learning, change, and communication. The levels of change are outlined below:

Purpose and spirituality: This is where one feels that they can be involved in something larger than themselves. This can be ethics, religion, and other systems. This level represents the highest in change.

Identity: This is the person you perceive yourself to be. The scope of identity is large and may include the roles and responsibilities that you play in life.

Values and beliefs: This level includes the things that matter to you and what you believe in.

Skills and capabilities: This level encompasses all you can do and the abilities you have.

Behaviors: these are the specific actions that you perform.

Environment: The environment is the lowest level of change and includes you, the people around you, and the context or setting.

The purpose of each of these logical levels is the organization and direction of the information that falls just below it.

As such, when you make changes in the lower level, it may trigger changes in the higher levels. Making changes in the higher levels will also often cause changes in lower levels.

NLP in Therapy

In therapy, NLP holds that reality and belief are usually different. As such, as a person, you operate and see things from your own perspective rather than from objectivity. As such, the beliefs of everyone in the world are limited, distorted, unique, or a mixture of both. Therefore, if a therapist is supposed to treat a patient, then they have to understand the map perception of the individual they are dealing with as this perception may have a bearing on how the person views the world.

The individual's map of perception shall then be formed through the data received through their senses. Senses include sight, touch, smell, and taste, and as such, information can come in through any of the senses. The difference in information occurs on the basis of quality and importance, and each person receives their information through a primary representational system. For the therapy to be successful, the therapist must try to match the patient's primary representational system so that they can use their map to help them navigate a situation. Neuro-linguistic programming practitioners believe that you can access the primary representational system using cues such as eye movements. By doing such, they are able to understand the thinking and behavioral patterns of these individuals.

Supporters of this approach claim that it produces fast and long-lasting results that are effective at improving understanding of behavioral and cognitive patterns.

Applications of the Neuro-Linguistic Programming Technique in Today's World

Neuro-linguistic programming has come a long way since the 1970s. Today, it is applied in a wide array of fields and in different ways. Below we explore a way in which NLP is applied:

In alternative medicine: Alternative medicine is an evergreen field that integrates various techniques to ensure positive outcomes for clients. Over time, NLP has been used as a tool in alternative medicine that can be used in the treatment of diseases such as Parkinson's and even cancer.

Chapter 19: Finding the Pressure Button and using it to Your Advantage

Everybody has a weakness or something that they struggled with, and the moment you are able to gain knowledge of that weakness, if you apply it correctly, you can use it to your advantage. For me, my weakness was anger. I have always been very open about my struggle with anger issues, and that is the reason why I am more than happy to share those experiences. While I am not particularly proud of the mistakes I made in my past, I would say that I am humbled and excited by the progress I have recorded on my journey so far. When I found this quote by Ethel, it resonated deeply with me for many reasons, one of them being the fact that I had experienced this first-hand during my early years. Or should I say, during the years that I struggled with anger at my workplace, I think I had issues with everyone except this particular guy. It was hard to pinpoint what it was about him that made it difficult for me to relate with him on the same level that I did with everyone else. Even my bosses or people that are considered superior to me at work were not exempted from my treatment. But for some reason, this guy (and I am going to call him Charles) seemed to be immune to my anger. It was almost impossible for me to be angry at him. It wasn't a deliberate effort on my part. It certainly wasn't like I consciously try to avoid being angry at him. It was just that he knew something about me that he used to his advantage. And that thing was a phrase. When I think about it now, it is ridiculous. Because it was just a silly word that would act like a deflator. Picture a balloon that has been pumped full with air. This balloon represents me at my worst. Now, picture the pointy end of a needle. This medal represents that phrase. Using the needle on this balloon was how that particular phrase was to my anger. And Charles knew that phrase. So, when we are having a heated conversation, and he notices that my temper is about to flare, he uses that phrase, and all of a sudden, the air goes out of me. I find myself giggling and unsure as to why I was even getting angry in the first place.

Finding a person's special button kind of works like this. Of course, there is the flip side to it. There are buttons that you press that send people over the edge, and so you refrain from pushing those buttons. But I think using the knowledge that you have in this manner is cruel. However, in a relationship, when you are trying to work things out to your advantage, it is important to know those triggers that can get you what you want without adversely affecting the other person. Communication is a two-way street and therefore it is not all about you. And in the following few steps, we are going to look at how are you can find a person's pressure button, and more importantly, you will be provided with an understanding of how to use that knowledge to your advantage.

1. Be Observant

Short of asking a person out rightly what their weaknesses are, there are ways you can gain access to that information without waiting for a response from them. And being observant is top on that list. People give clues to their inner struggles with their actions. No matter how closed a person is, if you pay attention, you would notice certain elements that reveal who they are. I would recommend directing your efforts towards observing what they do when they think that no one is watching. In FBI profiling, they have something that they call a cluster of gestures. Pay attention to these little activities that are carried out in a sequence or series. They may appear to be unimportant, but the odds are high that in those kinds of details, you would find the clue that you are looking for.

2. Establish a Baseline and Look Out for Deviations

A lot of people are creatures of habit. No matter how adventurous or spontaneous a person says they are, in certain areas of their lives, if you observe closely, you will find that there are patterns of behavior that have been established over the years. This is what you would call your baseline. For your colleague at work, you look out for the times that they are coming into work or when they go out to eat. Now please note that in the course of trying to establish a baseline, you should avoid behaviors or activities that make it seem as though you are stalking this person. The goal here is to simply try to establish what their routine is. You don't have to follow them all around or especially outside the zone where you relate with them. Just observe how they do certain things. When you feel like you have enough information that can enable you to predict their routines, look out for deviations from those routines. Those deviations are you clues to their weaknesses. People don't give up things that they have consciously or subconsciously worked on over the years for nothing. It is usually for something that is important to them, and this thing could be the weakness.

3. Look at Their Areas of Inadequacy

A person may successfully create an image that makes them seem as if they are perfect. If you fail to observe closely, you would buy into the story that they are trying to sell. Admittedly, some people are very gifted at hiding their true emotions and experiences. One way to clue in on what their weaknesses are is by discovering their areas of inadequacies. You can also redirect your focus to discovering what their fears are. We know that no matter how tough you are on the outside, there is just that one thing (or many things) that can reduce you into a mumbling blob because of fear. Your fears are your weaknesses, and since we are on the hunt for those things, discovering people's fears can also help you discover whatever their weaknesses are. Now that we have figured out 3 non-threatening ways to discover what the weaknesses of other people are. It is time to look into how you can apply the knowledge that you have gotten because it is possible to abuse the knowledge. Remember that knowledge is power, and with power comes the responsibility of ensuring that you are not controlled by it. That said, it is important to prepare yourself in order to be a person who is responsible with the information. Knowing a person's weakness in a certain way gives you power over them. But you have to understand how not to abuse that power.

4. Be Direct About it

I feel like this is the best way to go about it because, this way, you are now setting the person aside to have a direct conversation with them about your discoveries. This will open up the line of communications and clear out any general misconceptions you may have about the person at the same time. If you are able to get the tone right, you could end up strengthening the bond in that relationship. However, in your decision to be direct, you have to learn to apply tact as certain issues may be too sensitive to just approach with brutal honesty. Be delicate when you are discussing certain subjects, especially when it has to do with a person's weakness. You should try to exude empathy and genuine concern if you are going to go this route. Because anything less basically puts you in that ugly blackmail category. When people feel as though you sympathize with where they are coming from, they are more likely to give in to your demands. Hostility and brutal honesty, on the other hand, will only earn you a slammed door in your face. This method is about knowing their weakness, understanding where they are coming from, and then confronting them with this weakness without being mean or hostile. If you are able to maintain this balance, you would earn their trust, respect, and in the long run, their confidence. This benefits you very much in that relationship.

5. Put Them in an Environment Where They Can Thrive

As you will come to learn shortly, your weaknesses do not have to define you, and this also applies to the people that you have in your circle. When you are able to discover their weaknesses, the following step is to turn it around for your own benefit. All you need to do is plant them in places where those weaknesses can be nurtured and groomed into becoming strengths. This is particularly applicable if you are in a work setting where you have to work together with people as a team. When a member of your team has a weakness, it reflects on every other person. And to identify that weakness is one thing, to spin it around you as an advantage is another matter entirely. My recommendation is to ensure that you give them tasks where their weaknesses may not be utilized, however, it can be channeled for the greater good of the team.

A person's weakness does not have to be the red flag that sends them into outcast territory. You can manage this information and leverage the knowledge by ensuring that the person gets the help that they need. In addition to this, you can also work towards providing the resources needed to ensure that they are able to build on those weaknesses. If you are able to help another person achieve this feat, there is a very strong possibility that you can earn their loyalty. This kind of loyalty is often given for life.

6. Fill Their Emotional Need

With the knowledge you have gained, you can now fill the gaps that you have discovered to be missing in their lives. The only problem I see with going this route is the fact that you may have to bear certain responsibilities, and if you are not ready for that, you shouldn't attempt to fill that role. Filling the emotional need of a person strategically positions you in a place of trust. When a person trusts you, you are in a unique position to influence their decisions. Now, if you decide to fill that role as I said earlier, you are going to have to play certain roles. For instance, a person with an absentee father might be looking for a masculine input when they get into the adult years. If this is the kind of weakness you discovered, you may have to take on a more masculine role in order to fill that emotional gap.

The obvious fact is, as long as you are clear on the goals for the relationship and you understand that both parties deserve the joys and benefits of being in a relationship where communication is clear and consistent, the effort you take into ensuring that this happens is justified. Whichever way you choose to look at it, communication is about understanding and expression. From understanding, you are able to find expression.

Chapter 20: Influence and Leading without Authority

This is the capacity of having others follow you minus any form of power. It is the way you influence people; it does not matter if you are at a place of authority or not. To lead in other terms or words can be used to mean influence. To lead in many occasions has been used interchangeably with influencing. In this context, we could just have an overview of the situation where one is obligated to lead without any form of authority or power. There are questions that one may come up with because in typical circumstances, whenever a leader is chosen or appointed or elected, there must be a set of rules and regulations which govern his way of leadership.

In a country, we can talk about the constitution that hs been laid down to help leaders in their governance. However, whenever rules are set in any given institution, they must be followed strictly, and also they must be ell explained to the members of that organization whatsoever to avoid conflicts of interest. On the other hand, there are situations where you can be assigned the role of leadership, yet no principles to govern your leadership strategy.

Tactics to Influence Without Authority

1. Creation of a Mutual Setting

By creating an environment that is more collaborative than stand-alone, mean that you need to act on some aspects. You need to leave the sense of self at the doorway. In this, we mean that sometimes people or leaders would always want their subjects to know their nature of the operation and how strict or tough or time-bound they are. However, that only happens in an environment where there is room to exercise power or authority. Many are times where you could hear leaders saying statements like, "they must know who I am today!" such sentiments only apply where there are traces of authority given to its leaders.

But in this format, you need to be selfless for you to be effective.

Again, passion is very crucial. You need to have passion for whatever you are doing. You need to have an interest in the people you are, leading. When you have a passion for them, I mean that you will definitely love them and like what they are doing. In the long run, they will also love you You need to come up with a single form of authority. Not everyone under you should exercise authority. You could instead come up with a specific unique structure which will help you in your governance.

2. Preparedness

You must be able to define your audience in advance. This helps you have courage in your roles as a leader. It takes away the fear because you will have gotten used to the people you are leading.

In the same way, you need to devise answers to the underlying questions within the setup. This helps eliminate unnecessary doubts from within the multitudes, hence paving the way for your effective leadership. It is imperative to plan ahead of time. Things may become very challenging if you do not plan for them ahead of time. This helps solve the puzzle of time wastage and also alleviating the inevitable as they come up. Else if you do not organize yourself very well, you risk failing.

3. Be a Facilitator

You need to be a team leader who is as well a team player. This motivates the audience to follow the trends and gives them courage in what they are doing as well as confidence.

Whenever you facilitate the exercises, you will be motivating them and also communicating with them in a manner they feel appreciated and loved. However, you shouldn't overreact to events. This will lead to overinvestment in you in terms of outcomes. They will tend to rely on your ability for every result they get. They will tend to imagine that all results were influenced by you and, as such, heavily rely upon your input for their performance.

How to Criticize Without Being Hated

Feedback in any organization is vital and must be there for systems to work perfectly well. Employees need to receive feedback regularly as far as their jobs are concerned. And more especially, as far as their overall performance is concerned. It has been a trend in many organizations to relay the criticisms or feedback to employees in a more formal way every time it arises. However, sometimes, this may not work depending on the nature of the feedback. In a recent survey as indicated on the Harvard Business Assessment blog, in one of the postings, it was noted that some employees would opt to get their feedback, however negative they are, in a more constructive criticism way rather than very positive feedback. This is associated with their belief that it would improve their job performance. We have found out that most people do not like receiving negative feedback; however, negative feedback is important as long as it is packaged and delivered well. It is good for improvement.

a) **Feedback should be given on the basis of real behavior, not imaginary stories**. When giving feedback, constructive feedback is based on actual facts and figures, not general assumptions of how a person perceives the other. For example, if an employee is deemed to be underperforming, as a leader, you need to point out the exact causes leading to underperformance like late submission of reports, and not allegations like you are very lazy.

b) **Avoid beating about the bush**. Good leaders will always precise, specific, and straight to the point. This drives the point home easily; else, the employee may become confused and fail to understand your objective. The employee may feel that you were too personal with him.

c) **Suggest relevant examples and possible alternative ways of improvement**. If the employee knows where he erred, he should be given as well possible remedies to the same. It motivates him most.

d) **Tone**. While passing the information concerning the negative feedback, learn to use a proper tone that does not mean to harm.

Even though the boss is very annoyed with the employee's performance, he needs to use a socially receptive tone that seems friendly to the employee in question. This will help alleviate the problem than molding it.

e) **Identify the proper timing of the real event. Timing is very important.** Constructive criticism can yield good fruits if delivered at the right time as far as the recipient is concerned. The managers should not as well delay so much in issuing out the constructive criticisms, for they will tend to forget the basics and hence embark on another objective making the whole exercise unfriendly.

f) **Medium of communication.** Managers need to embrace the so tempting face to face conversations. As tempting as it could be, it still carries the day. The employees will be so encouraged that they will also be given room for explanation. Continuously, in turn, builds confidence in the employee towards his bosses as opposed to a very frustrating and embarrassing phone call or email.

Different Types of Influences

There are different types of influences that can be used to achieve the same results as above. We will look at each one of them briefly in the text format.

i. Positional Influence

Positional influence is very key in delivering constructive feedback to the organization. As the top boss or the CEO of a company, you need to act as the role model to the workers. Assume you are the one in that position of your worker. Handle the worker as your equal but not in a light manner. Be user-friendly. Let the employees know that you are aware of the performance positions of every employee and that you are concerned with their well-being. Do not be so harsh or react in a manner that depicts that you are the overall decision-maker

ii. Expertise Influence

Whenever you have that level of expertise, it is good to assume that not all employees have a similar experience. Handle the cases in a more professional way.

Correct practically as if you are teaching them for the first time. They will want to associate with the person who has some expertise in the right field for the term to be challenged.

iii. Resources Influence

Use the available resources to pass the communication to the employees. Resources are vital because if you use the resource influence to take constructive criticism, then it is easier for the employee to grasp the content and become more resourceful to the company.

iv. Informational Influence

If you have access to various types of information within the organization, it is perfect to merge this information as relates specific issue or person for better results. Knowledge is power. Always when trying to pass information, use the right means, and always aim at resolving conflicts.

v. Direct Influence

If you have a direct link with the employees, be sure what you relay to them. If you are involved directly in what they do, you should act as a guide to them and not as a supervisor. They will want to listen to you much when being guided, as opposed to when being criticized.

vi. Relationship Influence

A relationship is significant to any organization. It determines how good you can work with one another. Whenever you create a good relationship with the employees, they can be so willing to associate with you, and as such, it is easier to rely a message on them, whether good or bad depending on the nature of communication.

Chapter 21: Kinesics

Kinesics is a fancy psychological name for body language and defined as the study of gestures and facial expressions. We cannot effectively read people without a basic understanding of Kinesics (studying gestures and facial expressions). The Kinesics theory states that 'gesture, movement, and expression are all part of communication.' They can express intent and meaning. Kinesics is still a budding science, and you won't suddenly become a wily human reader by merely studying it. However, you will begin to read, interpret, and understand people by being attentive to specific signals like body posture.

The Basics of Kinesics

Kinesics, or Body language as it's called, has been divided into five classes, namely, Emblems, Illustrators, Affect Displays, Regulators, and Adaptors. We will learn about each of them in turn.

Emblems

Emblems are signs that are 'solid' and have an established meaning in a specific context/culture. For example, a thumbs-up gesture is interpreted to communicate 'approval, 'satisfaction' while a thumbs-down sends a 'rejection' or 'failure' signal. Note that Emblems are culture-sensitive, and different territories may have different meanings for the same emblem.

A group of people may have signs that are specific to them. It is typical for a gang or a squad to develop signals as a salutation gesture or to identify those who are part of the group. You likely had one of such emblems as a child. It is not unusual for School children to pass 'secret messages' to one another during lectures without attracting the attention of the teacher.

Illustrators

Illustrators are movements or gestures that help to express and overstress what a person is saying. Illustrators are utilized when we are trying to describe something, like moving our hands to illustrate direction, shape, or size. It includes pointing. Emblems are usually consciously controlled than Illustrators. When a person makes demonstrations with Illustrators, it could mean that the person is highly engaged, even though they are not so conscious of their actions.

On the other hand, if a person isn't displaying any Illustrator, it could mean they are not enjoying the conversation, or they are not engaged in the discussion. However, Illustrators may not convey our real intention. When we say something but feel or think differently, the use of illustrators may betray us, because they can send the wrong signal. If I say something is small and illustrate that it is big, or say 'turn to the right' but point my fingers towards the left, I present two opposing layers of information. Any contradiction between our speech and our demonstrated illustrator may give an impression of dishonesty. A very common illustrator is a chopping motion (one palm landing in the other open palm perpendicularly as if one is chopping vegetables). It demonstrates forcefulness and assertiveness. If a person displays this illustrator, they often believe strongly in what they are discussing. It could also mean they are aggressive or have a desire to be.

Placing a palm over your heart is another illustrator. It conveys an 'I am very emotional' kind of message or that what you are listening to or saying is heartfelt. However, it may also come across as sarcasm, especially when making an apology. It is essential to understand the messages each illustrator portrays since they are unconscious acts – you may send out signals you had no intention to give and turn people off.

There are so many examples of illustrators, too many to be covered in a manuscript. Nevertheless, try to start identifying them everywhere you go and see whether you habitually display them (or if the people around you do).

Lastly, please note that illustrator should be used moderately — a person who gestures perceived as 'impulsive' and one who has no control over his acts.

Affect Displays

In the world of psychology, affect is used to mean emotions. Thus, change displays are gestures with the sole intent of projecting a specific feeling: be it happiness, anger, fear, sadness, etc. Emotions are shown through our faces. Therefore, most affect displays are facial expressions. They come naturally and are rather spontaneous. Generally speaking, most gestures have feelings attached to them; it all depends on the contexts in which they appear. Affect displays include hand gestures that have the principal purpose of revealing a particular emotion (they are different from illustrators)

One typical example of affect display is slow or fast rubbing of hands. The slow rubbing of hands can be associated with expectancy and self-gain, usually at the expense of other people. He probably is planning to overthrow a king or dominate the world, whatever it is, he is most likely not up to any good. This gesture may be a warning sign that a person isn't truthful, especially when it happens during negotiation. On the other hand, fast rubbing shows anticipation and excitement. The person anticipates that something good is about to happen.

Rolling up the sleeves is another example of Affect Displays. It is an action that shows that the hands are ready to work – it could fight, to do some manual labor, or make a presentation. It passes a message of 'confidence,' 'hard work' and 'readiness to swing into action.'

Another example of Affect Displays is 'shaking fists.' A fist is a natural weapon against our opponents. The act of holding and shaking the fist while speaking denotes 'Anger' and 'Aggression.' It can also be used to show conviction and determination in achieving your goal.

Affect Displays are quite hard to handle because they are spontaneous actions. However, it is vital to learn how portrayed and how to respond to them.

Regulators

Regulators are non-verbal gestures that help control/moderate the flow of a conversation. Shaking one's head or nodding, for example, communicates disagreement or agreement, which allows the other members of a conversation to know what to say. Other regulators may include raising a finger (to denote 'silence please') or just walking out of a conversation (or starting to walk out).

When a conversation lacks regulators, people begin to interrupt each other, trying to overtake the conversation. It always ends in catastrophe. If you regularly interrupt other people, it could mean that you are not paying attention to the regulators other people are making.

If you receive a signal that the other person in a conversation is becoming impatient, then it's probably time to stop talking. Such messages communicated through gestures are like shuffling the body or fidgeting. It may also include leaning forward or sitting with mouth open (as if one is getting ready to speak). Illustrators or emblems are regulators.

Likewise, if people seem uninterested or disengaged from the conversation, it could mean that you are not giving them sufficient room to contribute. Generally, it is safe to prompt other people to speak, and you listen, especially if you suspect that your speech may inhibit the conversation through the non-recognition of regulators.

Adaptors

Adaptors are habits employed by people at low levels of self-awareness, which may demonstrate how they feel at the moment. These movements include biting your lip, pulling at your hair, fidgeting with stationary, bouncing on chairs, scratching at itches, etc. These actions are not borne out of a conscious desire to act, and they are habitual responses. Adaptors are fascinating because they do not have an intentional meaning, triggered by stress or anxiety. We develop adaptors in our early years, and it can be displayed many times when we feel more anxious. Since they are dependent on Environmental factors, adaptors can differ significantly between different people.

Adaptors are useful in revealing lies and moments of nervousness. If someone is lying to you is making up a story with the intent of deceiving you, they begin to feel stress and worried than usual. They don't want to be exposed. They may start to display adaptors.

If you have mentioned a subject of conversation that makes other people uneasy, you may notice that they begin to display adaptors. However, it is essential to note that not every Adaptor has a meaning attached to it. Not everyone becomes restless due to anxiety –their other reasons. We have to be sure we do not misinterpret harmless gestures.

How You Can Benefit by Understanding Different Gestures

People can pass across different types of information at varying levels of understanding. The process of communication does not consist of spoken or written language only. While trying to give a message across to someone, sometimes you succeed or fail other times — not because of what was said or how it was said — because the message received is based on the degree of the listener's empathy for your non-vocal communication. A husband who turns his back on his wife and slams the backdoor without saying a word is sending an important message. It is, therefore, essential to know the benefits of understanding non-verbal language since we can communicate the same message in different ways. Note that your gestures, mannerisms, emotional relations, and habits are distinct from those you meet at a party or a business conference, at a bar, or a ballgame. Studying and being aware of gestures is quite simple, but interpreting them isn't as straightforward. For example, the gesture of covering one's mouth while speaking is most likely a clue that one is uncertain of what he is saying. When listening to an individual who suddenly starts talking through his hands, you begin to wonder if he is lying. Or if he is unsure of what he is saying? It could be any of these. But before you jump to conclusions, try to recollect if the person has spoken in that manner before. What were the conditions? Could it be that he just had dental work, which makes him self-conscious, or he has a bad breath? If he regularly closes his mouth while speaking, you may continue to the second phase of the analysis. You may test what he says by asking,

"Are you sure?" Such questions answered with either a 'yes' or 'no.' It could make him defensive, in which case you will know if he is unsure of what has just said. As it is with verbal understanding, you must consider more than the individual unit. Congruencies, alternative verification, Experience are essential ingredients. However, in a situation where the usual methods of confirmation cannot use, a consensus is needed to determine the meaning of the hand-over-mouth gesture: Many law-enforcement agents identify that the gesture indicates that the person is unsure, lying doubtful, or distorting the truth.

Chapter 22: Differences between Men and Women When Using Body Language

There are inherent differences between men and women, which are not only physiological ones. The psychological differences are as important as the physical, and they affect our view of life, our behavior, and our way of communicating – both verbally and non-verbally.

There are three reasons for the differences between men and women: the specificities of the male and female brain, the different hormones' functions and cultural and social differences.

The main difference in the brain functions is that, in women, both cerebral hemispheres are equally developed and can function simultaneously, while men can use either the right or the left hemisphere at any given time. This is due to the longitudinal fissures that serve as connections between the two hemispheres. Women's brains have more of these, and that is why they can do a few things simultaneously. At the same time, this creates something like chaos, while men's brains are organized; everything is classified according to categories and subcategories.

The second physiological difference lies in the hormones. As we all know, hormones are those substances in our body whose overproduction or underproduction and normal levels, more or less, determine our behavior. The main one of these is testosterone in men and estrogen in women.

Testosterone affects aggressiveness, competition and rivalry, independence, and confidence. Most men, in their communication, manifest all of these separately and in different clusters of behavioral traits that can be seen in both speech and non-verbal communication.

Estrogen, on the other hand, is responsible for feelings such as satisfaction and peace of mind, etc.

Due to the specific structures of the male and female brain and the levels of the hormone characteristic to men and women, we can analyze and explain the differences in behavior.

One of the first things we can discuss here is the ability of women to switch from one topic to another extremely quickly, while for men this process is slower and more difficult. Women are much more emotional than men, and because of this, they are able to switch from one mood to another rather fast, and those who have problems with hormonal levels – even quicker. There is also the fact that women can perceive reality with almost all their senses at the same time. Men, for their part, perceive mainly with their eyes. It is also true that women evaluate situations more closely, they see the details, while men evaluate the problem from a more global perspective.

Men need order, a rule that can be followed, and this is how they explain reality, how they perceive it. On this basis, he can try and change the reality towards an end that is more to his goal. Men's emotions are subject to reason, to rationality. That is why, more often than not, men are better at controlling their emotions, especially in front of people and especially in a business environment.

Women, on the other hand, experience rather than analyze and rationalize everything. Their behavior is almost always based on intuition, on details that can stay hidden from eyes.

Naturally, these characteristics are rather general and are a small portion of all that has been researched and defined. However, they are more than enough to draw some basic conclusions on the differences in communication.

Men communicate directly, in one direction, and usually based on logic, reason, and impartiality. During their communication process, verbal, vocal, and non-verbal, they exude vigor, perseverance, sometimes impatience. In general, body language may express aggressiveness or total composure, depending on the conversation, the counterpart, or the goal they are pursuing. Men usually sit quite still; they are calmer and more together than women. Despite their logic and reason, they cannot read p emotions and body language well. During communication, men use eye contact less often than women and prefer to perceive through their ears. They listen to their counterpart and may catch something in the tone, but rarely pay attention or take under serious consideration the body language of their partner. Of course, this is something that can be learned, there are courses and records that can help develop this "reading" mindset.

Contrary to that, women are somehow born with it. Because of their emotional character and the way they communicate, they are much better "readers" of human behavior. The intuition is one of the things that helps them, but also the fact that women usually use gestures and mimicry much more than men. That is why it is much easier for them to recognize something they also use quite often.

One of the main differences she lists is the position of the body and the fact that usually, men's sitting posture is more relaxed than women's'. They sit back in their chairs when they concentrate on listening, while women lean forward and nod to show they are paying attention to their counterparts. What is more, men change the position of their body more often than women. She gives an example of lecturers. According to her studies, men who read lectures or make presentations move more around the room than women do in the same situation. This comes to show that despite the fact that men are much worse than women are in reading body language, in cases of public speaking, they use body language quite efficiently. To occupy the space during speaking and using movements and gestures shows you feel comfortable; it shows composure and confidence.

Another interesting remark concerns the listening process. Men usually lean their head a little bit to the side, which shows interest and/or attention. Women usually look straight at the face, and their head doesn't go to the side.

The differences are infinite and are subject to a lot of research. However, in today's modern world where women chair big meetings and preside over multinational corporations, they can act and react as men do due to the environment which is still dominated by males. Body language and mirroring are important factors in high business circles, and behavioral psychology will change some of the aspects of the differentiation formula of men vs. women.

Common Myths About Body Language

It's evident that body language is one of the most telling signs that a person can use in the accurate analysis of another person. Most of the time, the body language and non-verbal communication cues that you pick are right, and trusting them will help you make credible inferences. That notwithstanding, it is imperative to learn about some of the most common myths that surround body language and non-verbal communication to help you to perfect your craft even more.

Myth 1: Liars Don't Make Eye Contact

This is one of the biggest myths that result in the wrong conclusion about a person. While it is true that some liars, children especially, may find it difficult to make eye contact while lying, you must keep in mind that there are professionals out there. Conmen, narcissists, and other pathological liars know how to get their victim to trust them in entirety, and you can be sure that they will look at you in the eye as they spew out their lives without flinching.

The only problem with their strategy is their likelihood to overcompensate. Therefore, while a regular truthful person may just look at you briefly, liars will tend to look at you for longer to try and forcefully establish trust. If you notice someone using this strategy, hold your stare too and see how they react once they are done speaking. Some liars are bound to get nervous when you stare back without talking, and they may look down after finishing or continue "bluffing" unnecessarily.

Myth 2: Moving Hands is a Sign of Uneasiness

Some people find it easier to express themselves using hand movements than using any other means. When a person moves their hands too much, it is not necessarily a sign that they are nervous. Rather, that may be just how they communicate with others.

Myth 3: You Can Tell What Others Are Thinking by Analyzing Them

Analyzing people and their body language is not a superpower. You cannot be able to tell exactly what someone is thinking by looking at them. However, you can tell their emotions and catch any signs of deceit and lying. Therefore, do not expect to know people's thoughts by simply analyzing them. It will not happen.

Myth 4: Knowing Analysis Methods Can Help You to Disguise Yours

Most people who know all about analyzing others through the methodologies we have deliberated think that they can disguise theirs. The major problem presented in this situation is that you will use a lot of conscious effort to disguise your feelings, prompting other body cues that can be picked by others. You can also tell when someone is trying to disguise their body language, and it is not possible for one to cover all of their tracks no matter how smart they are.

Chapter 23: Understanding People's Outward Personality

At that moment when you meet a new person, the simple truth is that there are lots of things you don't know about them. All you have to go on at that moment are the outward clues you can pick out; their choice of clothing, physical appearance, speech pattern, and gait, for instance. In addition, you can also try to know more about people by watching the kind of people they mix with, their interactions with them, their social life, and tastes. All these combine to form a mental image of the person's character profile within your mind.

In evaluating people, it is of utmost importance to be objective so that you do not just jump to preconceived conclusions. Most times, one sign is not enough to attribute a particular character trait permanently to an individual. You need an aggregate of complementing attributes to reach such definitive conclusions. In fact, it is not advisable to reach a conclusion based on just observable traits and remain unyielding to contrary signs. Your conclusions are there to guide you even if they are correct a vast majority of the time. Outward attributes you see does not precisely indicate the personal qualities of those around you.

What You See

However, from their outward appearance, some important indicators that tell much about a person's personality are revealed. Part of these indicators includes the cloth they wear, hairstyle, perfume, and some other grooming habits that can be very useful in gaining the right perspective about a particular person. The thing is that many people make use of their style for their outward expression. Although there are some instances in which people dress in a particular way to change their look and probably make some impression that may not correlate to what they are going through internally.

A person that has taken the time to look good, presentable, and neat has demonstrated attention to personal appearance to a reasonable extent. On the other hand, people that have an unkempt appearance display ill social grace.

Does that mean we can judge a person by the kind of clothes they put on alone? No! You need to consider the other variables before you make an erroneous blanket judgment. The only thing is that you can use that to form an initial opinion pending confirmative signs.

What You Hear

The way people speak can betray their emotions and show the sort of people they are. People who speak using a steady intonation and a constant, smooth flow of words are typically identified as being self-confident and are at ease in the present circumstances. On the other hand, if you observe that a person has a shaky voice or stutters while addressing you, this can probably indicate the fact that they feel uncomfortable or lack confidence in what is being said. In addition, rapid speech may signify anxiousness or panic.

Apart from the speech pattern itself, there are other variables that can be drawn from how active an individual is during a conversation. The thing is that some people spend most of their time talking and give the person they have a conversion with little or no time to make their own points. Such people may be overconfident, arrogant, or outright rude. They usually have the belief that what they have to say is much more important than what the other person has to say. Other times, it may be the feelings of insecurity that make them feel they need to overcompensate.

Interestingly, some research studies show that people that have a loquacious or extroversive nature appear to be more intelligent than they are. But then the supposed intelligence is going to fade out when they make a remark that looks absurd or does not at all appeal to common sense. People that give room for others to express their view have shown reasonable consideration, and the assumption should not be made that the outward projection that is the exact reflection of their internal processes.

What They Listen To

There are no definitive explanations for why this is so, but research carried out over the years has shown you can have an idea about the specific traits a certain person has when you check their musical preference.

In a particular study at Heriot-Watt University, the following general traits in people who listen to a specific category of music over a long period of time were theorized.

Rock: These set of people tend to be creative, gentle, introverted, low self-esteem

Hip Hop/ Rap: They are not prone to aggression and violence

Pop: The fans tend to be conventional, honest, high self-esteem, and extroverted, the only "but" is that they have relatively little creativity

Country Music: This set of people are emotionally stable

Dance: They have an assertive and outgoing personality

Classical: The listeners are introverted, but then they are comfortable with their skin and have high self-esteem

Blues/jazz; They tend to be creative, intelligent, and extroverted

N.B

By all means, trying to judge a person's traits based on his musical preference is as unscientific as they come. I have included it here mainly for trivial reasons. There is little to suggest that fans of rap are non-violent individuals. Even if the research has shown that most fans of a specific musical genre have certain attributes, not all of them have that trait. Again, nobody has been able to explain the presence or prevalence of certain traits in fans. There is no conclusive evidence that listening to a particular genre will give you certain traits. There is no scientific proof either that having a particular character trait predisposes you to like a particular genre. Cross-sectional studies have shown that certain traits appear more in certain people, but nobody can say for sure what the relationship is. This is one piece of information for the back of your mind. Have it, but its practical value is not high.

Habitual Behavior

As Warren Buffet said, "the chains of habit are too light to be felt until they are too heavy to be broken." The sum total of a person's habits is probably the best indicator yet of their character. After all, our character profile reflects our average attitude and actions.

The habit that a person portrays is the most significant indicator of the kind of character they have. For instance, a naturally helpful person may come across as being generous and selfless from the start if they offer to help you out. That alone can communicate that such a person may be empathetic and genuinely caring.

Someone who prefers to stay indoors almost all day may most likely turn out to be highly introverted. That would definitely not be surprising if you find out they enjoy their own company much lot than social gatherings. Someone who literally enjoys hanging out and socializing may be able to make friends more easily than someone who does not. Habits dictate the things we like to do. They facilitate our hobbies and help us avoid boring chores and situations. So, being able to discern a person's habits will give you a huge helping hand in determining just how they think or act.

Another thing to be put into consideration is the particular kind of entertainment that the person enjoys a lot. Some people enjoy sports and games; others are movie freaks, art lovers, etc. The kind of entertainment a person gets to enjoy can set the tone for his character. A lover of the latest online trends may absolutely love getting new costumes at any cost. The same goes for all the entertainment categories. They can absolutely tell you the hidden truth you want to know about the person.

This highlights how much of an impact the company and relationships we keep have on us. To analyze someone, your work may be made simpler if you know the traits that their closest friends and associates possess. A lot of our habits are picked up subconsciously from the people closest to use. Their traits rub off on us and show up in our own life by default. For instance, if you find yourself in the midst of a tightly knit, outward group of friends, that may likely be because you are outgoing yourself. Even if you are not, though, it could mean that you find that trait about them intriguing enough to want to give it a try.

By way of conclusion, there are several pointers that can help you better profile the stranger standing in front of you. If you are able to pin multiple of these pointers in the same direction with regards to certain traits, then you are on safe ground. However, you must be careful not to allow preconceived notions to impede your judgment.

Chapter 24: How to Read a Lady's Sexual Language

Does she flirt? Is she smiling? Does she make contact with her eyes? How can you collect flirting signals from her? It has never been easier to understand her erotic body language. Here are some hints:

1: She Starts Preening

Otherwise, it's known as making sure she looks her best. Standing up straight, tucking in their tummies, and pushing out their breasts are spontaneous and instant gestures that show a woman is interested. This would be followed by smoothing her skirt or dress, playing with her hair and jewelry, and then disappearing for once into the ladies' room. It is an excellent sign of body language flirting with changing and testing appearances. If you catch her inspecting your butt when you're on the way to the bar, or when you turn your back, and she starts fixing her makeup, then you know she's sexually interested.

2: Eyes

Her eyes say everything. Usually, a flirting woman sends you three sidelong glimpses. You'll get a second look to indicate that they've enjoyed what they've seen and a third if they're talking to you.

The four seconds. For 3 seconds or less, we're looking at uninteresting people. A sure indication of interest is when the woman continues to look your way for at least 4 seconds.

How the flirting girl breaks your attention. This is even more significant than the way she looked at you. You've lost her interest if she looks to the side or around the room. You have a chance if her eyes drop to the floor before looking back to meet yours within 30 to 60 seconds. Downcast eyes followed by a preening gesture, such as playing with her hair or flipping her head, demonstrate that she likes what she sees.

If you look at her and lock your eyes, a flirting woman will often slightly and quickly raise her upper eyelids. This is a very subtle movement to open the eye that says, "I'm looking at you." Zero eye communication means zero connection — time to move on to another man. Usually, a raised eyebrow indicates some issues. The more you look someone in the eye, the more attractive, confident, and truthful you appear to be.

3: Foot

Feet may be a great indicator of the true feelings of the flirting woman. Few people subconsciously notice what they're doing with their feet because they're so far from our faces. This puts them a long way up on the credibility scale.

The flirting woman is saying that you are welcome to join her party by pointing a foot towards you.

If she has one leg crossed over the other, she is slightly defensive, but while one foot is still pointing at you, she still looks all right. It's a better sign that she loves you when she uncrosses her legs and begins to imitate your foot pose.

Her foot between your feet is a precise movement in the sexual language of the body. Better yet, if she's bending her knees and touching her knee or leg while both of you are standing. Both of these reflect clear signals of romantic flirting.

4: Body Posture

The flirting woman pulls back her arms and thrusts out her breasts. One hand placed on a sexually jutting hip for you to join her is a flirting signal. It can also be a gesture to put a hand on the back of a hip to emphasize her tiny waist. Arching her spine in the shape of a 'C' showing both her breasts and her bottom is flirting with the body language, inviting you to check it out.

As she starts to lean back, she brings her arms closer to her chest, draws her breasts together, and deepens her cleavage, a highly sexual body language signal.

Another unconscious flirting act is to play with her necklace. Her fiddling with her jewelry at the neck invites you to look at her breasts as a definite erotic signal that she flirts when she begins to stroke her throat, neck, or upper chest. When she blends the stroking with a neck arch, the message is even greater. By tilting her head to show you more of her neck, she means she has begun to trust you. Throats and necks are "lover's zones," where we are not touched by anyone else. Her neck or chest stroking draws her eyes to her breasts as well.

5: Playing with Her Hair

Flapping her head, running her fingers through her hair, and flirting with the best sign of body language, and flipping her hair. All these are designed to show you that she's there.

6: Her Legs

Women sometimes cross their legs while sitting, looking attractive, lady-like, or just showing off. The higher over her thighs that she crosses her legs, the stronger the sexual signal. If she also smiles at you, this is a compelling sexual body language, showing eye contact and resting one hand in her lap. Smoothing hands over her thighs is another common preening sign for women when they find themselves sexually attractive in the company of someone.

By sitting on one side with her legs, she makes an apparent attempt to make her legs look longer and look suitable for anyone watching. The more often she crosses and uncrosses her legs in front of you, the better your chances are. The more she exposes, the more likely she is to be hot for you.

If you're in a barefoot situation, if she thinks there are attractive men around, she'll start walking on tiptoe. This makes her legs look longer, her body slimmer, and she looks more feminine overall.

7: Her Wrists and Palms

Somebody, if they're interested, will flash their wrist at you. As she plays with her hair or fiddles with an earring, test to see if her wrist is turned to face you with her hand. When she flashes it at you, she is saying, "You can get close to me."

8: Will She Kiss You?

If she does any of these, then probably the answer is YES!

Licking her lips, someone licks his or her lips when faced with something exciting.

Suggestively eat and drink, suck and brush hands — All different ways their skills can be promoted.

She continues to cover her mouth. As someone gets turned on, the lips get swallowed up, making us more conscious of them and more likely to play with them.

Putting her head close to yours: This is an invitation to kiss almost always

Tilting her head: Getting to a subconscious level position

9: Would She Like More?

With this little test, you can check out her intentions towards the end of the encounter. Step back from her, and then step back quickly. If she's interested, she'll step forward now to close the gap without realizing that she's doing it.

Trying to lower your voice to a whisper is another trick. When she sits where she is, screaming at you that she can't hear you, and then she won't get closer.

What the Color of Her Clothes Means About Her

Red: She is delighted to be the center of attention and is not ashamed of her feelings.

Black: Stylish, original, and chic.

Beige: Doubtless.

Navy Blue: Business suit.

White: Look at me.

Blue light: Composed.

Hot Pink: She wants the crowd to stand out.

Pink light: Fragile.

It has never been so easy to understand the art of flirting and interpreting sexual body language. Never again misread the situation! Apply these tips for dating and go out now!

Chapter 25: How the Brain Controls Body Language

The reason nonverbal language never lies is that it happens unconsciously. We have the ability to consciously control the things we say in order to lie or share half-truths, but the body will still show the truth, why does this happen?

Humans have evolved to communicate in a nonverbal manner. There is an ancient system that lives inside our brain that understands and conveys intentions or emotions through physical movements. This part of the brain is what is called the limbic system. It works in a precise manner. The amygdala is the key player in the limbic system and is located in the medial temporal lobe. It works by helping us to process emotions.

There is an interesting evolutionary story that explains how the limbic system came to be. It takes us through how water-dwelling creatures became land roaming and continue to turn into walking, talking, and hunting humans.

Something that is hard to believe for most is that creatures have evolved from common ancestors. These ancestors lived in the water 360 million years ago. The struggle to survive and climatic changes forced them to move to the land. Their fins turned into limbs in order to walk, and their skin became tougher in order to handle the harsh climate.

About 320 to 310 million years ago, the reptile evolved. This was when the limbic system began to develop. The reflexive system of the breed, feed, flight, and the fight began. The part of the brain this created consisted of the cerebellum and brain stem. The behavior of the reptile is predictable, but it is what helped them to survive. Emotions didn't exist until mammals evolved.

When mammals emerged, they had a deliberate social behavior, unlike their reptile ancestors. The reason for this could be connected to their habitation, bonding, nurturing, reproduction, and changed metabolism. A mammal's offspring grows inside of them until they reach a certain stage. They are fed by secretions from the mammary glands, and they control their temperature in order to adjust to different climates.

The new brain structure, called the cortex, for mammals was built upon the reptilian complex. This new brain section consisted of the insula, orbital frontal cortex, cingulate gyrus, hippocampus, and amygdala. Even though mammals were superior in their survival, they naturally used the fight or flight approach, which is a reptilian act. They created other ways to work around this fight or flight approach through planned movements, expressions, and behavior. Emotions were a great gift, as well as being able to smell different things and being able to remember them. This helped mammals to endure different circumstances. This caused them to spread across the planet.

Finally, the common ancestors of apes and humans appeared the primate. It is possible that they evolved from mammals that were more skilled at climbing trees for shelter and food. The primate's brain developed more complex parts to help them adapt to new environments and social challenges. They have better systems to coordinate movements on the ground and in trees. They had the ability to plan and think. Their vision also improved, and they could recall scenes.

As the climate changed, parts of these primates remained in wooded areas, leaving in the trees. Others were forced to start roaming the ground when their trees were replaced by brush. These primates start to walk on two legs with the hands-free to farm, fish, and hunt, make tools, and gather food. They start to build and live in fixed shelters.

This ability to walk on two feet changed their movement and behavior patterns and how they communicated. Making different sounds, gestures, and facial expressions became helpful in express their feelings to the other people in their group. Through various civilizations, this continues to be a diverse part of their lifestyle and communication. This created their cultural and social norms and ethics.

For us, modern humans, the neocortex is the most advanced part of the brain. This rests above all of the old brain sections. This section of the brain is the reason why we can solve problems, figure out math, navigate our way around, perform introspection, learn other languages, use our imagination, and reason things. This is also the area that helps us to regulate our emotions, harbor feelings, and control a few of the impulses of our limbic system. The limbic brain is what controls all of our nonverbal communication, and we can't completely control it with our neocortex.

Emotional and visual memory has the ability to cause us to act in ways that our ancestors would. We feel comfortable in favorable situations and uncomfortable when in danger or distress. When we are placed in a threatening situation, we are still going to act like other mammals or reptiles.

Who Should Know Body Language and Why

Body language is a very important part of communication that only a few people study, yet it takes up most of how we communicate and is normally more accurate than the meaning of words.

You've heard that actions speak louder than words, and this couldn't be truer because there are some things you can communicate without saying a word. A shrug of the shoulders can tell somebody, "I don't know." A raise of the eyebrows can say, "Did I hear that right?" With palms up and shrinking a little it says, "I don't know what else to do." Pointing to your nose can mean, "That's right."

The way we use our bodies helps to reinforce the things we say. You can simply say, "I don't know," or you can add this gesture; turn your palms face up in front of you, raise your eyebrows, frown a little, and stick out your bottom lip. At this point, you have also made somebody laugh and taken some pressure off yourself or anybody who was nervous.

Why do people bother with the imprecise and hard work of trying to figure out body language? I mean, we are an expert at it already with the unconscious mind, and our unconscious mind is already better, faster, and immensely more powerful than our conscious minds. Why should we take the time and do the hard work of moving out unconscious expertise to our conscious mind, make it worse, struggling with improving it, before pushing it back down into our unconscious mind once we stop focusing on it in our awake brain?

The reason we should do all of this work is that it allows us to develop the skill of reading the body language of others and how to control our own. Learning this skill will allow us to become better communicators that use intent instead of leaving communication up to chance.

For example, when we meet a person for the very first time, our unconscious mind starts trying to develop answers to certain questions that evolution has taught us are important. Are they a friend or an enemy? Are they more or less powerful than I am? Are they a potential mate? Do they understand what they are saying? And then, as the relationship deepens, the big question is, can I trust them?

By communicating with intent, can you use body language to create some form of trust with another person more quickly and reliably than leaving it all to the unconscious mind? This is a question that salespeople are very interested in, but this is true for speakers as well, since an audience wants to trust the person on stage, and the answer to this question is going to determine if they buy into whatever you are trying to tell them.

A great way to improve the likelihood and speed of trust building is to mirror what the other person does. This is a very well-studied phenomenon in the body language world. You can look around and see co-workers, friends, and lovers unconsciously mirroring each other and agree on things easily, which is our body's way of telling others, "Hey, we act alike, we agree on the same things, we are working on the same page."

A person can consciously mirror a complete stranger, which will greatly improve their rate and depth of trust-building. This should be done subtly and carefully, but it is pretty rare for a person to notice this happening unless you become extremely hyperactive in mirroring every single twitch they make.

But how does this help speakers? How could a speaker possibly mirror an audience? There are quite a few ways. First, align yourself with them by moving into them and turn to face the stage like you were an audience member. Second, when you get the chance to interact with individual people, possibly during a Q and A, you can mirror that person. Thirdly, you can act out something and then have the audience participate. Just make sure it is relevant. You are only going to cause more questions if you start making everybody do jumping jacks for no reason.

The conscious study and use of body language for psychological purposes is hard work, but what you get in return is being about to make stronger connections with those around you.

Some people like to clear their throat, change the pitch of their voice, or stutter a lot when lying. They may try to pull your attention to something to distract you or stall the conversation to come up with a plausible explanation. Additionally, tapping their foot, bouncing, rubbing their face, blushing, looking away, or raising their shoulder could be an indicator that they aren't completely comfortable in the conversation because they aren't truthful. These are only a few examples, and we will go over more later on.

Something else that body language helps with is expressing our feelings. When you pay attention to nonverbal signs, it helps you to figure out how the person feels about the things they are saying. For example, somebody could agree to do something, but their body language tells you that they don't want to. This can be helpful if you are a manager or in a leadership position so that you can figure out who would be the best at an assignment. If somebody's heart isn't in it, then they probably won't do the best job.

When it comes to job interviews, body language is sometimes the determining factor. If the applicant conveys confidence and is calm with the subject matter through their body language, they have a better chance of getting the job. Body language can cause somebody to seem out of control or uncomfortable. These types of traits cause a job applicant to come off as less comfortable and confident.

When you are having a conversation with a person, their body language can let you know if they are paying attention to what you say or if they could care less. When they lean forward, they are saying they are interested. Leaning back could mean that they feel superior or aren't interested. If a person is standing close to another and leaning forward while they talk, they could be trying to persuade the other person or dominate the conversation. If somebody is talking and you don't make eye contact, then you look like you aren't listening and just waiting to get to talk. This makes you seem like you don't care, and they may be less likely to listen to you when you do talk.

Chapter 26: Guilt Body Language

Guilt body language is not easy to detect, and it is not for several reasons. The first is that guilt is not a basic emotion. Only the basic emotions are clearly reflected in the micro expressions of the face and body posture. Guilt, on the other hand, is a more complex formation that involves the participation of reflection and can involve several emotions at the same time.

On the other hand, a person who is guilty does not always recognize his guilt. It is possible that, for example, someone steals feels that they have the right to do so, because, according to him, the other person does not need that object that he or she took from him or acquired unfairly. Therefore, you will not feel guilty and obviously will not reflect it in the guilt body language. Likewise, in basic emotions, there are movements and postures that are impossible to control voluntarily, at least for a few seconds. Instead, there is a strong component of rationality in guilt, so it is also possible to exercise deliberate control over the movements that reveal this feeling. In conclusion, guilt body language is more difficult to detect, although not impossible. These are some of the features that characterize it.

The Essential Gesture in the Body Language of Guilt

A person who feels guilty, but does not want to take responsibility for what he did wrong, often happens to live in a state of alert. He is aware that he is hiding both the damage he did and the resulting remorse. Hence, in those cases, you have relatively broad control over your body language.

However, according to anthropologist Desmond Morris, there is an unconscious and involuntary movement that would be part of the body language of guilt. It's about blink. As much as the person pretends to have everything under control, when asked or hinted at an aspect related to that feeling of guilt, an intermittent and rapid blinking will appear.

The increase in blink frequency is considerable and noticeable, but those who feel guilty do not immediately notice it. This gesture denotes that the person feels vulnerable and has an intense desire to regain control of the situation. It is usual for it to be accompanied by head movements in different directions.

The Look and the Expression

Another aspect to look at in guilt body language is the gaze. It is very usual that when a person knows that he has acted against his convictions and his values, he has difficulties in looking at the face. The most common thing is that he looks elsewhere, always with his eyes downcast. The chin does not necessarily tilt downward, but the gaze does. However, this is relative. It does not always happen because some people know that this gesture gives them away. Sometimes there is also a strong conviction that what was done was bad but necessary or convenient. Therefore, the person does not experience guilt as such, even though he knows that he inflicted harm.

In this second case, it is common for the person to show excessive control over the expression on their face. What he wants is, precisely, not to reveal anything with him, that's why he keeps his muscles tense and tries to gesture as little as possible. He does not take his eyes off the other, because he wants to be aware of this. It seeks to maintain control over the situation.

Coverings and Difficulty Speaking

Except that this does not apply in all cases, another of the habitual gestures in guilt body language is the tendency to cover your mouth or face. Sometimes the person puts his hand on his lips or on part of his face. He does not want to give himself away and, without being aware, he tries to cover himself.

In the same way, some noticeable speech difficulties may appear. The guilty person clears his voice too often or stutters a bit. The tension and stress of maintaining your role makes your mouth dry, which is why you drink frequently. You may also have difficulty building coherent sentences.

Signs of Emotional Connection with a Person

The people with whom we maintain an emotional connection make us feel calm, comfortable in the interaction. That connection makes us learn about life, recharge our energy, and be happier.

1. Understanding

Two people with this link will achieve very high levels of understanding. An understanding based on empathy that encourages, for example, support, listening, or comfort.

2. The Instant Connection

To establish and sustain an emotional bond, you don't need to develop the relationship first. Personalities should suit perfectly from the start. The relation is immediate and can be strengthened over time.

That doesn't mean that when you first meet someone, if you don't have an emotional bond that means you will never get between those two men. Instantness is a characteristic of emotional attachment, but it doesn't determine its growth.

3. Personal Growth

People with emotional ties grow together emotionally and spiritually faster. Via that relation, these two people know exactly what the other's problems are and share them generally. This fosters a supportive atmosphere that allows all experiences to evolve.

This has everything to do with contact. Dialogs between emotionally-connected people are also relaxing. They never stop learning, whatever the subject of conversation.

4. Peace of Mind

People with an emotional bond always feel at home here. It's very easy to distance yourself from issues and see them in perspective. The tranquility gives way to optimistic feelings, if not to a new perspective to solve a certain question.

5. The Company

Link is a strong isolation antidote. The emotional bond includes a feeling of business, irrespective of the distance that divides us. Linked to tranquility, we believe we are present in the other's feelings; we live outside our physical limits.

Especially in times of crisis, this feeling helps find solutions. Without asking for help, the person will do anything to be with you, listen to you, and support you when you need it most.

6. The Fascination

We're intrigued by the people we're so especially related to. We still find them fascinating, and we're their biggest followers. Any victory of people with an emotional bond is honestly exchanged, without jealousy, without judgment.

It doesn't mean that people with this relation can't see the other's defects. In reality, they are the ones who see them most, thinking about each other transparently. Like other cultures, though, it's very easy to talk about the other's flaws and develop as an individual as we've seen.

7. Empathy

The last important trait of emotional connection is empathy. As we have already seen, people who share this bond do not always need to verbalize their concerns: they are able to extract the emotional needs of the other through conversation. The ease of putting yourself in the other's place strengthens the relationship.

Chapter 27: The Power of Body Language over the Spoken Word

The power of body language becomes very clear in political speakers, who, with certain gestures and facial expressions, give more weight to the spoken word and emphasize its great importance. The spoken word only has a significance of seven percent. In contrast, 93 percent use non-verbal signals or body language, which creates an optimal basis for manipulating other people with gestures, facial expressions, posture, arms, and hands. The body language shows whether the person opposite feels comfortable or not. With the combination of voice, body language, and posture, the inner attitude is quickly revealed. A person who knows the power of body language knows exactly how to use the expression, speech rate, pauses, and body language to get you in the desired direction and influence you in that direction. The appearance provides an overall picture. The beauty of it is that you can train body language and use it for your benefit.

In the same way, you can also use body language to expose yourself to him when he is telling you lies. There is even some scientific evidence for this. In a conversation, you will quickly discover the lie if the words and body language are in a tense relationship. The untruth can be recognized by the symmetry. If the truth is told, an asymmetrical picture emerges. If an attempt is made to tell you a lie, the body image is thrown unbalanced and becomes asymmetrical. You can recognize the lie or a half-truth by sloping shoulders, inflated nostrils, and eyes. The interviewer avoids your gaze and cannot look you in the eye.

Those who have a correct command of body language and thus give the spoken word even more power can manipulate. Inviting gestures are used, as well as facial expressions, micro-impressions, and body constitution.

Interpret Body Language and Decipher Different Gestures

Even when not a word comes from your lips, your body speaks. And when it is spoken, you always speak two different languages — once the words are spoken and meanwhile the body is talking. Body language can be a vicious betrayer if what you think and feel is not put into words. Your body brings out your real emotions and thoughts in posture, facial expressions, and gestures. You curl your lips, raise an eyebrow, inflate the nostrils or wrinkle your nose, and the person opposite you knows your true thoughts and emotions. A harmonious overall picture is only created if the body language matches the words spoken. Authenticity and credibility are the results. In communication, body language is of great importance, whether in conversations with colleagues, at job interviews, in negotiations, or in contact with customers. Even in small talk, attention is paid not only to the words said but also to the language of the body. To detect manipulation, it is important that you correctly interpret and decipher facial expressions and gestures. This will help you to quickly recognize what the person you are talking to wants to achieve with their words.

Body language is seen as a success factor since gestures have indescribable power. However, when it comes to body language, the spirits are divided into two camps. One camp believes that the hype about facial expressions and gestures is greatly exaggerated, and the effect is often overestimated. Voices from the other camp, on the other hand, think that body language is an important factor for effect and individuality.

They practice and train hard because in their opinion, their success is closely linked to convincing body language. Somewhere in between lies the truth about body language. In the same way, the statement "You cannot "not" communicate" by Paul Watzlawick is correct. Because gestures and posture speak for themselves, even when no words are spoken. There are so-called high-status gestures, which are also called power poses.

Not only do they have a great effect on other people, but they can also increase your self-esteem. The following gestures express a very high status and especially a lot of power:

- An upright and still head position

- A powerful voice

- Elegant and slow movements

- Open, uninhibited smile

- Smooth movements

Various gestures are used in the game of recognition and status. If these are used in a controlled manner, it is much easier to win over other people for yourself. However, body language has two very different sides. One side is even very dangerous. The hidden signals that are sent out with posture, facial expressions, arms, and hands are aimed at manipulating you and winning you over for your cause. People who can manipulate correctly do not need words to make you feel bad and to influence your thoughts. Be aware that body language is manipulative. In this way you will encounter obvious signals, but also those that are much more subtle.

They have a hidden influence on your thoughts and perception. You have no control over this influence. Always remember that you are influenced by everything you perceive. Because the brain not only records the words you say but also the gestures and facial expressions. If a stimulus is strong enough to upset the balance of ions in the cell membranes, a very special reaction occurs. This refers to the biochemical process that processes sensory impressions. As soon as a reaction is triggered in a cell by a stimulus, a hidden influence is established. If the stimulus did not exist, there would be no manipulation.

Not only are you being manipulated by body language, but you are also manipulating yourself. For example, other people can read the current mood from your posture. The signals that you send out trigger stimuli in other people. You, for example, use these stimuli to get the most out of them. Therefore, body language can manipulate. However, it cannot be used to elicit a particular reaction that does not correspond to your interests, values, or innermost desires. That is why manipulation through body language alone is not so effective because inner values have greater power.

Manipulation through body language only works if there is already an inner inclination in this direction. This is especially true for advertising. For example, you can watch an advertisement for beer for hours without immediately feeling the desire for a beer. But if you watch an advertisement from Zalando or About You, there is no stopping you.

Always remember that body language is largely unconscious. Or have you ever thought about your posture, the movements of your hands and arms, or your current facial expression? This gives other people a deep insight and allows them to read your thoughts and emotions unfiltered. If you want to prevent another person from manipulating you, you should learn to become aware of body language and use it in a way that you can benefit from it.

This makes it difficult for a manipulator to force you into the role of a victim. By now you have learned so much about how to protect yourself from manipulation by saying things. Now it's just a matter of using body language correctly. The following tips will help you do this:

1. Get to the same level as you are opposite. This is meant literally. This is meant because it enables you to compensate for differences in height and ensures that what is said is perceived correctly and is no longer twisted. As soon as you are at eye level with the other person, the threatening, superior effect disappears. If someone tries to manipulate you, starts rumors about you, and you want to confront this person, you should not look up or down. Because you will weaken your position.

2. A true multi-talent of body language is the smile. And the best thing about it: you can use it consciously and purposefully. This way you radiate self-confidence, inner strength, and self-assurance.

3. Just like facial expressions, gestures, and other aspects, body language also requires a certain distance, which should be respected. In plain language this means: Do not let anyone get too close to you and keep the distance from the other person.

4. Are you aware of your body language? To use body language perfectly, you need to understand its effect on others. That is why you should find out what signals are sent through your body language. Those who feel small and have little self-confidence express this through body language. Manipulators who are looking for a new victim will find you immediately.

How to Control Your Body Language

Body language can enhance your communication skills in a great way. You can have effective communication skills only if you can control your body language. Before, we look at the most used body language for manipulation. It is important to know how to take charge of your own body. Can we base these with the quote that, 'Charity begins at home?' Yeah, you cannot have an interest in understanding how to manipulate other people positively, yet you do not know how to take control of yourself. Let us kick off with understanding and having control of our body language.

Chapter 28: How to Take Control and Manipulate Your Body Language

Research has shown that, when you are aware of the happenings of your own body, you can manipulate it by training yourself to have control and even mold it to have effective communication. Further research recommends that you take some breathing exercises before going into a meeting or presentation. It will help you calm as well as have the ability to take note of your posture and gestures while on presentation. As you have noted by now, mirroring is a good technique. Always try to be keen on what the next person is doing non-verbally and copy that. It will help you become more effective in your communication with them. They will understand you better because this tunes your mind to the ability to communicate more truthfully at a place of relaxation. However, you should be careful while shaping your body language. This is to ensure that the body language that you portray matches with what you are trying to present. A mismatch may bring confusion and may not be relevant at the moment. The person you are in conversation with makes a mistake by saying something contrary to what they intended. The secret to having control of your body language is to take your time to learn it, to be aware of your non-verbal cues while you apply what you learn.

The Body Language That Will Help You Take Charge of Your Space

Effective management involves individuals being able to encourage and have a positive influence. In planning for an important appointment, maybe with your employees, management team, or partners, you are focusing on what to say, memorizing critical points, and rehearsing your presentation to make you feel believable and persuasive. This is something you should be aware of, of course. Here is what you should know if you want to take control of your position, at work, at a presentation, or as a leader.

Seven Seconds is What You Have to Make an Impression

First impressions are essential in market relationships. When somebody psychologically marks you as trustworthy, or skeptical, strong, or submissive, you will be seen through such a filter in any other dealings that you do or say. Your partners will look for the finest in you if they like you. They will suspect all of your deeds if they distrust you. While you can't stop people from having quick decisions, as a defense mechanism, the human mind is programmed in this way; you can learn how to make these choices effective for you. In much less than seven seconds, the initial perceptions are developed and strongly influenced by body language. Studies have found that nonverbal signals have more than four times the effect on the first impression you create than you speak. This is what you should know regarding making positive and lasting first impressions. Bear in mind several suggestions here:

Start by changing your attitude. People immediately pick up your mood. Have you noticed that you immediately get turned off after you find a customer service representative who has a negative attitude? You feel like leaving or request to be served by a different person. That is what will happen to you too if you have a bad attitude, which is highly noticeable. Think of the situation and make a deliberate decision about the mindset you want to represent before you meet a client, or join the meeting room for a company meeting, or step on the scene to make an analysis.

Smile. Smiling is a good sign that leaders are under using. A smile is a message, a gesture of recognition, and acceptance. "I'm friendly and accessible," it says. Having a smile on your face will change the mood of your audience. If they had another perception of you, a smile can change that and make them relax.

Make contact with your eyes Looking at somebody's eyes conveys vitality and expresses interest and transparency. A nice way to help you make eye contact is to practice observing the eye color of everybody you encounter to enhance your eye contact. Overcome being shy and practice this great body language.

Lean in gently the body language that has you leaning forward often expresses that you are actively participating, and you are interested in the discussion. But be careful about the space of the other individual. This means staying about two ft. away in most professional situations.

Shaking hands This will be the best way to develop a relationship. It's the most successful as well. Research indicates that maintaining the very same degree of partnership you can get with a simple handshake takes a minimum of three hours of intense communication. You should ensure that you have a palm-to-palm touch and also that your hold is firm but not bone-crushing.

Look at your position. Studies have found that uniqueness of posture, presenting yourself in a way that exposes your openness and takes up space, generates a sense of control that creates changes in behavior in a subject independent of its specific rank or function in an organization. In fact, in three studies, it was repeatedly found that body position was more important than the hierarchical structure in making a person think, act, and be viewed more strongly.

Building Your Credibility is Dependent on How You Align Your Non-Verbal Communication

Trust is developed by a perfect agreement between what is being said and the accompanying expressions. If your actions do not completely adhere to your spoken statement, people may consciously or unconsciously interpret dishonesty, confusion, or internal turmoil.

By the use of an electroencephalograph (EEG) device to calculate "event-related potentials"–brain waves that shape peaks and valleys to examine gesture effects proofs that one of these valleys happens when movements that dispute what is spoken are shown to subjects. And, in a rather reasonable way, they simply do not make sense if leaders say one thing and their behaviors point to something else. Each time your facial expressions do not suit your words, e.g., losing eye contact or looking all over the room when trying to express candor, swaying back on the heels while thinking about the bright future of the company, or locking arms around the chest when announcing transparency. All this causes the verbal message to disappear.

What Your Hands Mean When You Use Them

Have you at any point seen that when individuals are energetic about what they're stating, their signals naturally turned out to be increasingly energized? Their hands and arms constantly move, accentuating focus, and passing on eagerness.

You might not have known about this association, however, you intuitively felt it. Research shows that an audience will generally view individuals who utilize a more prominent assortment of hand motions in a progressively ideal light. Studies likewise find that individuals who convey through dynamic motioning will, in general, be assessed as warm, pleasant, and vivacious, while the individuals who stay still or whose motions appear to be mechanical or "wooden" are viewed as legitimate, cold, and systematic.

That is one motivation behind why signals are so basic to a pioneer's viability and why getting them directly in an introduction associates so effectively with a group of people. You may have seen senior administrators commit little avoidable errors. At the point when pioneers don't utilize motions accurately on the off chance that they let their hands hang flaccidly to the side or fasten their hands before their bodies in the exemplary "fig leaf" position, it recommends they have no passionate interest in the issues or are not persuaded about the fact of the matter they're attempting to make.

To utilize signals adequately, pioneers should know about how those developments will in all probability be seen. Here are four basic hand motions and the messages behind them:

Concealed hands - Shrouded hands to make you look less reliable. This is one of the nonverbal signs that is profoundly imbued in our subliminal. Our precursors settled on endurance choices dependent on bits of visual data they grabbed from each other. In our ancient times, when somebody drew nearer with hands out of view, it was a sign of potential peril. Albeit today the risk of shrouded hands is more representative than genuine, our instilled mental inconvenience remains.

Blame game - I've frequently observed officials utilize this signal in gatherings, arrangements, or meetings for accentuation or to show strength. The issue is that forceful blame dispensing can recommend that the pioneer is losing control of the circumstance, and the signal bears a resemblance to parental reprimanding or play area harassing.

Eager gestures - There is an intriguing condition of the hand and arm development with vitality. If you need to extend more excitement and drive, you can do it as such by expanded motioning. Then again, over-motioning (particularly when hands are raised over the shoulders) can cause you to seem whimsical, less trustworthy, and less incredible.

Laidback gestures - Arms held at midsection tallness and motions inside that level plane, help you - and the group of spectators - feel focused and formed. Arms at the midsection and bowed to a 45-degree point (joined by a position about shoulder-width wide) will likewise assist you with keeping grounded, empowered, and centered.

In this quick-paced, techno-charged time of email, writings, video chats, and video visits, one generally accepted fact remain: Face-to-confront is the most liked, gainful, and amazing correspondence medium. The more business pioneers convey electronically, all the more squeezing turns into the requirement for individual communication.

Ability to Study Body Language

More business administrators are learning how to send the correct sign, yet also how to understand them. The most significant thing in correspondence is hearing what isn't said."

Correspondence occurs more than two channels: verbal and nonverbal, bringing about two unmistakable discussions going on simultaneously. While verbal correspondence is significant, it's by all account not the only message being sent. Without the capacity to be able to read non-verbal communication, we miss critical components to discussions that can emphatically or adversely sway a business.

At the point when individuals aren't installed with an activity, pioneers should have the option to perceive what's going on and to react rapidly. That is the reason commitment and withdrawal are two of the most significant signs to screen in other individuals' non-verbal communication. Commitment practices demonstrate intrigue, receptivity, or understanding while separation practices signal fatigue, outrage, or protectiveness.

Active participation sign incorporates head gestures or tilts the widespread indication of "giving somebody your ear," and open-body poses. At the point when individuals are locked in, they will confront you straightforwardly, "pointing" at you with their entire body. Be that as it may, the moment they feel awkward, they may edge their chest area away – giving you "the brush off." And if they endure the whole gathering with the two arms and legs crossed, it's far-fetched you have their upfront investment.

Additionally, screen the measure of an eye to eye connection you're getting. Generally, individuals will look longer and with more recurrence at individuals or things that they like. A large portion of us are alright with an eye to eye connection enduring around three seconds, yet when we like or concur with somebody, we consequently increment the measure of time we investigate their eyes.

Separation triggers the inverse: the measure of an eye to eye connection diminishes, as we will generally turn away from things that trouble or get us bored.

Conclusion

We have learned many important things about our own and other people's body language. The better you get at this, the better you can build relationships, prevent yourself from being the wrong end of a liar's tale, or land an opportunity you are striving for.

There is so much that is shared nonverbally through body language. The most important applications of body language are to be able to model your own nonverbal expression to better communicate, observe, and analyze that of others and use both factors to persuade and convince more effectively.

By following the guidelines outlined, you will be well on your way to understanding the true thoughts and feelings of others beyond what they are saying. In addition, with a little practice you'll soon be on your way to making your body language work for you, which in turn will allow you to connect better with others and give a much better account of yourself. The key is sensitivity; be observant, and you will soon develop the instinct to pick up signals and respond accordingly.

Through practice, you will also be able to differentiate if a signal means something or not. Most of our body movements are a result of habit, mannerisms that do not mean anything at all. If you prepare yourself in reading body language, you will be able to ignore meaningless body signals. Rather, you will only choose and absorb the ones that have an effect on your life at the proper time. And since you have more focus, you will be able to read people better. Life is a game and knowing body language gives you the advantage. You can choose to win, change partner, or play an entirely different game.

Body language experts are quite as positive. They believe that even if you are introverted and shy, there are some things that you can do to show that you have strength behind your nerves.

Besides making sure you hold on and pull tight, you should also keep your body facing the other person to show that you are listening and open. When you shake hands while standing, it seems more positive, which is tried for women and men, but you have to keep eye contact. A person is seen as rude if they reach for a handshake when the other person clearly has their hands full. If you are at a party, you should keep your drinks in the left hand to keep your right dry and warm, ready for a handshake. This will also keep your hand warm and dry.

According to some cultural norms, a person is who of higher standing, like an elder or teacher, should be the one initiating the handshake instead of a person of lower standing. If you are about equal with the other person when it comes to job and age, offering the handshake is a way to make yourself look confident, and you won't be surprised if the other person initiates one.

When you see world leaders shake hands, look for the person who appears the most relaxed and confident. A rule of thumb is, if you stand on the left in pictures, you will give off a better impression than standing on the right, where you come off as submissive. You will also have the upper hand in the picture.

Making sure that you have the right amount of pressure during the shake plays just as big of a role as the shake. Men tend to squeeze harder, especially if you are trying to make a deal, show more confidence, or to provide a warm greeting. The important thing about pressure is to have the appropriate squeeze for the situation. Being firm in your handshake, without crushing their hand, comes off as confident and is always better than a limp shake. Limp handshakes won't build rapport.

PART 2

PERSUASION TECHNIQUES

Introduction

Do you know that persuasion occurs much quicker than influence? You will usually come up with a strategy for persuasion before as well, where influence might end up happening without even trying. In order to be good at persuasion, it is something that you have to practice. Since sometimes you only have one shot, you have to make sure that you are not going to ruin your chance to be persuasive.

Influence can make it easier to convince someone of something or to recover when you have failed to do it. If you persuade someone to do something and get caught and labeled as a manipulator, it can ruin your credibility. Not all forms of persuasion are bad, but some people are wary that you might be trying to control them, so if done in the wrong way, it can make them turn away from you.

Even a thirty-second ad can be persuasive. There is no time limit that says how quickly or how slowly you can persuade someone. You might have a year to persuade someone to move to a different neighborhood, or you might only have a minute to persuade them to sign a lease for a new apartment.

In either scenario, the right persuader would have no problem trying to convince the other person to do what they want. If something takes too long, however, it might turn into a form of influence, or you might just have to find a different way to be persuasive.

Sometimes you do not even have to say anything; just a look can be enough to persuade. Someone might be trying on a certain outfit, and without saying that it makes them look bad, the look on your face can be enough to make them realize they should choose something different.

At the same time, we also have to look at how not saying anything can persuade someone to make a certain decision. If someone talks about wanting to do something, and you give them a simple head shake, they might be persuaded not to follow through with it at all and pursue something else instead.

Even though it can be short term, moments of persuasion can have long-term effects. If you did persuade someone to sign a lease within a short period of time, that lease could be for twelve months, and that person is now committed to a certain apartment. Before you attempt to persuade, you have to ensure that it is going to be mutually beneficial for both parties.

You do not have to have a close relationship with the person you are persuading. Sometimes we can persuade the sales clerk to give us a discount, or we can persuade a customer to go through with a larger sale. While influence requires a longer-term relationship, persuasion can be accomplished from the moment you meet someone.

You must be a persuasive person in order to carry through the motivation for a choice one way or another. If you come off as untrustworthy or someone who is not authentic, it is going to be harder to be persuasive. Persuasiveness comes naturally for some, but it can certainly be learned by even the most suspicious-looking people.

Influence occurs with people who might have been admiring the influencer for a while, so it is easier to become influenced by them. Persuasion requires a little more work. You do not have that trust to fall back on, so you have to make sure that you are building an authentic case for yourself.

Chapter 29: What is Persuasion?

Persuasion is something that we experience on a daily basis. We are going to be persuaded by friends and family to help out on occasion. We are going to see a ton of advertisements from companies that want to persuade us to purchase their products and not form the competitor. We see persuasion so often that it is sometimes hard to realize that it could be bad and that a manipulator could try to use this against us. How does one get people to think and behave in a different manner and to follow their path? There are going to be a lot of subtle ways that you can press your agenda without turning everyone off and making it seem like you have some bad agenda in the making. When it comes to persuasion, Robert Cialdini is well respected for some of his ideas on persuasion and how to do it successfully, whether your intentions are good or not. According to Cialdini, there are six principles that can be used to help out with the ideas of persuasion, and these six principles are going to include:

- **Reciprocity**: This is where you will do a small favor for someone, and then right away ask them to do one back.

- **Commitment and consistency**: This one holds the target of doing something because they have done it in the past.

- **Social proof**: This is when you convince the target to do something because it is popular, and everyone is doing it.

- **Authority**: Your target is more likely to do something if they believe you are an authority on that topic.

- **Likeability**: If you can become likable and they see you as a friend, they are more likely to do what you ask.

- **Scarcity**: This is the fear that an item is going to be in short supply, so they want to get it.

Understanding Persuasion and its Significance

The main aim of every negotiation is to come to an agreement regarding an issue. In coming to that agreement, a major skill you need is persuasion. You should be able to persuade and convince the other party to agree with you.

Being good at persuasion is a vital part of a successful negotiation. It is a very important skill that you and everyone who intends to have fruitful negotiations or who intends to wield some influence over others should have. Persuasion is effectively marketing and selling your point of view to the other party. You have to persuade the other party to understand your viewpoint and to even accept it.

As an entrepreneur or an individual going into a negotiation, you should be able to convince others to accept your ideas or your stance. For example, it is persuasion that would help you get your employer to increase your salary when you are negotiating a salary raise, and this would only happen if you can convince your employer about how valuable you have been and how a salary raise for you would be beneficial to both you and the company.

Persuasion is mostly giving people reasons why they should do something in a way that they would be convinced to do it.

Contrary to what people believe about persuasion being a talent, it is a skill that can be learned and can be honed through practice. If you are still in doubt about why persuasion is important in negotiation and why you need to learn how to persuade people, here are some reasons.

Changing Mindsets

This appears to be the most apparent benefit of persuasion; however, because of how important it is, it needs to be reiterated.

When people come to the negotiation table, they come with their beliefs, mindsets, and attitudes. Now, sometimes, these beliefs or mindsets do not favor you, and this means you have to change them through persuasion.

The mindsets or beliefs do not even have to be about the negotiation or the issue at hand. Sometimes they are about you, and you can use persuasion to change the way the other party views you.

For example, a former negotiation with an earlier client earned you a bad reputation in the industry; the status of a shrewd business person who everyone should be wary of when transacting business. Now, when people have to do business with you, they are so careful, and they are always on the defense so much that the negotiation process rarely goes smoothly. With persuasion, you can convince the client that the reputation is false. You can influence them to stop being on the defense, and you will end up having a smooth negotiation process and getting the best possible outcome.

Dispute Management

Paul is in a negotiation between the IT company he works at and a prospective client. A tactless colleague at the meeting has just said something the prospective client finds really annoying. Tempers are flaring; words are being exchanged.

Paul decides to step in and do something. At the office, he is known as a tension diffuser who is able to influence people to do his bidding. He calmly speaks to the client and then to his colleague. Apologies are exchanged, and everyone goes back to doing what they were doing earlier.

When you have the ability to persuade people as a skill, you will be able to deal with any disputes that arise while you are negotiating. Sometimes, deals do not go through because they are open or latent disputes or rising tensions, and the two parties have gotten to a point where their judgment is clouded by their emotions. It takes the skill of persuasion to handle this and ensure that everyone goes back to the negotiation table and that the deal is made.

This benefit of persuasion is particularly important because you should build relationships that leave room for further negotiation and business transactions after the initial negotiation.

Greater Sales

Stella is a businesswoman looking to sell her products. However, she is experiencing a drought when it comes to getting customers to buy the products she is selling. Also, there is the problem of the existence of competitors who have established brands in the industry getting most of the patronage. Stella wants customers to patronize her business. She wants customers to buy her products. Not only is Stella looking for new customers who have not purchased a similar product, but she is also hoping to get some of her competitors' customers. She needs to convince these customers to buy her products.

When you are promoting your product or service to a customer, your ability to persuade them to see reasons why they should patronize is a vital part of you making any successful sale. You need to be able to convince your target market that you understand their needs and that you know how to provide great solutions to those needs.

Persuasion during sales will help you show the customer the merits of giving you their money. Persuasion is important for negotiating even the price that will be paid by the customer. If you want to make a sales deal happen, learn how to be persuasive.

Career Advancement

Everyone wants to grow. Whether it is transitioning to a new job or getting a promotion and a corresponding pay raise, career advancement is always welcome.

Career advancement also involves some negotiation. From negotiating your salary to negotiating with the management of the firm you work for a promotion and a pay raise, you need to have good negotiation skills to get your desired outcome.

When it comes to getting your desired outcome in terms of advancing your career, persuasion plays a significant role. If you are applying for a new job, you should be able to persuade your prospective employer to increase the initial offer that was made and to pay you either the amount you are asking for or something close to that which would still be favorable to you. If you already work at a firm and you would like to take on more responsibility, you would like to be promoted, or you want a pay raise, you need to be able to convince the management of the firm to get the desired outcome.

One good thing about persuasion is that its effects are not limited to a single person. You can use it for large audiences. If you are trying to pitch a product or service to a room full of potential investors, beyond persuading one person to invest in the product, you can persuade all the potential investors to make you great offers.

After discovering how persuasion can be beneficial to you, you should learn the types of persuasion. Learning the types of persuasion is a step in the right direction when it comes to learning how to wield persuasion as a valuable skill while negotiating.

Chapter 30: Human Behavior

Human behavior concerns the full spectrum of emotional and physical behaviors that humans engage in that include social, biological, and intellectual actions and are impacted by attitudes, culture, ethics, rapport, and genetics, among other considerations. Human behavior is a complex interplay of cognition, actions, and emotion.

Correspondingly, actions are behavior as actions capture everything that can be observed. Actions can be captured through eyes or through physiological sensors. An initiation or transition from one state to another is an action.

When viewing emotions as behavior, emotions are considered as a relatively brief conscious experience marked by intense mental activity and a feeling that is not influenced by either knowledge or reasoning. Emotions normally happen from a positive to negative scale. Increased arousal can cause other aspects of physiology that are indicative of emotional processing, such as enhanced respiration rate. Emotions can only be inferred indirectly, akin to cognition, through monitoring facial expressions and tracking arousal, among others.

Understanding Human Behavior from a Psychological Viewpoint

Investment Model

Human behavior can be understood in terms of work effort focused on creating change. For instance, whether Hilda is headed out due to the need to watch the movie or wants to be with her boyfriend, the act of going to the movie is a form of investment. In this manner, human behavior occurs due to the need to get a particular outcome. The return of this investment can be found in the movie Hilda watches or a kiss from her boyfriend at the end of it.

In this aspect, behavior involves making consideration of the investment in terms of calories, time, risks, and opportunity costs. The motivation of where to invest our actions in spurring a particular behavior to emanate from evolutionary influences that have made us prioritize sex, food, safety, territory, and higher social status over other states of affairs.

Genetics also impact certain behavioral traits, such as dispositions and temperaments. For instance, extroverted people find stimulating social situations more satisfying compared to introverted people. Against this backdrop, the learning history of an individual impacts the investment value system. For instance, if Hilda loved the first two Star Wars movies, then we can expect her to show a strong desire to see the third.

An illustration of the investment model of human behavior is where one is seated on the couch watching television when an advert of a cookie activates in you the desire to pour a glass of milk. You have had a long day, and you are feeling worn out. In your mind, a small computation takes place where you weigh on the value of getting up and pouring yourself a glass of milk. Eventually, the thirst wins out, and you decide to go get a glass of milk from the refrigerator. Unfortunately, a quick look in the fridge indicates there is no milk, which makes you take a glance at the trashcan where you notice the empty milk container.

In detail, the investment model for understanding human behavior views behaviors in the form of work effort committed to realizing a particular outcome — the behavior costs in the form of time and energy computed in the form of benefits and costs. Human behavior is largely a cost-benefit analysis according to the investment model of animal behavior. Most animal documentaries on the behavior of animals can help you realize how inherently animals make the cost-benefit analysis. Take the case of wildebeests in African savanna plains that need to drink water and cross the river that is infested with hungry crocodiles. In this environment, water and grass are scarce, and wildebeests desperately need water and grass. At the same time, the wildebeests have to watch out for marauding crocodiles lurking under the surface of the water, ready to devour the wildebeests.

Eventually, wildebeests have to invoke an investment model of behavior to maximize the possibility of living, drinking water, and crossing the river to graze. Under this model, most wildebeests cautiously approach the river, ensuring that they near the river bank when drinking water, which would enable them to retract sporadically at the slightest hint of danger.

In this manner, human behavior is a sort of commerce with the environment. The human being actions are primed to maximize benefits from the environment. The mind is a critical component of behavior as it stores a history of what has desired outcomes as well as computing the cost-benefit analysis before one acts. It can be argued that the investment model of behavior affirms the assumption that human behavior is conscious and well-thought. Additionally, actions lead to lost opportunities, and one has to pursue an action that best maximizes the intended outcomes. For instance, if an animal spends time defending a territory, it is losing out on finding food.

Social Influence Model of Human Behavior

Human behavior can be viewed from the understanding that a human being is a social animal. Human behavior happens in the context of a social matrix. A social influence entails the actions that influence the investment of another person. For instance, when Hilda was going to the movie, did she ask her boyfriend out, or the boyfriend did ask her out. In most cases, social influence processes involve cooperation, cooperation, and whether the transactions move people closer or make them drift apart. Social influence also manifests as a resource. As a resource, social influence concerns the capacity to move other people in alignment with our interests.

Social influence in this context refers to the levels of social and respect value other people show us and the degree to which they listen, care about our well-being, and are willing to sacrifice for us. For instance, if Hilda is attracted to his boyfriend, and he agrees to go to the movie with her, then this indicates social influence as a resource. If the boyfriend breaks up with Hilda, it is a potent indication of a loss of social influence.

Additionally, social influence is determined by the amount of attention from other people. In line with this understanding, the actions of a person will seek to attract attention from people or sustain the attention of people. Probably you have colleagues or public figures that consistently act to attract and sustain admiration from other people. On a personal level, one is likely to act in a manner that invites admiration from colleagues, friends, and other people. The behavior and likely behavior of an individual is likely to optimize admiration from others.

Furthermore, within the social influence model of human behavior, people are likely to act in a manner that invites more positive emotions than negative emotions from others. In a way, the need to attract more positive emotions from others is related to attracting admiration from others, but it is highly related to emotional intelligence. One can only enhance the likelihood of getting a positive emotional reaction from others if he or she has requisite emotional intelligence levels.

Through emotional intelligence, one learns to show empathy and pay attention to how others are feeling. Against this backdrop, human behavior is likely to be reactive to how others are feeling, or it is likely to be highly considerate of others for the motivation of attracting positive emotions from them. Then there is the degree to which others will sacrifice their interests for the sake of another person as a mark of social influence. People with big social influence will have tens to thousands of people willing to sacrifice their interests for the sake of the person. The behavior of the individual with great social influence is likely to take into account that there are tens to thousands of people who are willing to forego their interests for the sake of the influential figure. On the other hand, the followers of the influential people are likely to take the actions of the individual as guidance or a message of how one should act and live.

Justification Model of Human Behavior

First, human behavior requires justifications by legitimizing it. For instance, when you shout at someone, there are chances that one will qualify the behavior by stating that they were upset. In reaching a justification, one assesses the behavior and the ideal outcome. For instance, the ideal outcome may have been attracting admiration from others, but one ended up embarrassing themselves in public. Expectedly, the individual will feel angry for not only failing to attain an ideal reaction from the audience, but also degrading the status quo. In this state, the individual will justify subsequent undesired behavior by drawing attention to the disappointment he or she got earlier on.

Using the Hilda and the movie example, Hilda may have felt justified to make her boyfriend tag along to the movie and allow the boyfriend to show romance because of this what lovers do. The justification of her behavior and the boyfriend's behavior emanates from observation and learned patterns of what lovers do and not necessarily of how each of them individually feels. Justification of behavior can be simply that is what others do, and so the individual is obliged to emulate the same. Try watching court proceedings for you to realize how people place significant value on justification for their behavior.

At the corporate level, organizations have invested significantly in assessing human behavior during recruitment stages and as well as assessing workers. Human behavior is complex, and organizations seek to have the best bet in recruiting and retaining fairly predictable workers. Most of the personality tests administered during hiring and appraisal processes are meant to help profile workers and have a predictable look at how each of the workers may behave. There have been attempts to determine a formula for human behavior as a simple system, but it has been satisfactorily concluded that human behavior is dynamic.

Chapter 31: What We Can Get from the Power of Persuasion

Have you ever asked yourself why there are some people, and even situations, which can persuade us so much more than others? But here is one thing that most of us do not know. How persuasive a person has something to do with the kind of state in which they are in. if you are all alone, hungry, tired, or just in need of something very important, then you can be more persuasive? It is easy to have a desperately thirsty man do anything you need just in exchange for a glass of water. Therefore, ensuring that your primal physical needs and emotions are met in a satisfying manner puts you at a position where you are less quick prey to being conned by those who appear to just offer empty promises. These people might also be expecting too much in return for the little favor they might have given you.

Anybody or anything that appears to meet the emotional need within your whole being will also appear so persuasive to you.

You will be wrong to think you can easily notice when someone is attempting to persuade about something, but a good number of these needs are very subtle, and we are usually not so conscious about them. According to Robert Cialdini, who was one of the best psychologists, there are six principles of persuasion. These principles make the whole point that being persuaded is not necessarily a bad thing as others might think. If you are able to persuade a person to wear a safety belt when in a car or not to drink and drive, then persuasion can honestly be a great thing. However, when we take time to consider some of the awful things that people have been persuaded to do by their leaders, then it becomes apparent that understanding the psychology that is behind persuasion is very important for all our sakes. But the truth is that the six principles that were introduced by Cialdini should be employed in a dishonorable way. Those who are savvy can make full use of the six principles of persuasion in an ethical way to make society great and to give the willing donors some fulfillment.

To prove the truth in this, a questionnaire was sent by the Stanford Social Innovation Appraisal to the consultants and executive directors of various non-profit organizations. In the questionnaire, they were asked which among the six rules were most relevant in their fundraising works. The results of this survey, as well as the other interviews that followed up, suggested that at least 4 out of the 6 rules give special opportunities for non-profit development. The four principles that were identified included the following:

Reciprocity – People will always try to pay back, with lots of kindness, what they have been offered by other people. This is the same rule that prompted the gift that Ethiopia gave Mexico.

Scarcity – The fact is that opportunities will appear more valuable when they are not available in high numbers.

Authority – Human beings will defer to decision-making authorities as a shortcut for making lasting decisions.

Consistency – Once a person has taken a stand or made a choice, they will encounter interpersonal and personal pressures to behave in a consistent manner with the commitment.

Despite the fact that the use of the mentioned principles will optimize influence, they are optimally employed by just a fraction of those who could easily benefit from them. A number of nonprofit leaders always hesitate to use any of these principles because they don't understand them or even know how they can harness their main force. There are also others who are much aware of what the principles are and even how they operate, but they still dishonestly import them. They end up achieving just short-term goals while leaving their main target in a manipulated state.

Non-profit leaders who are successful in their lines of work understand so well the rules of influence and even employ them in an ethical manner.

Instead of placing people in a hammerlock kind of situation, they go ahead to uncover all the affinities that are pre-existing.

Here are the principles of persuasion that make up the power of persuasion:

Reciprocity

The first principle of persuasion is known as reciprocity. We always feel obliged to do something back to those who do good things to us. At times, we consciously do not realize this. Some of the common phrases that we use when someone does something great to us include the following:

• I owe you something.

• I am much obliged.

A person who is trying to persuade the other may use this particular principle by doing something, no matter how small it is, to the other individual first. This explains the origin of the widespread use of a free sample in the marketing spaces. While working on the report that contained the six principles, Cialdini quoted out the instance where Ethiopia offered thousands of dollars to Mexico in humanitarian aid after having experienced an earthquake in 1985. The reason why this is a great example was that Ethiopia was also, at the same time, suffering from civil war and a crippling famine. Unknown to many, Ethiopia was reciprocating for the diplomatic help that Mexico offered when they were invaded in 1935 by Italy.

It is a fact that people do some good things to others nearly all the time without making conditions to have the same favor back. However, you shouldn't forget that the feeling of being beholden to some individuals is one of the most powerful influencers. Each one of us has learned to live up to the rules of reciprocation, and we are also fully aware of the social sanctions that the violators of this golden rule risk undergoing. A portion of the power of reciprocity is based on the fact that an individual can decide to trigger an indebtedness feeling of doing a favor that is not invited. But people will always feel obliged to repay the favor, whether they have been asked or not. A number of nonprofit organizations follow this golden rule when they send free gifts through the mails and expect a donation back.

Self-Consistency

Self-consistency is the second principle of persuasion. According to Cialdini, those who commit either in writing or orally to some goal or idea are more likely to either strive for the goal or hold the idea. This is due to the fact that commitment, in itself, establishes the idea as a self-image congruent. Even if the original motivation or incentive is taken away after the agreement has been made, they will still continue to honor the agreement.

Human beings have this tendency to present a consistent image of what we are made up of to the world and even to ourselves. It is dangerous to role-play or be in the character of an individual who doesn't subscribe to your school of thought. This is because you will be very sympathetic to the idea, even if you are sure that you are just role-playing.

Two Canadian psychologists discovered something very interesting about people who are at the racetrack. The duo discovered that people at a racetrack are usually very confident once they have placed their bets. Nothing about the horse changes. The track also remains the same. However, in the mind of the bettor, the prospects of the horse shall have greatly improved. This dramatic change is brought by a very common tool of social influence that is found within people and directs their actions with very silent powers.

The Social Proof

This is also another powerful principle of persuasion. The quote that million people can't be wrong can have some adverse effects. Since we are herded creatures, we just do certain things because others are doing it. This is so evident in the fashion industry where people just wear certain types of clothes because others are doing it. People will just do things they have seen others do even if they are not so sure of the outcomes. Because of the principle of social proof, testimonials have become so powerful.

This, however, does not dismiss the fact that there are better reasons why people do certain things. There is still what has been defined as the madness of crowds, and this is what pushes people to do things they haven't tried before. The madness of crowds is a tendency to believe or do certain things just because lots of people are in it. One of its dangers is that it can actually stop us from thinking for ourselves.

In all the circumstances that we always find ourselves in, we look at behavior as way much correct to the level we see other people enacting it.

This explains why in situations that are difficult and awkward, people have this tendency of looking across the room at the other people before behaving in a certain way. We do this just to make sure that our reaction is socially correct or accepted, especially when we step out. Nobody desires to be the odd one out in everything. Social proof is very crucial to us due to the fact that we might make some fewer mistakes as we go along with the crowd. Even though there are pitfalls to going with as opposed to going against the grain, like the bystander effect, those who are skilled at persuasion have exhausted the main idea of social proof by alluding to the fact that everybody is doing it, and so there is nothing wrong about giving it a try.

The Perceived Authority

Perceived authority is the fourth principle of persuasion. We assume that something is just fine because the teacher or the scientist has said so, or because it is an order coming from the president. Little known to us is that there is usually a dark side of all this. A typical example is the ex-Nazis who were asked to explain the cause of their actions, and all they could say was that they were just following the orders. According to famous experiments that Stanley Milgram undertook in the 1960s, normal people can be forced to carry very cruel and highly objectionable acts just because of the universal principle of making a blind response to the authorities without thinking twice. The major problem is that it is so easy to fake authority by just putting on certain right trappings, which is a uniform or a type of behavior or speech. This is one of the things we all fall for overtime. For another time, we hand over our sole responsibility of thinking for ourselves to another person just because they are wearing a badge.

Likeability

This is also another common principle of persuasion. Likeability can appear all that sinister, but the problem lies with liking. It is a common fact that likable people can get persuasive. So, it is not surprising when various studies state that we will easily purchase from some people we like as opposed to just buying from random people. That explains why salespeople are usually very likable and attractive. And that's where the power of persuasion comes in because we will be easily persuaded by people we adore.

Chapter 32: Advanced Persuasion Techniques

After taking a look at the different types of persuasion and what they all mean, you may be able to see why dark persuasion is such a bad thing and can be harmful to the victim. Being able to recognize the different techniques that the manipulator may use can make it easier to understand when it is being used on you.

So, how exactly is a dark persuader able to use this idea in order to carry out their wishes? There are a few different types of tactics that a dark manipulator is going to use, but some of the most common options include:

The Long Con

The first technique that we are going to look at is the Long Con. This technique is kind of slow and drawn out, but it can be really effective because it takes so long and is hard to recognize or even pinpoint when something went wrong. Some of the main reasons that some people have the ability to resist persuasion is because they feel that they are being pressured by the other person, and this can make them back off. If they feel that there is a lack of rapport or trust with the person who is trying to persuade them, they will steer clear as well. The Long Con is so effective because they are able to overcome these main problems and give the persuader exactly what they want.

The Long Con is going to involve the dark persuader to take their time, working to earn the trust of their victim. They are going to take some time to befriend the victim and make sure that their victim trusts and likes them. This is going to be achieved by the persuader with artificial rapport building, which sometimes seems excessive, and other techniques that will help to increase the comfort levels between the persuader and their victim.

As soon as the persuader sees that the victim is properly readied psychologically, the persuader is going to begin their attempts. They may start out with some insincere positive persuasion. The persuader is going to lead their victim into making a choice or doing some action that will actually benefit the persuader. This is going to serve the persuader in two ways. First, the victim starts to become used to persuasion by that persuader. The second is that the victim is going to start making that mental association between a positive outcome and the persuasion.

The Long Con is going to take a long period of time to complete because the persuader doesn't want to make it too obvious what they are doing. An example of this is a victim who is a recently widowed lady who is vulnerable because of their age and from their bereavement. After her loss, a man starts to befriend her. This man may be someone she knows from church or even a relative. He starts to spend more time with her, showing immense kindness and patience, and it doesn't take too long for her guard to drop when he comes around.

Then this man starts to carry out some smaller acts of positive persuasion that we talked about before. He may advise her of a better bank account to use or a better way to reduce any monthly bills. The victim is going to appreciate these efforts and the fact that the man is trying to help her, and she takes the advice.

Over some time, the man then tries to use some dark persuasion. He may try to persuade her to let him invest some of her money. She obliges because of the positive persuasion that was used in the past. Of course, the man is going to work to take everything he can get from her. If the manipulator is skilled enough, she may feel that he actually tried to help her, but the money is lost because he just ran into some bad luck with the investment. This is how far dark persuasion can go.

Graduality

Often when we hear about acts of dark persuasion, it seems impossible and unbelievable. What they fail to realize is that this dark persuasion isn't ever going to be a big or a sudden request that comes out of nowhere. Dark persuasion is more like a staircase. The dark persuader is never going to ask the victim to do something big and dramatic the first time they meet. Instead, they will have the victim take one step at a time. When the manipulator has the target only go one step at a time, the whole process seems like less of a big deal. Before the victim knows it, they have already gone a long way down, and the persuader isn't likely to let them leave or come back up again. Let's take an example of how this process is going to look in real life. Let's say that there is a criminal who wanted to make it so that someone else committed the crimes for them. Gang bosses, cult leaders, and even Charles Manson did this exact same thing.

This criminal wouldn't dream of beginning the process by asking their victim to murder for them. This would send out a red flag, and no one in their right minds would willingly go out and kill for someone they barely know. Instead, the criminal would start out by having the victim do something small, like a petty crime, or simply hiding a weapon for them. Something that isn't that big of a deal for the victim, at least in comparison.

Over time, the acts that the manipulator is able to persuade their victim to do will become more severe. And since they did the smaller crimes, the persuader now has the unseen leverage of holding some of those smaller misdeeds over the victim, kind of like for blackmail. Before the victim knows it, they are going to feel like they are in too deep. They will then be persuaded to carry out some of the most shocking crimes. And often, by this point, they will do it because they feel like they have no other choice.

Dark persuaders are going to be experts at using this graduality to help increase the severity of their persuasion over time. They know that no victim would be willing to jump the canyon or do the big crime or misdeed right away. So, the persuader works to build them a bridge to get there. By the time the victim sees how far in they are, it is too late to turn back.

Masking the True Intentions

There are different methods that a persuader is able to use dark psychology in order to get the things that they want. Disguising their true desires is very important for them to be successful. The best persuaders can use this approach in a variety of ways, but the method they choose is often going to depend on the victim and the situation.

One principle that is used by a persuader is the idea that many people are going to have a difficult time refusing two requests when they happen in a row. Let's say that the persuader wants to get $200 from the victim, but they do not intend to repay the money. To start, the persuader may begin by saying that they need a loan for the amount of $1000. They may go into some details about the consequences to themselves if the persuader doesn't come up with that kind of money sometime soon. It may happen that the victim feels some kind of guilt or compassion to the persuader, and they want to help. But $1000 is a lot of money, more than the victim is able to lend. From here, the persuader is going to lessen their request from $1000 down to $200, the amount that they wanted from the beginning. Of course, there is some kind of emotional reason for needing the money, and the victim feels like it is impossible to refuse this second request. They want to help out the persuader, and they feel bad for not giving in to the initial request when they were asked. In the end, the persuader gest the $200 they originally wanted, and the victim is not going to know what has taken place.

Another type of technique that the persuader can use is known as reverse psychology. This can also help to mask the true intentions during the persuasion. Some people have a personality that is known as a boomerang. This means that they will refuse to go in the direction that they are thrown and instead will veer off into different directions.

If the persuader knows someone who is more of a boomerang type, then they are able to identify a key weakness of that person. For example, let's say that a persuader has a friend who is attempting to win over some girl they like. The persuader knows that the friend will use and then hurt that girl. The girl is currently torn between the malicious friend and an innocent third party. The persuader may try to steer the girl in the direction of the guy who is actually a good choice, knowing that she is going to go against this and end up going with the harmful friend.

Leading Questions

Another method of dark persuasion that can be used is known as leading questions. If you have ever had an encounter with a salesman that is skilled, verbal persuasion can be really impactful when it is deployed in careful and calibrated ways. One of the most powerful techniques that can be used verbally is leading questions. These leading questions are going to be any questions that are intended to trigger a specific response out of the victim. The persuader may ask the target something like, "how bad do you think those people are?" This question is going to imply that the people the persuader is asking about are definitely bad to some extent. They could have chosen to ask a question that was non-leading, such as "how do you feel about those people?"

Dark persuaders are masters at using leading questions in a way that is hard to catch. If the victim ever begins to feel that they are being led, then they are going to resist, and it is hard to lead them or persuade them. If a persuader ever senses that their victim starts to catch what is happening, they will quit using that one and switch over to another one. They may come back to that tactic, but only when the victim has quieted down a bit and is more influenceable again.

The Law of State Transference

The state is a concept that is going to take a look at the general mood someone is in. If someone is aligned with their deeds, words, and thoughts, then this is an example of a strong and congruent state. The law of state transference is going to involve the concept of someone who holds the balance of power in a situation and can then transfer their emotional state onto the other person they are interacting with. This can be a very powerful tool for the dark persuader to use against their victim.

Initially, the influencer is going to force their own state to match the state that their target naturally has. If the target is sad, and they talk slowly, the influencer is going to make their own state follow this format.

Chapter 33: How to Resist Persuasion

Did you know that one of the best ways to not allow what someone says affect you is simply by not listening? You don't have to be rude, just don't home in on the words they're saying and maybe nod along as if you're listening. In the end, when they deliver their ending pitch, "So, just sign here, and we'll get this party started."

You can shrug. "Nah. I'll pass." And walk away without looking back. Because if you did look back, you'd see one agitated person who just realized how much time and energy they've just wasted on you.

You can take these secrets and use them for the times you want to use persuasion on others. This way, you will see the signs a person gives when they're not being affected by what you're saying. You can cut your time short with these people as you will not penetrate their mental boundaries. The key to not listening is to not listen to a word they say. As you know, there are those hot words that can seep into your brain without you realizing it's happening.

You know that the key to getting people to do what you want them to is to put the pressure on them, time wise. If you agree to something at record speed, you best take a moment or two to reconsider what you've done. Most decisions are better made when you give yourself time and educate yourself on whatever they are selling or trying to get you to agree with. It's okay if you fell into the trap. But get out of it as soon as you possibly can.

Of course, the best thing is to avoid getting sucked in altogether. There are a lot of unscrupulous people out there who will sell you their junk and put a no-refunds policy in their paperwork. So, be smart and never sign anything that will end up costing you lots of money until you take a day to think it over and research everything you can about the purchase.

Seeing as how you now have advanced knowledge of persuasive techniques; you have been forewarned about this type of thing. Consider yourself lucky at this point.

Being forewarned about this type of thing means that you have a defense mechanism already in place inside of your head. Whenever you see something that you recognize as persuasive techniques, bow out before they can even start bombarding your psyche with their nonsense.

Be on the lookout now for things that might be meant to lead you to a place you wouldn't go before or on your own. And watch out for people who say things about others that you might not agree with.

So many people nowadays want everyone to think the same way that they do about most things and people. Take politics, for instance. It used to be considered bad manners or rude to discuss politics anywhere but in political rallies and conventions. Nowadays, that topic is front and center wherever you look.

If you listened to what each person had to say on the subject, you might want to blow your brains out by the end of it all. That's because most people have one mindset; you're either with me or against me. This isn't true, but a lot of people think in these terms now.

So, if someone comes up to you, stating some so-called facts about any political figure or even one of your neighbors, either don't listen or take it with a grain of salt. Make your own decisions about people; don't allow others to make them for you.

Another train of thought in fending off persuasion is inoculation. This refers to the way we use a bit of disease to give us immunization to a full-on attack from it. Since you do know about persuasion, you can delve into it a bit more than others can. You can go into an argument with a mind that's accustom to these things. The thing about arguments is this. When you are prepared for them, you will rarely find yourself in one. That's because the other party can see that you will volley everything, they say right back to them. It's like a tennis match where you already know where the ball is going and continue to put it right back into their court.

The only way to gain this knowledge is by getting into a few arguments yourself to know where people are going with theirs. It's a lot easier than it sounds. People only have so many ways they can argue, and once you understand those things, you will always win.

Persuasion is different from mind control in the way that it doesn't restrict your decisions. It is restricting it, but it doesn't look that way.

Most people, when told what to do, will not do it. They will do just the opposite most of the time. If you want someone to do the opposite and you're well aware of how they take it when someone tells them to do something, then, by all means, use that.

But if you spot someone doing this to you, don't let your ego or will allow you to fall into their scheme. No matter how hard it might be, don't react in your typical way.

The person who is attempting to persuade you might give you the idea that you've got the free will to make your own decisions, which you don't have at all. If you feel gently pushed in any direction, this is persuasion, and it's best to avoid it at all costs. You need to make your own decisions, after all.

There is a technique called Counter arguing and bolstering. What you must watch out for here is the help brought in by the person who's trying to persuade you to their way of thinking and using dirty tricks to do it.

There may be people planted in the group or audience who are supposed to join your side of the argument and make you think you've got the support you need to prove that you're right. And that's what the persuader wants. Sneaky, I know, but it happens.

Another thought on resisting persuasion is that it only serves to make more resistance. If you are resisting and the person doing the persuading is just coming at you harder, then you are in this little scene. Again, the best way to avoid being manipulated this way is to walk away or turn your mind off completely to what they're saying.

You must remember this; there cannot be an argument if you refuse to do your part in it.

Most of us grew up hearing our parents give this reason for most things they told us to do, "I'm your father, and you will do it because I said so."

When we were little children, most of us just did what we were told to do after that was said. But that isn't the case anymore. I've heard very young children ask their parents why they want them to do something, and when given that lame reason, they rebel.

You should also rebel when someone uses their authority to tell you what to do. If it makes no sense, that is. If you were speeding in your car and a police officer pulls you over, then you shouldn't argue the point that you felt like speeding, so you did it. There are times when you must concede to authority once you've broken a law that you were aware of.

But if you don't believe you broke any law and you were pulled over anyway, you can try to speak respectfully to the officer, explaining that you didn't know about the law you broke and now that you know about it, you won't do it again. You can hope that would get you out of receiving a citation over it.

If the officer won't budge, there's no reason to get upset about it and cause yourself to insult the officer and perhaps get yourself thrown into jail. You have an alternative way to argue your point or case. You can take that citation and see a judge about it. There, you can argue your point and see if the citation can be dropped. But those are extreme examples of persons in authority using it to make you do something you don't want to do. What if your boss came to you and told you that he wanted you to hurry down to the grocery store, pick up some meat, and barbeque it for all one hundred employees that very day? And you still have to get all of your work done too?

Now, this is a point you could argue or turn down. If he was to fire you over something like this, then you can always fight that by going to your human resources department or even the workforce to see justice taken on your behalf.

But let's say that you're a parent on the opposite side of this thing. You want to be able to get your kids to do whatever you want them to without any resistance.

With the introduction of television and the internet, the children of today have so much more access to what other people think and do that it's unimaginable. A parent's influence used to be about all a kid had. Now, they can be influenced by the world, and there's not much you can do about that.

We pay the price for technology – always has – always will.

If you think back, you will remember a time before cell phones when we were kids, and you had to be home before the streetlights came on each night. A little later than that, and you might be grounded or spanked.

Then cell phones came around, and the kids just had to keep in contact with their parents through that. They began to stay out and go further from home when they did leave.

And with that, parents lost a bit of the hold they'd always had on their children. They no longer needed to hold your hand, lest they get lost. Now, they could let go of your hand and run free, just as long as they had enough charge on their cell phone.

Technology comes at a price; it always has.

Another thing you must be sure of is that you are alert when someone is trying to talk you into something. When we're tired, we tend to agree to anything just to be left alone so we can rest.

Just like you shouldn't be hungry while you've got to go grocery shopping, you shouldn't be tired when faced with any decision. You can always sleep on it and face that decision the following day when you are well-rested and alert.

You wouldn't go dog-tired to see a used car salesman, now would you? Don't try to discuss anything with any manipulator when you're tired.

Breaking people by sleep deprivation is a proven mental manipulation technique that you must be aware of and not fall for. Especially an exhausted parent who has a kid who is begging for just one piece of candy before bed.

If you fall for this, you are sure to be even more exhausted when the kid finds himself wired up and unable to fall asleep the way you need him to if you are to get some much-needed sleep yourself.

The bottom line is this – if you feel the least bit like you are being persuaded or manipulated in any way, get away from the person who is doing it.

Chapter 34: Mind Control and Dark Psychology

The concept of mind control has existed for as long as psychology has been studied. You have probably overheard a person express their fascination or fear concerning what would happen if there was ever a chance that someone was able to control the minds of others and make them follow his or her commands. Similarly, there have been multiple conspiracy theories running around about powerful people or authorities utilizing their positions to force small groups of people to do certain things. There have even been court cases where the accused people blame "brainwashing" for causing them to commit their crimes.

However, the form of mind control that people seem to define is that which has been portrayed by the movies and media, which, unfortunately, is just the tip of the iceberg. Mind control exists in many forms, and people appear to understand very little about it. This pushes the need for a definite understanding and description of what exactly is mind control. If we take the words of psychologist Philip Zimbardo, mind control is defined as a process whereby the freedom of action and choice of an individual or a group is compromised by agencies or agents that distort or modify motivation, perception, behavioral and/or cognitive outcomes. In summary, mind control is a system that disrupts a person or groups at their core, that is, the level of their identity (which includes behaviors, decisions, preferences, beliefs, and relationships, to mention but a few) and creates a pseudo personality or pseudo-identity.

The above descriptions make it clear a person might be wrong to assume that they are forever in charge of their actions and thoughts. By now, you should already know that our minds are not solely at our discretion since they are susceptible to influence and control. Let us take a very common example. When you are watching an emotional movie, the directors utilize camera shots, lighting, color, music, and other enhancements to control your emotions. In as much as you are aware that what you are watching is not real, your brain still plays along, and you find yourself engrossed in the movie. Some people weep at sad scenes, whereas others jump or cringe when watching horror movies.

Now, think about it; if your brain can respond to a prompt which it clearly understands is not real, how would it react to hidden (covert) prompts? This brings us to covert mind control, which is the form of mind control where the victim is not aware that some distortion is being applied. Covert mind control is the most brutal form of control known to psychologists today. This is because if a person realizes that they are being controlled, then they can try to escape the situation, unlike in covert mind control, where one never gets to know it. The result is the controller takes full charge and might drive the victim to destruction without them realizing it.

Mind control can be ethical or unethical. You might wonder how having your mind shaped by another person can be good for you. Well, a good example of ethical mind control began when you were growing up. When your parents were bringing you up, they applied a lot of mind control. In fact, you are the person that you are today because of this mind control. Most of the beliefs, values, and behaviors that you possess, though you might have altered some, were passed onto you by your parents. Let's get a little more practical: when you wake up, your immediate actions include brushing your teeth, taking a shower, jumping into fresh clothes, applying makeup, and having breakfast before anything else. Where do you think this routine came from? Obviously, it was passed onto you by your parents or guardians.

The Process of Mind Control

A mind controller approaches the victim with the sole intent of cloning themselves, which is making the other person think like them. This is a complicated thing to do, so, to achieve it, one has to possess an inflated ego, lack doubts about themselves, and have a high sense of entitlement. All of us are susceptible to manipulation, and what matters is how much effect the mind control will have on us.

Psychologists studying mind control have found out that the entire process seems to adhere to a common structure. This conclusion was made after a study was conducted on multiple marketing and networking companies which used mind control to persuade clients to purchase their products. One of the outstanding similarities is that all new members joining the companies underwent a pre-planned training on how to recruit more people and convince potential customers to buy their products. The training sessions are meant to make the employees think like the company wants and use a form of mind twist to convince people.

Let us now look at the mind control process in detail.

Step 1 – Understanding the Target

Before anything else, the manipulator will seek to establish a bond or connection with their potential victim. Good intent, or friendship, will be the first step because it makes the victim lower all their social and psychological defenses. Once the controller gains the trust of the target, they now start reading them so as to devise the most effective method to invade them. The aim of the reading is to tell whether their victim is susceptible to their manipulation. Just like any project manager, they do not like wasting time on a subject they suspect might outsmart them and lead to failure.

There are multiple clues that are used to scan the victim. They include verbal style, body language, social status, gender, emotional stability, and so on. A person's traits can be used to decode the strength of their defenses. All this time, the manipulator will be asking themselves questions like, "Are you introvert or extrovert?" "Are you weakly?" "Are you emotional?" "Are you self-confident?" Humans give a lot of information about themselves when interacting with each other, and this is something that the controller knows all too well

Step 2 – Unfreezing Solid Beliefs and Values

Each one of us has some beliefs and values engraved deep within. Most of them are the principles that were instilled in us since childhood, and others have been acquired from experiences are we grow older. We rarely let go of them, but revise them as we proceed.

Most of them are what make up our identities, so we do not like them being interfered with. If at any point in time these principles are threatened, contradicted, or questioned, our natural reaction is to defend them through all means possible. However, if a good-enough reason is given to us, so we voluntarily question them ourselves; we undergo a process known as "unfreezing."

Tons of reasons can lead us to unfreeze: a breakup, the death of a loved one, religious interference, getting evicted from our houses, to mention but a few. These situations force us to start seeking answers to complex situations, and this goes as deep as questioning our sole beliefs and values. Take this, for example:

When I was a teenager, we had some family friends who were solid Christians. It so happened that my best friend, who was my exact age, came from this family. His name was Sam. Sam used to tell me about the Bible and its teachings, trying to convince me to accept salvation and live according to its teachings. I remember asking him why he was so insistent on this issue, and he would respond that with salvation, all problems were solvable and that life was much easier and happier. Fast-forward about fifteen years, Sam's mother was diagnosed with breast cancer. They tried all forms of treatment available at the time, but cancer would grow back. One day, while talking to him about the issue, he looked at me with a pale face and said, "I think what they say about Christianity is not real!" Unsure about what he had just said, I asked him why he thought so. His response was that they had met tens of spiritual leaders for prayers, but his mother's cancer was only getting worse. What's worse, she would not live for more than a year.

Sad as Sam's story is, it makes us realize that some situations in life might force us to question the strong principles that we grow up with. In this case, my best friend had come to doubt the very same religion that he once felt had automatic solutions to all of life's problems. In the very same manner, a manipulator will dig deep into their victim's life to understand their vulnerabilities and exploit them fully. These people will say anything they think their targets would love to hear. Once the victim swallows the manipulator's comfort, there is a shift in power dynamics, and the target is now ready for the manipulation.

Step 3 – Reprogramming the Mind

The mind control process seeks to separate the target from their initial beliefs and begin reprogramming their mind. The reprogramming is meant to install the manipulator's beliefs and values into the victim's mind. Apart from distancing the initial principles, the controller also tries their best to make them look wrong or bad, or the cause of past mishaps in the victim's life. If the victim absorbs this reprogramming, their defense is literally lowered to zero, and they now become a robot that is ready to accept any operating system that is offered.

During the reprogramming phase, the attacker will try to ensure the victim has minimal contact with the outside world. They make everyone else to appear insignificant to the victim because this raises their opportunity to deposit their malicious principles into them. This behavior is common in cults, which are mostly crafted to sway their followers from mainstream human life. Some cults go as far as controlling the food intake of their followers as a way of weakening them. The psychology behind this idea is that a weak person will always turn to the person they feel has the power to protect them or alleviate their suffering. The same happens in relationships, where one partner plays the controlling role, and the victimized one has no choice but to adhere to the other.

Once the victim has been re-programmed, the manipulator moves into the final phase of the mind control process known as "freezing."

Step 4 – Freezing the New Beliefs and Values

Once the victim has been fed with contrasting principles by the offender, the offender applies tactics aimed at cementing the new beliefs into their brains. This is what psychologists call "freezing." The freezing bit is necessary because the controller is aware of the person's new beliefs that might clash with their initial ones. As such, they need to force the victim to choose their malicious principles over their old ones. To do this, they might apply any of the following methods.

One of the methods is using the reward/punishment approach. When the victim acts according to the manipulator's demands, they are rewarded. Hopefully, you see the similarity between the freezing process and dog training. The dog is given treats when it follows the trainer's instructions. The trainer aims at solidifying the new skill in the dog by rewarding it. In the future, if the dog is instructed to do the same thing, it will not hesitate since it has been made to think that obeying the command is good and attracts a reward. The same applies to mind control; when the victim obeys, they are made to feel that what they did was right and deserves a reward.

Punishments are the second most-applied approach in the freezing process. If the victim deviates from the controller's commands, they are punished. If we go back to the scenario of a cult, they usually have defined punishments for violations of terms.

Chapter 35: Speed Reading People

The concept of speed reading is described as the manner of quickly distinguishing and understanding sentences or phrases on a page all at once rather than identifying words one by one. Speed reading is also described by researchers as any of the methods that help one's ability to read faster. The average person can identify small images flashed on a monitor for only two micro-seconds. Humans had been reading slowly before the present time. However, researchers' consistent desire to increase reading speed has paid off, and they have discovered that the motion of the hands and eyes are vital in determining speed. They discovered that the smoother one's hand moves over a manuscript page, the faster they read. They, in effect, use the hand as a pacer.

It is no news that the information we process daily seems to be piling up each day. This information includes social media, reports, articles, textbooks, email, among others. The likelihood that we will want to quickly get through this bulk of information is very high. On average, most people read at the rate of two hundred and fifty words per minute. This is not to say that some are not quicker than others.

There are a lot of arguments and misconceptions about speed. Some are premised on the clash between understanding and speed, reading and flipping through. The arguments have been further strengthened based on the fact that a person whose understanding level is below fifty percent is deemed unacceptable by educationists. After a lot of controversy over a magical way to read faster, it has been resolved that there is no magic way other than a constant practicing of reading and the on-going usage of language. It is clear that speed reading is essential in picking up the key parts from texts or materials, be they school texts or files read for the fun of it. However, there are certain skills that guide us in how speed reading is to be done. Without the mastery of these skills, attempts at speed reading will end up futile. Let's get to the thick of things.

Speed Reading Basics

Never Talk to Yourself

This thing happens to almost everyone who reads; we talk to ourselves or mouth the words while reading. This helps one remember the ideas in the material, but it is a major hindrance while learning how to speed read because it slows you down. However, there are a few ways to stop talking to oneself. They include humming or chewing gum while speed reading and holding a finger against one's lips if one mistakenly starts mouthing words while speed reading.

After Reading Words, Make Sure You Cover Them

As stated, when we read, our eyes go back to words we have read before. Most times, these movements are short, and they don't boost comprehension. In order to speed read, after reading words, cover them with a card to train your eyes not to keep going back to them. Sometimes our eyes go back to the things we have read before if we do not understand what we have read properly.

To Speed Read, Try Speed Reading Software

If you discover that you have been trying hard to speed read with little to no results, or naturally, and you are learning things at a slow rate, take a look at Rapid Serial Visual Representation, a very potent speed reading application. With this application, the computer, or mobile phone, you are using flashes one single word at a time. This enables you to choose if you want to read at a fast or a slow rate. However, raising the reading speed too high will prevent you from understanding the details of what you are reading. Raising the reading speed may come in handy when trying to get a quick summary of a newspaper article.

Software exists that increases reading speed by training one's reflex actions, followed by consistent practicing until the brain adapts to the advanced speed. You can learn speed reading since the brain adapts to repeated actions over time. Using this method, you might understand more after a few days if you are intentional about increasing your speed to an extreme level.

Here's how you can do it:

- Use your pencil as a pacer to read about one thousand words in a minute.

- Spend one or two minutes reading at the pace at which the pencil is taking you. If you cannot understand anything, concentrate on the material and keep moving your eyes for the entire two minutes.

- Rest for four to five minutes. Then repeat the process again using your pencil as a pacer. You will find out that you will soon be going at the pace of the pencil. Consistency is key!

Be Knowledgeable in the Why the Eyes Move

It is a known fact that you can only read when your eyes are not moving. Therefore, if your eyes move at a slower rate, you will most likely learn faster. However, you need to be careful as research has revealed that this method impedes the way those who read English typically see. Your eyes move jerkily, stopping on some words and skipping others. Therefore, training the eyes to speed too much will result in skipping the details altogether. To learn speed reading, you can use your eyes to read nine letters to the left and four words to the right. This way, you can read roughly three to four words at a time. Also, you may notice eight to fourteen spaces to the left but cannot read them clearly. Normally, people who read do not understand the words on other lines. Training one to skip lines and understand the words seems difficult but is achievable.

Chapter 36: Influencing People

Talking to a person in authority, such as a preacher, professor, boss, or supervisor, can be quite unnerving. You want to catch their attention by seeming knowledgeable and competent on the subject, but not so much that you come off as a suck-up. Finding the right balance between the two can be quite tricky.

The following points will make it easier to influence persons with authority:

Overcome Your Fear

The first and most important thing to do is to get over your fear of speaking with the authority figure. Of course, it's easier said than done, but it is not as complicated as many of us assume. You must first realize that it is in a preacher's or professor's job description to speak to people like you; they expect it even.

You see, the secret to gaining favor with a person in authority is to keep off giving your opinion unless the authority figure asks for it. Unsolicited advice often comes off as pride and arrogance, and this will do nothing to better the relationship you have with the persons in authority. Therefore, ensure that you have all the available information on the subject, take a deep breath, get rid of all the butterflies and jitters, and march on. Whichever direction the talk takes, whether good or bad, you will be glad you did it.

Conduct Research to Identify the Person's Achievements

Persons in authority love it when juniors humor their ego a bit. Therefore, take to the internet and get to know all that your employer, professor, or pastor has done. Carefully study his professional history and see the people that he or she knows in your current field or in the area you hope to get into in the future. Read the files the person has authored and if possible, source the person's theses and research to know more about the things they are passionate about. The knowledge you are getting here will be excellent jump-off points and will show the authority figure that you did your homework before your conversation.

Be Prepared

While it is essential to know what interests the person you will be speaking with, know that flattery and knowing their backgrounds will only help you build a rapport, but what will get them interested in you and in what you are saying is the concepts and new information you intend to discuss. If you want to ask a question about the content you are learning in class, ensure that you have read through the assigned reading and done the assignments issued.

Even if you want to speak to him on a different matter, you might be surprised to see your professor asking class-related questions, and this will require you to be well-read and prepared on these matters too. You are not going to 'wing it'; this situation needs preparation on all fronts.

Be Practical

I cannot stress it enough that you should never postpone a discussion you were planning to have with an authority figure. The first reason is that it is very irresponsible of you to wait around for the problem to become worse just because you were scared of speaking to your supervisor, your professor, or any other person in authority. If you wait for long, the authority figure may be so disappointed and may not treat you with as much kindness and sympathy as he would have had you presented the issue earlier.

He will see you are irresponsible for allowing the problem to progress so much, and you could lose your job, be forced to repeat your class, or any other negative outcome. Therefore, at the first sign of trouble, schedule a meeting with the authority figure and get them to resolve the problem early on.

Be Respectful

Our upbringing and the hierarchies in society have conditioned us to address people differently, according to their relative authority. Therefore, ensure that you show respect to authority figures. However, do not talk to the seniors sycophantically with phrases like 'to be honest' and 'with all due respect' because they sound condescending.

On the other hand, do not let the seniors people silence you or dominate the conversation. There is always a temptation to shut people up or to keep quiet and let the opinions of authority people take the day, even when they are erroneous. However, if you are continually taking orders without considering your thoughts, the executives will not respect you either. The best way is to present to them your best ideas, and if you need to correct the authority figures, do so respectfully.

When addressing your juniors, accord them the same respect you give to the seniors. Be attentive to what they say, acknowledge their views, and add on to their ideas when the opportunity presents itself. Forcing your opinions on them or communicating with them forcefully is a sign of disrespect. If you genuinely believe that your opinion is better, give it to them respectfully and allow them to take up your idea themselves, having seen that it is better. Let the decision be theirs.

Be Willing to Challenge Them

Experts who have interviewed various leaders from different spheres of life report that the leaders often say that they value thoughtful input that creates an engaging debate. It would be boring if all people followed their bosses' opinions. However, an atmosphere in which people challenge each other and present contrary views promotes growth and creative thinking. That's the reason they look out for unique talent anyway; they want diverse creative ideas because that is what gives their companies a competitive edge over the competitors.

When you present your critical thoughts to the table, ensure that you do it in a way that invites discussion, critique, and collaboration. Whenever you challenge ideas presented, don't just say, 'that's wrong' or 'I disagree.' Instead, acknowledge the idea by saying, "I see your approach to the problem, but perhaps we could also approach it from a different angle by doing ..." If you agree with the idea presented but have a different method of reaching the same goal, say, "Your method would work well, but I believe that we could achieve the same goal, more cost-effectively, if we approach the problem from this angle..." Approaching issues in this way will yield more productive results rather than having a combative dialogue or staying quiet.

While you should keep in mind the above points when relating to people in authority, the issue at hand, and the relationship you have with the authority figure will matter. Always remember the role that the authority individual plays in your life, and keep in mind the havoc that it would wreak if you were at odds with the person.

Sycophancy will come off as being 'thirsty' and insincere; therefore, only be polite and respectful. Maintain an upright posture, make direct eye contact, and speak confidently in your normal voice. If you are meeting the individual for the first time, let your handshake be firm, but don't overdo it. While you may want to impress, do not smile too often or too excessively. Do not also nod too much. Be likable and ensure that your manners are proper. Your goal, when speaking to the authority figure, should not be to get them to like you; it would be better if they respected you because they will come to trust and depend on you.

If you are asked questions, such as in a traffic stop, answer the questions briefly and truthfully. Address the police officer respectfully by referring to them as 'sir' or 'madam,' but don't overdo it, lest you sound insincere.

How to Put Your View Across to Someone in Authority

While the traditional hierarchical leadership setup is disappearing from the corporate sector as many organizations open up opportunities for employees to lead and contribute their ideas freely, the reality of superiority and power has not disappeared, and juniors are still expected to honor those ahead of them in power and treat them with respect. Your boss may be open to having his meals with you, playing games with you, engaging you in discussions, and other forms of socialization outside the work environment. However, despite the cordial relationship, keep in mind that he or she is in a position of power and that they could influence the direction your career takes. Here are tips to help you steer out of trouble areas as you engage with your bosses and other persons in authority in the society:

Be Resolute In Regards To Your Convictions

Sharing your ideas with others always seems like an uphill task, especially when the persons in questions are colleagues you esteem, people outside your team, or persons in authority like bosses, prospective clients, police officers, and senior executives. The idea of sharing your opinion in itself might make you feel like you are going over your head. However, if you don't share your opinion, how will they know? How will they know that you have something useful to bring to the table? You must muster courage and indicate that you have something to contribute.

Avoid Sitting on the Fence

Sitting on the fence in regards to your ideas refers to being undecided about whether the ideas or the points you want to present are worthwhile. Undecided opinions start with words like, "I'm not sure that this idea will work, but we should give it a try," or "I'm sorry if you are already aware of this but..." In cases like this, your modesty too could be taken as uncertainty. Avoid starting your statements with words like, "I might be wrong..." or "I guess that could work..." or "It could be that..."

With every conversation you have with your superiors, you reaffirm their decision to hire you. Therefore, when you speak, don't begin planting doubts in their minds, making them wonder whether they were right to hire you.

Defend Your Ideas

It may turn out that in some instances, you will have to defend your ideas. Explaining and defending your view can be tough, especially if you have to defend them against contradictory ideas raised by persons in authority. However, be strong and engage them because the ideas that are worth sharing, the kind that is likely to bring transformation, will be controversial to some point.

Challenge Other People

In the same way, other people challenge your ideas, and test theirs too. This is not done on a revenge mission, but it allows you to explore an idea and examine it from all possible angles before implementing it. By asking questions, you and others listening with you will also get clarity on the issue at hand, and from there, you can even come up with better ideas than the one being presented.

Have an Open Mind

You cannot control how other people think and respond to your ideas, but you can control the reaction you give, whichever response you get. The best way to do this is to have an open mind; be ready for anything. You could receive a positive or a negative report, but whichever way the conversation goes, it is crucial that you maintain your cool.

Chapter 37: Hypnosis

Hypnosis is a condition that is human Involving concentrated attention and an improved capability. There are currently competing concepts describing associated phenomena and hypnosis. State notions that modified the view of hypnosis as an altered frame of trance or mind distinct from the state of consciousness.

By comparison, hypnosis is seen by non-state theories as a kind of role enactment, a redefinition of an interaction with a therapist, or a sort of placebo effect.

During this, an Individual said to have concentration and focus. Subjects thought to demonstrate an elevated reaction.

Hypnosis starts with an induction between a collection of hints and directions. The use of hypnotism for therapeutic purposes is known as "hypnotherapy," while its usage as a kind of amusement to get an audience is called "stage hypnosis." Mentalists often perform stage hypnosis. Hypnosis for pain control "is very likely to reduce chronic and acute pain in many people."

The use as a type of treatment integrates and recovers the injuries is controversial within the psychological or medical fields. Research suggests that hypnotizing someone can aid the creation of false memories and that hypnosis "doesn't help people remember events more accurately."

Myths of Hypnosis

Myths are untruths or exaggerations regarding the definition, process, and purpose of something. I will list some myths along with their refutations about hypnotism.

#1 Is Hypnosis Sleeping?

No. The hypnotic trance is a modified state of consciousness called the Alpha state. In this state, other than physiological sleep, there is strong electrical activity in the brain due to the very high level of concentration that the subject is performing. Simplifying hypnosis to the maximum, we can define it as monoideism, that is, absolute focus on the imagination.

#2 Hypnosis Is Conditional

A trusting partnership between the hypnotist and subject is required, so if the subject does not want to be hypnotized, they will not be. In the old days, it was said that the hypnotist became the operator of the mind of the hypnotized subject, but I would say that the hypnotist is another facilitator of the trance. He bridges the conscious mind and the unconscious, thus allowing the subject to access a state of consciousness which allows the subject to experience the full potential of their own mind.

#3 Hypnosis Works

If this is true, 100% of the people who can pay attention are mentally weak. After all, if you "dream awake," have fun reading a good manuscript, "travel" listening to an interesting story, or go to the movies and get emotional about them, you go into a trance. Have you ever encountered a person who has a lost, seemingly distracted look, and when you catch her attention, she takes a little fright? This person is not distracted; in fact, she is hyper-concentrated, that is, in a trance. The truth is that once in a while, our brain "hibernates" for a few minutes to save energy. Have you ever wondered if you needed to be aware of everything you do all the time? Consider someone who drives a car, when he was learning, he found it all complicated – steering, gears, brakes, throttle, clutch, and all at the same time!

But now, he operates so unconsciously (or automatically) that he even commits himself to reckless talking on a cell phone while driving. Basically, if a human being is able to concentrate and obey the instructions, he can be hypnotized.

#4 The Hypnotized Subject Will Do Whatever the Hypnotist Says

The human mind is not "mother's house." There are particular moral principles of each person, and these principles are obeyed and protected by the subject's unconscious mind. Thus, it is true to say that a hypnotized person will do nothing against their moral principles (religion, family, values, and physical integrity), that is, if you would not perform an action while "awake," you will not do so while hypnotized.

#5 The Hypnotized Subject Will Tell All His Secrets to the Hypnotist

Topic # 4 answers that one.

#6 Hypnosis is a Physiological Phenomenon

It is a legitimate neuro-physiological phenomenon, where brain functioning has very special characteristics, such as muscle relaxation, anesthesia, dilation of the pupils, and memory enhancement.

During the trance, there are actually changes in the brain, and this has already been confirmed in a study by examination of volunteers using an encephalogram. Perhaps in mysticism, there is a little hypnosis, but in hypnosis, there is nothing mystical.

#7 Can a Person Not Return From the Trance?

Back from where? You're not going anywhere. The advantage of being hypnotized is that you can travel the whole world without leaving your body, just with your mind.

Finally, hypnosis is a safe method for both entertainment (street, stage) and clinical applications (hypnotherapy and the like). If you believe in God, see the ability to be hypnotized as a divine gift for your self-improvement, but if you do not believe in a deity, see hypnosis as a very powerful tool that nature has given to the human being to accelerate positive changes in life.

Hypnosis Techniques

There are 3 main techniques of hypnosis used in clinical treatment. Clinical hypnosis, that is, hypnosis performed in the office by a trained professional, can follow different methodologies or concepts, depending on the line of work of the hypnologist. Today, we will present the three most known lines and their main characteristics:

Conditional Hypnosis

Created and patented by Luiz Carlos Crozera, conditional hypnosis is a technique used to rid the patient's mind of blockages that directly interfere with his physical and emotional health.

In this technique, deep body relaxation is done so that the patient has a decrease in his brain frequency and, with the purest mind, can be led by the hypnotist to the traumatic records that accompany him. At this point, the professional removes the registered emotional charge, disassociating the trauma from the given situation.

Upon returning from the trance, the patient already has an important behavioral change when faced with what caused him anguish. Thus, the hypnotist uses the post-hypnotic suggestion, a technique that executes the commands inserted during the trance, in order to achieve the best possible results. In conditional hypnosis, the patient does not interact with the hypnotist.

Eriksonian Hypnosis

In this technique of clinical hypnosis, described by the American psychiatrist Milton Erickson, the patient is suggested to seek within himself new learning that leads to a reformulation of thoughts and truths. Thus, the patient is led to the trance and suggested to relive, in a metaphorical way, the situation that causes him pain and suffering but with a completely different outcome, aiming for the trauma to be forgotten.

The idea is not to change what has been experienced but to give other responses to the trauma since it is believed that the patient has all the resources necessary to solve his own problems.

Classic Hypnosis

This method is mostly in disuse because it presents less efficient results than the other methodologies. Classic Hypnosis consists of searching in the memory of the patient for the facts that bring him suffering and making him understand that it is part of the past and should no longer reach the present.

Chapter 38: Types of Persuasion

The Pull Style of Persuasion

The pull style of persuasion involves obtaining information from the other party in the negotiation, understanding their point of view and why they want the outcome; they are seeking and developing an agreement that is beneficial to all the parties involved. This type of persuasion is perfect for situations where the parties involved intend to establish a relationship that allows them to do further business both in the near future and in the long term.

The Push Style of Persuasion

In the push type of persuasion, you offer information about yourself and your stance to the other party. You try to get them to understand your position on the issue and why the outcome you are seeking is important to you. You persuade them to believe that they have the upper hand and that they are exhibiting goodwill when they understand your stance and try to work on a mutually beneficial outcome. The push style of persuasion is perfect for situations where the other party has more power than you do or when they are not so interested in the deal. There is yet another type of persuasion, and this type has not gained popularity because of the method it employs. This type of persuasion is called the punch or aggressive kind of persuasion. Every good negotiator advises against its use because it employs methods that involve threats, manipulation, and coercion. Such methods rarely ever produce a successful negotiation. The technique might actually work for you, and the other party might accept the terms. However, the agreement is not mutual, and it is challenging to build a business relationship based on fear and coercion.

Now that we are done addressing the importance of persuasion during negotiation, and the different styles of persuasion, let's take a brief look at how you can make use of persuasion skills to influence the way a negotiation goes.

Recognize the Importance of Self-Confidence

The way persuasion works involve convincing other people to see things from your point of view enough to agree with it. However, it is difficult to convince people when you do not believe in yourself and your point of view. First, you need to be confident in yourself and believe in what you are pitching to the other party. Then, you should also be confident in your ability to convince them to go with your point of view.

Having self-confidence gives you a calm-headedness that allows you to see things more clearly and to gather all the facts you need to make informed negotiation choices and decisions. With self-confidence, you would be able to properly consider what options and outcomes would be in your best interest.

Be Always Ready to Counter Criticism

When preparing for a negotiation, never assume that everything will happen smoothly. Thinking that the other party will not raise any objections or that there will be no hitches is making a grave mistake. There are indeed some negotiations that are hitch-free; however, those are rare cases. What is typical and obtainable in most negotiations is getting some objections and criticism of your ideas from the other party.

You should anticipate the criticism from the other party. If you are prepared to receive such criticism, you would not be caught off guard, and you will be able to respond appropriately to it.

When you prepare for criticism, you will be able to understand the questions and misgivings of the other party and to provide a quick rebuttal to the criticism. You will then be converting what should be opposition to strengths you can build on to further persuade and influence the other party and to have a successful negotiation.

Promote the Benefits

In negotiation, you are trying to get the other party to see the merits of the offer you are making or of your stance. Hence, when you are using persuasion as a skill, you have to put the spotlight on the merits of what you are proposing to the other party. Your promotion of the benefits of what you are offering should satisfactorily answer the "what's in it for me" question, which is usually in the mind of everyone during negotiation. You have to clearly communicate how the offer is in the interest of the other party. When the other party can clearly see how the proposal aligns with their interests, you have succeeded in persuading them, and you will most likely get the best possible outcome.

Chapter 39: Self-persuasion

Self-persuasion is one of the most powerful and one of the most challenging areas of persuasion. The reason is that, where the other forms of persuasion are applied from an external force, self-persuasion comes from within. So how can self-persuasion be used as a technique?

First, self-persuasion can be used as a method to persuade others indirectly. To be effective, self-persuasion must come from within. In other words, a person decides without being told what to think directly. Persuading someone using self-persuasion involves setting up a situation where the other person comes to the desired conclusion because of what they have learned. Given what they know, they can come to no other conclusion.

Self-persuasion is a useful technique to employ in association with some reward. If a person behaves in a certain way and receives a benefit afterward, they will begin to see that the behavior is beneficial and come to the conclusion that it must be right.

We'll look at the techniques of self-persuasion on others:

Personal Development

We all have parts of our life that we would like to improve. It's just human nature to want to get better, to want to strive for something more. But getting the change we want to see in our lives is difficult, because we find it hard to reason our way into the proper behavior. Persuasion techniques don't tend to work well when we try to use them on ourselves because we realize what we're doing. It's like trying to use persuasion tactics on another person overtly. If they know we're trying to persuade them, they tend to fight against what we're asking them to do.

Habit Stacking

This works the best with small tasks that can easily be combined so that you can treat them as one habit. The power of habit stacking is to make good and easy habits interlocked so that you always do one with the other. Eventually, the good habit becomes just as strong as the original habit because of the pruning of neuron pathways to favor what we often do and eliminate what we don't do often.

From Many Small Habits Come Big Change

This system of self-persuasion works best with small things that can be easily done along with something else. But what if we want to make a big change?

Divide and conquer is the strategy here. Take a look at the big change you want to make, and divide it into smaller components that all work together to reach the larger goal. Just like any complex project, you can take your bigger target and separate it into several smaller tasks. Those smaller tasks can be stacked together with existing habits you already have to make a larger, long-lasting change.

Recognizing Self-Persuasion Tactics

We all like to think that we are immune to the control of others and that we are free to make our own decisions. With the advent of the Internet and social media, the positive thinkers were calling this time the new age of Information, where all information would be available to all people all of the time.

Never would people again be without the valuable facts they needed to make the best decisions about their life. People would find peace and understanding as we all started to find much more central ground because we had a better sense of shared experience around the world. Each person would be able to make their voice heard.

Persuasion in Overdrive

Much of what you're seeing is persuasion in overdrive because of the Internet. As you've seen in the principals and techniques, we've given you for persuasion; communication is a key component for persuasion of all kinds. The always-on nature of communication today has just increased the communication channels we all have available to us ten-fold-times-ten.

Welcome to the Age of Selective Reality

The Internet is like a fire hose of data, so we need to curate the information we have time to receive. But according to this research, people are very adept at subconsciously paying attention to the communication that reinforces what they already believe and what reflects well on themselves, while selectively forgetting information they wish was not true. This bias serves as an excellent means of leading you to self-persuasion. Nobody told you to believe a certain way, but you came to the conclusion that was wanted because you were given only information that led you to think that way. Your freedom of choice led you astray.

The Advent of Fake News

The media doesn't help. What was once a fact-checked, attribution-required record of facts is now a re-tweeted, live posted, be-first-not-right mob of professional social media echo-chamber-makers. Reporters are people too. If they are putting their opinion on the screen, they also will gravitate toward that information, which makes them look good. They use the 6 Principles of Persuasion, either consciously or subconsciously, to keep getting you to click, like, and follow them. Facts are subjective, they say.

Once, only advertising was allowed to behave in this overtly persuasive way. But now, all information is fair game. This is about news as entertainment, and the communicators need your attention to keep advertising revenue flowing.

Have You Been Informed, or Persuaded?

Recognizing the techniques of self-persuasion as they are applied to ourselves is one of those times when a simple 'gut check' won't be a good indicator. When the information is all geared to persuade rather than inform, you need to apply conscious effort and logic to find the truth. Analyze messages you receive against the framework of the 6 Principles to see if new information you receive is something you can believe or if it requires a bit of independent fact-checking to get to the real facts.

Chapter 40: Techniques to Influence Human Behavior

Here are some techniques that can help you influence others:

Use an Anchor

This technique is based on comparison, specifically, creating the illusion of a positive comparison. Say you're trying to convince your friend to go on vacation to a certain resort, but you know they might be resistant to the idea because they think it's too expensive. In an effort to persuade them, you might tell your friend that these tickets would be double the price at any other time during the year, but now they are just inserting their preferred price here.

Ask for Something Outrageous

You know that method every teenager has used at least at some point when they have bad news? Give the parents some horrible piece of news and then just go, "I'm kidding," so by the time you tell them the real thing, they'll just be relieved? Well, if you've ever done that, congratulations, you were employing a psychological persuasion technique, and you didn't even know it!

Ask for Something Small

Now, this one is similar to the technique before, but the other way around. Instead of asking for something huge to then ask for something small, go in asking for something small that anyone is likely to say yes to, and then use that as an opportunity to get your foot in the door to ask for something else, usually a bigger favor. With a lot of these "tame" persuasion techniques, you've probably never even realized people are trying to convince you, but once you learn about them, it's like you can't "unsee" it. People pull this move all the time when they want to get something out of you, but they can't ask for a bold favor right away.

Use the Hive Mind in Your Favor

One of the great things about being human is that we're social animals, and thus, we live in communities. We need society to survive and thrive, and we're known to help each other out and build each other up. Whether it comes down to business or raising families (after all, it takes a village!), society is there to collectively help out. It imposes rules, standards, and expectations that help us all lead our lives in the right direction.

There are unwritten social rules we're not allowed to break, and you can spin that to your advantage.

Do Favors for People

Now, this one is a little sneaky but based on a fair principle. If you want someone to do something for you, then first do something for them. You don't just ask for things without offering anything in return, because that's unfair and possibly a little rude. You're putting someone out and asking them to go out of their way for you, but if you do something for them first, then the whole game changes.

You see, now they owe you. Or they feel like they do. You've been nice or generous enough to do them a favor, so now they'll either offer to do something for you, or they will be much more amenable to performing whatever favor you wanted to ask them. Think of it as an advanced reward that motivates them to help you; you were going to repay their time or effort anyway, but you just did it in a way that benefited you.

Make Use of Authority

People like it when they don't have to think for themselves, because then they don't have to make an effort or accept responsibility for their actions. It's easier to just follow a self-proclaimed leader and "let Jesus take the wheel," as they say. Plus, remember what I said about people being insecure and lacking confidence in their abilities? If they perceive that someone is better than them in some way, they are more likely to listen to them or change their mind about what they think.

Appeal to People's Emotions

You have no idea how much we've got to lose because we're emotional creatures. But other people's downfall is your gain, because of course this weakness can be exploited. Anything that elicits a strong emotional reaction, whether it be sadness, happiness, love, pity, etc. is incredibly attractive to people. We just love emotional highs, even when that emotion isn't positive, which is why people watch horror movies and go on rollercoasters.

To influence and persuade someone, it's not a matter of eliciting a positive reaction; you just need to create a strong reaction of any nature.

Take Care of the Thinking

It comes up time and time again that people don't like to think. It's difficult, it's stressful, and it's tiring. We're constantly plugged in, always thinking, always turning the ol' brain cogs to come up with solutions, to plan, to organize, etc. You don't even finish thinking about what you need today, and you're already thinking about what you need tomorrow. From time to time, people just want to not think.

Do you ever have those moments when you're so tired that all you want is to sit there and watch something stupid, so you don't have to think? That may be empty, wasted time, but it has value for you, because it allows you to just relax and stop thinking.

Drop Hints Constantly and Repeat the Same Ideas

Think about the most annoying song you heard this past summer and how often they played it. You didn't like it, it wasn't good, but still, it would play in your head constantly, just because you were exposed to it absolutely everywhere. That's called an earworm, and it can serve as a very efficient mind control technique.

One of the most effective ways to learn information, acquire a new skill, or get used to something is to be exposed to it all the time. Soon, it becomes normalized, and you don't perceive it as foreign anymore.

That also happens with that annoying song. Now think of what kind of results you can obtain by applying this same principle to people and ideas you can put into their heads.

Chapter 41: Honing Your Persuasion Skills

Below are the steps to honing your persuasion skills;

Take an Acting Class: If you want to be a manipulator, you first need to learn how to master your emotions and make others interested in your forced feelings. Now, if you desire to look more distressed than you really are or even want to apply a variety of emotional techniques to get what you want, then take an acting class since it will improve your persuasion powers. When considering an acting class, you need to note you should never tell people you are taking a drama class if you are learning how to persuade and control people's minds. This is because they may get suspicious over your skills rather than believing in you.

Taking a Debate Class

After you have taken acting classes and learned how to master your emotions when convincing others to get what you want, you need to take debate classes, which might also involve public speaking classes to learn more on organizing, presenting what you think and making you sound more convincing.

Pacing

In this step, you will learn how to establish similarities. You need to learn how to mirror your victim's body language and then see how effectively you can control your tonal variations and other body languages. The gentle and manipulative technique is the best when persuading your employer or fellow employees to get them to do something for you. In this case, you should NEVER be emotional since this is a professional setting.

Be Charismatic

Once you are charismatic, you will have the tendency to get what you want. In this step, you need to learn how to smile and light up a room. You should as well have approachable body gestures, so your targeted people feel willing to talk to you. You should be flexible such that you can hold up a discussion with anyone despite their age, body size, or profession. The following are other techniques you should apply to be charismatic:

- Making others feel special by maintaining eye contact when talking to them, asking them how they feel and what their interests are. Show them how much you care about knowing them even if you know you do not mean it.

- Love yourself and what you do by exuding your confidence. Have faith in yourself so others can take you seriously and fall into your persuasion intent.

- Be confident even if what you are saying is true or false. When speaking, be glib as this makes your target fall into your purpose easily.

Learn from Other Manipulators

Since you are still an amateur, you need to learn more from the masters. Look for your friends or family members who are persuasion masters and take notes. This helps in getting new insights on how to persuade and influence people, even if it means you end up being a manipulation victim. If you are interested in the art of mind control, you might also find yourself manipulating one of the masters.

Read People

You should also learn to read people as everyone has a different emotional and psychological composition and should, therefore, be persuaded for various purposes. Before you apply your latest manipulation skills, take time to learn your target by understanding what makes them tick, then evaluate which approach suits them. The following are the most proven factors you will come across when getting to know more about people:

• The majority are vulnerable to emotional responses. They are emotional themselves as they can cry while or after watching a movie; they love pets and are sympathetic. This means in order for you to persuade them, you will have to play with their emotions until they empathize and sympathize with you and give in to your intents.

• Others were raised in authoritarian backgrounds, hence have a guilt reflex. Since they are used to getting punished for every little wrong deed, they grow up feeling guilty about anything they do. As a manipulator, make them feel guilty for not fulfilling your demands, and within no time, they will grant your wishes.

• Other people are amenable to rational approaches. They are always logical-minded, tend to read the news every day, and they always ask for facts before deciding on anything. In this case, you will need to apply your calm mind-controlling powers to influence these people rather than using your emotions.

Getting Everything You Want

I. Your Friends

This is one of the final steps now that you have equipped yourself with the active manipulation steps. When it comes to your friends, it can be a bit harder since they know you well. But this does not mean you cannot manipulate them. You should never tell them you are trying to persuade them, as this might destroy your friendship. The following are the steps you should follow if it is in your friend's case:

• First, butter your friend(s) up. This is done by being friendly, doing small favors for them, and telling them how amazing they are to you, and this is done a week before you make a request for a straightforward indulgence. Do everything a friend is supposed to do without going overboard.

• Your friends should care for you, specifically when you are emotionally down, and this is a significant step to get what you want.

This means your friends will do everything possible not to see you upset. Use the skills acquired in your acting class to make you look more emotional than you really are.

• Remind your friends of how amazing you have been to them and how you have sacrificed substantial space and time to save the friendship.

II. Your Significant Other

This is the simplest step. You have to turn your partner on and then ask what you want because, in this state, they can hardly deny you what you want. There are also some other ways to persuade your significant partner than this subtle route. Look sexy when making the request, and they will grant your wish based on how cute you look.

III. Your Boss

This step requires you to apply rational and logical approaches. You should NEVER show up at your employer's desk crying or manifesting your problems as the likely result for this is getting fired. You should instead be logical with your employer and back up your request with detailed explanations. Therefore, you should:

• Be a model employee a week before requesting a favor. This can be achieved through working late, keeping a smile always on your face, and even bringing pastries in the morning.

• Request the favor in an offhanded way. This entails requesting support like it is no big deal. Rather than saying, 'I want to ask for something really important from you,' be casual as you request this, or you might alert the employer about your intents.

• Manipulate the boss at the end of the day or during breaks. In the morning, employers are stressed about all the work they have to do for that day. Persuading your boss during these mentioned hours has the highest probability of being successful, as the boss will instead grant your wish rather than waste their time.

IV. Your Teacher

This step works better if you combine professionalism with emotions. You need to:

• Be a role model to the other students by arriving in class early enough, reading ahead of the teacher, and being active in class work.

• Appreciate your teacher by telling them how great they are in a composed manner. Tell them how much you love the subject and how much you enjoy their way of teaching.

• Talk of how much you are suffering at home as this will make the teacher feel awkward and sorry for you.

• While talking about your private life, wait until the teacher gets uncomfortable, and for instance, offers to give you an extension to rewrite an assignment. Let your tone trail off and start crying. You can as well opt for walking on your way home as the teacher would not be able to withstand this and will end up granting your wish.

V. Your Parents

You have the right to maximum parental care and persuading your parents is also one of the easiest steps. If the parents love and support you, be a model son or daughter a while before making your request. Help out around the house as much as you can, then when you start persuading:

• Make your request in a reasonable way. Do not sit down and have a big talk about your request. Make it hard for your parents to say no to your request.

• State your claim while doing other household chores, such as folding the laundry. This reminds them of how good you are.

• Tell your parents about your friends, how their parents have granted the wishes of your friends and why your parents should feel okay too and grant the request.

• Make them feel guilty by talking about how you will get every detail of either a concert you missed or blame them for ruining your life by causing you not to have significant experiences in your life.

Having learned the steps for successful mind control and how easily you can influence your friends, parents, boss, teachers, or significant other, you should also know how effortless it is to manipulate someone hangs on the impressions you have of them. You should always be deceptive, use your emotions, and persuade using the waterworks approach in a public place, then finally use bribes where necessary.

Chapter 42: Methods of Persuasion

For some people, the art of persuasion comes easily. You can watch them talk to almost anyone, and it seems like they will always get the response that they want from the other person. On the other hand, there are those people who may have the best message in the world who couldn't convince anyone, even their closest friends, to do something. However, no matter where you fall in either of these groups, with a little bit of practice and hard work, you will be able to learn how to use persuasion to your advantage.

In terms of the process of using persuasion, there will usually be three parts that you need to follow, including the communicator, or the medium used as the source of persuasion

The Persuasive Nature of the Appeal

Each of these elements needs to be accounted for before you try to use persuasion on a higher level. It is always a good practice to look around you and check to see how many instances of persuasion are going on in your daily life. Some of these will be overt, but many of them will be pretty subtle. This can be great training for persuasion because you will be able to employ the same kind of tactics.

Let's take a look at some of the options that you can use when it comes to good persuasion and using the right techniques.

Foot in the Door

This one allows you to ask for a bigger favor after you have already been granted a smaller favor, especially if they are related in some way. You may start off with something that is pretty small, such as just borrowing a cup of sugar from your neighbor. Your neighbor will probably be fine with this because it's not that big of a deal, and most people, as long as they have it on hand, will have a cup of sugar to share with you.

Reversal Tagging

Another option that you can use is known as reversal tagging. This is a trick that uses simple and subtle sentence phrasing to get an agreement, or at least compliance, from the target in general. It will use two opposing structures inside the sentence, the first part being an affirmative statement, and the second one will be a tag question.

Reverse Psychology

This is a principle that can work well with those who like to have control, such as rebellious people or those who just like to do the opposite of what they are told to do. It is often called reactance theory, and it will describe the scenario where a person feels like they are losing control of things and they will try to grab that control back by doing the exact opposite of what they have been asked, even if it is not their best interest to do so.

Cognitive Dissonance

Have you ever been in a situation where you know that something seems a bit off about it, but you cannot figure out why it doesn't feel right? When there isn't something quite right about a situation, it is going to set off some dissonance in the mind and will trigger the person to try to make it all right. People who have OCD will often know this feeling because they will notice when little things are out of the normal.

Counter-Attitudinal Advocacy

It is pretty common for people to state a view on something, or even to support an opinion, even if that is not something that they believe themselves. This isn't necessarily that deceptive because the things that people choose to do this with are usually small, or they have the best intentions. For example, it is common for someone to tell a little white lie because it will help to protect the feelings of someone else. When this happens, we are attempting to reduce the dissonance that we caused by saying that our actions are still noble.

Perceived Self-Interest

If you ask anyone, they often believe that they are generous and pretty caring creatures. However, no matter how much most people believe this, as humans we are a self-serving species. There have been a lot of studies done on this over the years, and it has been proven over and over again. Even altruism is a self-serving act because it does help the grantor to feel good about themselves in the process.

The idea behind this technique is a pretty simple one to work with, but you will be spending your time on perception. If you can convince your target that they are doing something that is in their best interest, whether that is true or not, then the target is much more likely to go along with the whole thing. This can be apparent when you are trying to persuade someone who is higher up than you.

Hurt and Rescue Principle

This principle is based on evoking some discomfort or fear in the person from the start. When the person is assessing their options for a solution, you will be able to offer the perfect solution in the form of the thing you want to persuade them to. You need to be able to manufacture a level of discomfort here first, and being crafty enough to make this work can be hard.

Since you are trying to bring in some fear or discomfort with your target, you do need to be a bit careful with this option. It is not a good idea to come off as aggressive or intimidating in the process because this will just turn the person away from you completely.

Trial Ballooning

Another option that you can use is known as a trial is ballooning, or trial closing. This is the starting point, and it is relevant whether you are the seller or the buyer in the negotiation. The idea is to start out with the final solution that you would like to end up with. You will just put that information out there and see if the thing works.

Auction Model

This strategy is a good one to put in place if you are working with more than one buyer at the same time. Otherwise, it won't be the best one. With this method, you want to play one of the parties against the others so that there is a buying frenzy, and it is more likely that the price will be driven up, no matter what you are trying to sell.

Usage of Force

The manipulator may decide to use some degree of force to successfully persuade the victim into thinking in some specific type of way. However, this depends on the situation at that particular moment. However, this is seen to be deployed in instances where both the ideas of the manipulator and the victim do not seem to match up, the type of conversation they are having don't seem to bear fruit, or where the subject seems to be irritated or frustrated with the turn the conversation has taken. This may be classified as a scare tactic by most, since it gives the victim minimal time to think in a logical manner of the events that seem to be transpiring as opposed to when the victim is in a normal state of mind. A manipulator is normally inclined to use force as a method of persuasion is usually when at that particular, they may have hit a wall on their journey of persuasion. They may also result in this if the manipulator feels as though he is losing control of the grasp he had on the victim, or when the victim presents them with solid evidence of the manipulator contradicting them.

Asking Leading Questions

Another method that a dark manipulator skillfully uses is to ask leading questions. It could readily be considered one of the strongest verbal techniques because they ask the victims questions to obtain a specific set of responses. For example, a dark persuader may ask their target, "how bad you think these people are." This issue already means that the individuals at issue are certainly bad to a certain extent. Dark persuaders ask such skillfully these leading questions that they instantly feel the victim is whipped up to and leave the vessel and only go back to the questioning line when the victim appears to be in a relaxed position. Dark manipulators also use their real intentions to mask dark persuasion. To be easily exposed to dark persuasion, the dark manipulator hides from the outset his true intention otherwise, he will fail. Skilled persuaders may mask their real intentions in a number of ways, depending on the individual victim and circumstance. Dark manipulators have a gift for individuals reading. This implies that once you recognize certain kinds of personality in individuals and then reverse psychology becomes simple to get what you want.

Chapter 43: What is Dark Persuasion and How Is It Different from Regular Persuasion?

Persuasion is all around us. We see it all of the time based on what we do, what we watch, and more. For example, we see persuasion any time that a family member asks us to help them move something or when we see an advertisement on our favorite show. We recognize all of these different signs of persuasion, but we find that it is easy to ignore these types unless we are looking for the item in particular.

But then there is going to be the dark persuader. This person is going to be a little bit different. They are not just talking about a product that they want to sell or asking for some help with something and giving you the chance to say yes or no depending on your preferences. The dark persuader is going to work in order to make sure that you are going to feel stuck, or at least obligated, to do what they want you to.

First, let's take a look at what a dark persuader is. If you take a look at what the dictionary has to say you may find that to persuade is to prevail on someone to do or to believe something using any number of methods of advising and reasoning. This may sound similar to what we are going to find with regular persuasion, but the difference is the intention that is behind the persuasion that you use.

A persuader is sometimes gonged to attempt to convince their target to do something, and they aren't going to think much about the tactics or the motivation that they will use. They may not even have a good understanding of the target and who that person is before they try to do the persuasion. Maybe their target is more than one person, such as when a big company tries to advertise their product, and it is hard to know about each and every person who will fit in the target group.

In some cases, the persuader is going to be more concerned about creating as better as they can for as many people as possible. This could be a diplomat who wants to try and prevent two countries from fighting with each other and starting a war, so they will create some new political ties. A persuader sometimes has a plan, but other times they are just going to try things and see what sticks.

In all normal cases of persuasion, you will find that both parties are going to benefit. There may be times when the persuader is going to benefit a little bit more than the target. But the point is that both parties are going to benefit, and the target is not going to get purposely harmed or anything bad at the same time in order for the persuader to get what they want.

A dark persuader is also going to make sure that at all times, they are able to see and understand the bigger picture that is before them. This kind of persuader is going to understand the target they want to work with, what seems to motivate the target the most, and how far they are able to take the tactic (as well as which tactic they need to use) in order to succeed with this target.

There is a lot more planning that goes along with this kind of persuasion. They want to really know the person they are targeting. This helps them to see more success. This kind of persuader is often going to keep the relationship going with their target for a longer time than a big company will with their advertising, so really knowing their target on an individual basis is going to make a difference.

When it comes to the dark persuader, they are going to be unconcerned with the morality that comes with the manipulation that they are doing. This kind of person may see that doing the right thing is a cool perk sometimes, but it isn't their motivation, and if they have to do what is considered the wrong thing in order to get it done, and then they will. This doesn't bother them at all when they have to do the wrong thing in life, and they will do whatever works the best for them.

In the Venn diagram of self-gratification and morality, the actions that we see from the dark persuader is not always going to fall right into the area that overlaps, and they don't really care about that. A dark persuader is going to see the thing or the person that they want, and then they are going to use any kind of means that they can in order to get what they want out of it.

As you can see with this, there is going to be a big difference between the intention that is found between persuasion and dark persuasion. Those with regular persuasion are going to make sure that this relationship is going to be beneficial for both parties. They want to reach their goals, but they want to make sure that they are able to do so in a way that is not going to harm anyone in the process.

But with the dark persuader, this isn't a big deal. They don't care who gets hurt or how they are harmed in the process. They just want to make sure that they are able to get to their goals and that they are happy in the long term. While most of us may frown upon this, these people may not care, and if you have ever done something to get your way without worrying about the reaction or the harm of another person, then you have employed this kind of tactic in the process as well in your life.

Chapter 44: Elements of Persuasion

Just like other methods of controlling people, there are some specific elements attributed to persuasion. These elements will help you get a better understanding of persuasion and be able to easily recognize when the techniques of persuasion are at play. Richard Perloff, a professor of communication at Cleveland State University described persuasion as a symbolic process. He views persuasion as symbolic because people try to convince others by transmitting messages to aid in changing their current views and attitude about certain things in a free choice atmosphere (Perloff 2003).

The interesting thing about deliberate persuasion is what makes it different from other methods of control. The target is not brainwashed or forced, but allowed to make their own free choices on the subject matter. The methods of persuasion aim to shift the mind of the target in a particular direction. It is also why salesmen and marketers employ these techniques, which allows the target to choose if they want to purchase their product or not. It will all come down to the marketer or salesman to have strong enough evidence to change the mind of their targets. Persuasion is defined by multiple elements. The first is that "Persuasion is symbolic," meaning it employs images and sounds to transmit the points. And it usually involves two or more parties, where one methodically makes a deliberate attempt to influence the other party, which could be a single target or group.

This element of symbolic persuasion means that to persuade someone to change their attitude or perception, you will need to be able to show them why you think they should change their current views. This will include the usage of sounds, words, and images to get your points across to the other party. Some sounds can be used as an attention grabber and even target the emotions of the subject. Words are a great way to start your arguments, debates, and submissions, as well as drive your points. Images, on the other hand, are an easy way to display the evidence needed to convince someone to move towards the direction you want them to and accept your point of view.

The second key part of the process is the "self-persuasion" aspect. Unlike the direct technique of persuasion, self-persuasion entails putting people in positions where they are inherently driven to persuade themselves to change. More so, what sets self-persuasion is that you can't detect that any form of direct attempt is being made to convince you or anyone else.

This method can include the use of subliminal signals or even covert manipulation to get the target to think they are the ones motivating themselves into action or changing their standpoint about something.

When you want someone to self-persuade themselves, you can consider beginning the process with "hypothetically" or "supposedly." That way the target won't feel they have conflicting viewpoints with their current perception. You need to manage the process subtly and give them enough time to process your theories and hypothesis, then allow them to generate their arguments, that way you will get their best effort as well as their best self-influence.

For instance, you want to influence someone to self-persuade themselves, you can subtly ask them to set aside their own viewpoints just for a minute, then try and get them to create their own arguments for the topic which you want to make your point. And before long, you will see a change of mind. Whatever the narrative may be, once you can encourage the target to theoretically generate their own arguments outside their initial viewpoint, there is likely a high possibility of them changing their minds.

Meanwhile, the good thing is that it allows the target to make their free choice and retain some of their free will. The target will in most cases have to decide whether or not to take any action after the act of persuasion. For example, a target might listen to a commercial, watch several ads about the best deals and offers, and yet not go for it for whatever reasons. Therefore, it is different from other forms of mind control. Another example is that if a target is against something like abortion, no matter how many ads and persuasion they undergo, they are likely not to change their minds. Persuasion at the end of it all allows people the option of choice, which is usually not found in other forms of mind control.

While other forms of mind control such as hypnosis, brainwashing, and manipulation needs happen face to face, or in some cases, require the target to be in full isolation, persuasion can occur in different ways. There are other ways persuasion takes place, such as through normal discussions with someone, on television, on the internet, through the radio, and even other forms of messages that are nonverbal, including on a billboard, although they are not as effective when compared to the verbal means.

Principles of Dark Persuasion

Brainwashing: It is the practice of taking over someone else's capacity to think. Naturally, we all have unique thinking patterns, and we all have the power to think critically about what is going on around us. Brainwashing takes away this power, and it puts that power into the hands of whoever is doing the brainwashing. Cults use this technique heavily, as it allows them to recruit and retain members. Brainwashing has many different implementations, but the principle remains the same throughout. A person is first brought into the fold of the new scenario. They are told that they matter, that they are worthy, and that they have a place to be in the new milieu. They must be separated from outside society in order to do this. This is all part of the breaking down of the self. In order to make sure that the person adapts and accepts this new milieu, their sense of self must be broken down. In the case of cults, this will often already have happened when the person joins. Cults look for people who are weekend by loneliness, suffering, or isolation. When a person has a good sense of self, they are less susceptive to being brainwashed. Thus, this must be attacked and broken down in order for a person to convince that this new way of living is the best. Brainwashing might also employ guilt as a way to convince a person that they are in the best environment. Brainwashing will have people feeling guilty about their "past lives," and they will be presented with a solution for their guilt. Guilt and shame are very powerful emotions, and people will do whatever they think will work to get away from these emotions. Guilt and shame are what people feel when they are sad and ashamed of themselves. These negative emotions are what drive people to search out a solution, and often the solution can be manipulated by others in the form of brainwashing.

The brainwashers present the possibility of salvation. The possibility of salvation comes in the form of accepting the new ideas or format of the brainwashers. It comes in the form of accepting that they can be saved by this new person or group. Leniency is presented to the person. Rather than being told that their past transgressions are something that they will never be able to escape, they are told that they are able to escape it if they reach their new goals with the brainwashing. This, obviously, feels good, and it is hard to turn away from the possibility of salvation.

Another form of persuasion is hypnosis. Hypnosis works on a few basic principles. The first is the induction. Induction is where a person is helped along to a state of suggestibility or relaxation. This is a state wherein they are put at ease, and they are made vulnerable to messaging. The person who is being hypnotized is welcomed into this vulnerable state, and it is from there when they can be persuaded. After a person is put through an induction, their defenses are broken down, and they are able to receive suggestions. The suggestions may come in many different formats.

Some people seek out hypnosis to bring themselves away from bad habits, like smoking or other addictive habits. In this format, the person would go through the initial process of induction, and then the hypnotist will make suggestions to them about how to quit smoking and messages relating to why they shouldn't smoke anymore. The hypnotist's suggestion in this formula will include statements like, "You don't need to smoke. You don't have cravings. You don't have the social need to do it. You don't feel pressured to do it." And so on. The suggestion can be in any direction, and there are very subtle ways in which a person can be suggested towards any goals. A hypnotist might use positive messaging that might include positive feelings about the person's self or the world.

There is the military application of this process, which is fairly well-known. Initially, the soon-to-be-soldiers enter boot camp with their heads still in the mode of being back at home. Their goals are not formulated yet, and they are used to the comforts and privacy of home. They must be broken down first in order to be able to accept the messaging of the military. They enter boot camp, and they are put through rigorous physical training and emotional damage. Their first experience in the boot camp is that everything is crazy and uncontrolled. They are given the message that they are powerless and that everything is against them, except their fellow soldiers. They are thrust into a world that is pure chaos and evil. They are told that nothing will save them, that nothing matters except to achieve whatever goal they must work on in that very moment. This is the way that they are broken down: they must learn that they are worth nothing, that they are empty, and not valid. Then, of course, they are built back up. This is the classic formula of brainwashing and hypnosis. The first phase works as the breaking down, or the induction of the mind. This is where people are put into a state of suggestibility. Then comes the possibility of salvation. In the military case, what will save them is working hard and being tough, as well as bonding and working cohesively with their colleagues. The fellow soldiers, as well as the commanding officers, are the family and only friends of the soldiers. They are taught that they are worth less than dirt unless they are work-in toward a common goal with their fellow soldiers.

Chapter 45: Fundamental Persuasion Techniques

The main objective of persuasion is to influence and convince the target to adopt the point of view you want them to internalize, and your persuasive argument becomes part of their primary belief system.

There are several methods and persuasion techniques that can be adopted to influence people, such as punishment and reward systems, repetitive encouragement, and many more. Let's take a look at a few persuasive techniques that are highly effective.

Create or Coin a Need

The coin a need technique is a persuasion method that implies you create a need that is not formerly there or appeals to a need that already exists. This method targets the fundamental needs of a person, such as love, shelter, or self-esteem. This is a classic technique that salesmen and marketers usually employ to sell their products. For instance, there are so many commercials that suggest that in order to be happy, be admired, or perhaps to be loved, you may need to buy a particular product to succeed. They ensure that the need you have happens to coincide with what is advertised to you, or they ensure the need to purchase the product will be created by influencing, convincing, and reminding your mind of its fundamental needs.

Social Needs Allure

The social needs allure is an effective persuasion technique that appeals to the desires or needs to become popular, well-known, prestigious, feel good and important, or become similar to others (especially like celebrities).

This method can be used to influence people due to their desire for change. So many television commercials adopt this persuasion technique, which aims to encourage viewers to go for a particular product so that they can be more than they already are. Persuasive arguments like this are often done through television since most Americans spend hours watching it.

The Anchoring Bias and Adjustment Technique

This anchoring bias and adjustment technique are two methods that influence decision making. When people are in the process of making decisions, they usually have an anchor point that guides you to the choices you make. Psychologists suggest that people are inclined to depend on the first piece of information they learn about something. That very first piece of information becomes the focal point or anchor point and will then serve as a starting point or reference to their decisions on that subject, which can seriously impact the choices they make. This is known as anchoring bias. The adjustment part is when someone is influenced and guided to make a decision. This is done by presenting options to a person. The choice which the person will end up making is based on the customer's mindset, which has been anchored and adjusted. Anchoring bias can control how much you pay or are willing to pay for an item. For instance, you want to buy a new phone. While surfing online, you found that the average price for the desired phone is about $300. Then you go shopping at the local phone store, and the salesman offers to sell the phone for $280 instead of $300. You will quickly jump into accepting his offer; after all, you are saving $20 based on what you know about the price of the phone. However, the dealer across town sells the same phone for $220, which is about $60 less than what you have paid and about $80 less than what you saw online. When you find out what you have lost and how much you could have saved if not for your hasty decision, you might beat yourself up. The anchoring bias makes us favor that first piece of information, and since the preliminary research suggested that the average price of the phone is $300, the first offer we get will seem to be the best deal, and the need to get further information will be overlooked. This technique can be used to influence the decisions and choices of people. They are introduced to a particular piece of information to serve as an anchoring point in their mind beforehand, not knowing about the conditioning of their minds and perceptions.

Another instance where anchor bias can be really impactful is during negotiations. For example, you are to meet with your boss and discuss your salary increment, and you might not be quick to make the first offer.

Anchoring bias impacts your decisions on several other matters and areas of our everyday life. For example:

It can influence your decision on how much television time you allow your kids to watch every day. If, as a kid, you watched a lot of television, it might seem okay and acceptable for you to allow your kids to stay glued to the television for long hours every day.

What is the appropriate age for kids to be able to date? As a parent or guardian, your kids might debate that their peers are already in the dating business at the age of 14. Because you were brought up with the knowledge and belief that the appropriate age for dating is 16, the anchoring effect will impact your decision and guide your belief that the earliest age to allow a kid to date is at 16.

Anchoring can influence the judgment of a physician and their ability to diagnose an illness accurately and quickly after detecting the symptoms of the ailment. After coming in contact with a patient's condition and forming a first impression and creating an anchor point, when they meet similar cases, the initial anchor point will impact other subsequent assessments.

"Even If"

Everyone believes that they are unique. We are convinced and certain that we are very special, above average. In some cases, there is a strong belief that we are superior to most people. In psychology, this phenomenon is known by many names, such as above-average-effect, illusory superiority, the superiority bias, the primus inter pares effect, or the leniency error, which all relate to the same thing – that most humans assume they are actually better than others or most people.

A Door in the Face

The door-in-the-face technique, also called the reject-then-compromise technique, is a method in which the person doing the persuasion starts out by making an outrageous request while expecting to be rejected. While rejection is the primary aim of this technique, the target will be unaware that slamming the door in the face of the persuader will mean they have fallen into the trap laid. Once the door is slammed and the persuader is rejected, looking pitiful and sad, the persuader will now follow up with a smaller request, which will appear less outrageous to the target and even acceptable. The target will accept, not knowing that was the whole plan all along.

Chapter 46: Difference Between Persuasion and Manipulation

Visualize this: you are leaving the nation in 1 day, and you recognize that the toilet faucet is leaking. You'd love to have it repaired rather than worrying about flood the apartment building and leaving the house. You call the plumber, but he says now, he's too busy to get to your location and can make it in the following few days. Your excursion is mentioned by you, but claims you will persuade him to come over and to impress the person. Can you utilize exploitation or persuasion? Persuasion is an activity undertaken by people to alter the view of other people. With the attention of others in your mind with intent, and it is typically done. Persuasion suggests making their view is changed by somebody by assimilating the disagreements you're currently giving and taking in. You may direct that individual by assembling your arguments effectively.

The Idea of persuasion has been around since ancient times if the Greeks used to have disagreements from the public squares. The demonstration obtained the debate. Transparency is crucial when it comes to persuasion. People know others might feel the need to convince them. Parents will attempt to persuade their kids to prevent getting into strangers' cars, friends will try to persuade an individual to stop smoking, or an individual could convince a partner not to take a lousy job offer. The stone of Persuasion's arguments is the source of the disagreements in the other's intents. Manipulation suggests bending the truth to get somebody to do something different. It can be an action meant to find the person to do something valuable to among those parties, usually the one. Advertisers control people into believing they will need to remain hot and hip at any given age, and they require a solution. Everything goes when it comes to manipulation, and having any kind of advantage is a fantastic tool. Kids often manipulate their parents. Even for their mindset, they could relate their parents' attention from a young age, to get rewards or consideration of any sort, and they could pretend distress.

However, manipulation is utilized on all degrees in existence, not just in youth. Manipulation also feels pressured. There's a level of regarding it, coercion involved. The conversation might become personal when logical discussions fail. The individual cornered to a location where they feel, as there is not any other way except to select the alternative. The gap between manipulation and persuasion was a topic for thousands of years of debate. During the 4th century BC, in Greece, the father of belief, Aristotle, opposed a bunch of educators. Education provided by the Sophists, but became notorious. Aristotle clashed that they didn't care about the fact but could encourage any thought to get a fee. Aristotle claimed that the Sophists were participating in manipulation since they caused injury and deceived individuals. Nowadays, between manipulation and persuasion rages, many confess that it creates difficulty in differentiating between the two. Knowing the distinction is essential, as you will be guided by it in influencing other people and equips you with the understanding to recognize messages that what is manipulative.

Persuasion vs. Manipulation

The difference between manipulation and persuasion lies together with the intention behind the endeavor. Belief did do things -- to urge merchandise and the service, to produce the fit, to have an individual. Manipulation, on the other hand, is directed at benefiting only among the parties that were involved. Persuasion is all about presenting the right arguments all reasonably and considerably. Manipulation suggests bending the truth to satisfy the aim.

Although persuasion suggests doing the talking, somebody makes the intent behind it or makes it acceptable, and it is the clearness. Someone can convince a constructor who desired to push on a job to begin it earlier because they will need to move in the home. The arguments presented are actual, and the aim is precise. Manipulating the constructor would indicate stating the wife is pregnant and about to give birth even though there's no spouse. That is the reason for the stigma of exploitation. It is how individuals feel as they have been lied to and pressured into accepting something. The difference between the two lies in the fact that a person who has influenced to adopt a different view, convinced that this is the thing to do. They've awarded all the disagreements and equipped with everything they must earn a situation in favor of the choice. When manipulation is elaborate, there's sorrow after having consented. That is because no arguments are used, there is no evidence of motive, and the manipulator advantages for more.

Why Persuasion Is Excellent

To identify the distinction between persuasion, and it is crucial to comprehend. There are a few communication theorists, which have announced that belief is "ethically neutral." That's to say that this can be neither great nor bad, but only an impartial procedure. But this condition is not accepted. I'd argue that the opinion on persuasion isn't unbiased, however noble, is accurate. Aristotle stressed as it's among the ways through that persuasion is good. Throughout the efficient method, an idea is set forth with signs, and there has an individual permitted to decide to accept or reject, which appeal that is persuasive. Jay Conger wrote about this at the Harvard Business Appraisal, when he confirmed, "Persuasion does involve moving individuals to a position that they do not presently hold, but maybe not by yelling or cajoling. On the contrary, it entails careful planning, the appropriate framing of disagreements, the demonstration of brilliant supporting evidence, and the attempt to detect the right psychological match with your audience. The belief that persuasion is valid and an essential means of arriving seems in-fact it is the foundation for counseling clinics, economics, and the legal system. Persuasion is the basis of democracy. As Professor Raymond Ross writes, "Democracies utilize thoughtful, ethical conduct any time they choose leaders, set legislation, or attempt to secure their citizens" People who become familiar can't escape it. Persuasion is ingrained within communication. When collaborating, individuals unintentionally and intentionally promote such behaviors and beliefs. Persuasion isn't an issue of choice. Persuasion is the pursuit of reality. It is persuasion due to favorable change occurs. By way of instance, messages have demonstrated to prompt high school pupils to raise blood donations, to refrain from smoking, and protect against youth. Communication scholars Gas and Seiter repeat this notion when they claim, "Persuasion helps reestablish peace agreements between countries. Persuasion helps to open societies. Persuasion is essential to charities and organizations' attempts. Persuasion convinces drivers to refrain from driving or buckle up when driving once they have had a couple of drinks. Persuasion can use to convince an alcoholic or drug addictive relative to find assistance. Persuasion is an underdog team's the coach motivates the gamers to give their all to it. Persuasion is a tool employed by parents to advocate children not to take rides or allowing anyone to touch them. Persuasion is the cornerstone of numerous prosaic jobs. Very little of the virtuous that people see on earth can do without persuasion." However, the goodness of the fact and persuasion is embedded inside human nature. Isn't it? What causes people to fear? What causes stress in the event of persuasion's corruption? It can become manipulative, which can be harmful if persuasion twisted to be defined. Con artists, cult leaders and massacred millions, and even dictators have abused, enslaved. As deadly as misuse is also, it should not confuse with hyperactivity. Manipulation is the perversion of persuasion. It isn't concerned with truth, but deceit. Aristotle commented about this in his acclaimed work, Rhetoric, when he highlighted, "an insult of this rhetorical school can work great mischief, the same charge could bring against good things save itself. In addition, particularly against handy things like strength, health, wealth, and military ability. Rightly used, they function the best boon; and erroneously used, they function the best harm." Consequently, the question is, how do you Differentiate between manipulation and persuasion? Listed here are the three ways in which you may analyze whether there is a message manipulative.

Intention

The Intent is an element in estimating a petition is manipulative. They're participating in manipulation if someone tries to present an idea or behavior which isn't in the interest of another. It is so common. Individuals fall into the snare of others of what they want in the pursuit. Others are not seen by the root causes of the Machiavellian perspective. The philosopher Immanuel Kant wrote concerning this mentality when he implied the precept is treating a person of morality as a human being rather than as an object.

Withholding Truth

Manipulation involves withholding or distorting the facts. That can see employ fueling the benefits of product, idea, or behavior. It was this kind of exploitation, which prompted the term Caveat Emptor, which is Latin for "Buyer Beware," to become widespread. If vendors were liable, the term was general during these periods. The expression was a warning to prospective buyers to be sure they verified, and to be aware of those products or the grade of the item was identical to the promises. Most people have experienced advice about the advantages or the qualities of a service or product and. That is incorrect, as anything other than honest representation is manipulation.

Coercion

Coercion is the most visible and following part of a manipulative appeal. It's the elimination of the option or does it else. By comparison, persuasion involves sway, but not force. As a communication scholar, Dr. Richard Perl off writes, "a defining feature of persuasion is a free option. At a certain level, the person has to be capable of accepting or rejecting the situation that urged them." An invitation that you are not able to say is not persuasive but is manipulative and coercive.

Chapter 47: Principles of Persuasion

The Rule of Reciprocity

This rule is simple - you give something in return when you have been treated well. Humans, by nature, have an obligation to provide concessions or discounts to people that they have received favors from before. For many people, feeling indebted to others translates into stress, which they don't want to feel.

A classic example of reciprocity is when you are inviting people to your party, and your friends decide to invite your neighbor down the street. You don't really want him at the party because he disrupts everything, but since he invited you to his party a few months ago, you feel obligated to invite him over to repay the debt.

You are at work, and a co-worker asks you to help them over the weekend because they have a graduation to attend. You had your plans, but since he filled for you before, you decide to do it even without thinking.

In all the examples, we see reciprocity at work, whereby you do one thing for another just to fulfill a debt that you feel compelled to repay.

Why does reciprocity work in this way? Because just like all the other principles of influence that we shall look at, reciprocity forms a shortcut for making decisions, when making a decision, you need to understand that evaluating a situation critically in order to make a decision takes time and effort, which is why it is vital to know how to take shortcuts that help you make reliable and reasonable decisions.

The decisions you make usually make use of little information. For instance, if you are looking to make a decision on investing in real estate, you can follow the advice of an authoritative real estate consultant

So, with reciprocity, we make a quick decision whether to perform a specific action based on the prior experience we have with the person. If the person did something for us some time back, and then they ask for a favor, we automatically make a decision based on what the experience was.

You might think that reciprocity is just another theory of influence, but it isn't. Instead, it is so strong that many sociologists admit that all societies on earth follow this principle.

When used the right way, reciprocity can be a powerful tool to influence the decision you make. Many people cannot resist the temptation to return a favor that they were granted some time back. Even if the original gift waste asked for, the recipient would still return the favor when you ask the right way.

How to Make Reciprocity Work for You

When using reciprocity, you are working towards something after you have given another thing away. The item you give away should not necessarily be of the same value that you receive in return. The aim of giving something away is to create a sense of indebtedness in the other person, and when you ask for the thing you want in return, you set in motion the rule of reciprocity.

You can apply this rule to many areas of your life, from work to selling items.

So, how do you make full use of the rule?

Give Something First

Before you can ask for something in return and expect to get it, you need to be the first to give something out. The aim is to be in control of the situation, and the only way this can happen is to create a sense of debt in the person receiving the item. This is the situation you desire to create and then maintain it for some time till you make the request.

So, what will you give out? You can give anything, regardless of the value. However, it is usually crucial that you give something that the other person will remember a few years down the line. If you are a marketer, you can provide something that is related to what you are selling – a free pamphlet, a sample of the product, or a particular service.

As an example, say you are working with various insurance companies, and when changes happen, only one of the banks sends you private information regarding the effects a specific change in policy will have on your account, which bank will you do business with?

• **Offer Special Deals** – here, you give someone a special deal, for instance, a lower price when they initially refused your first offer on a product. For example, if the buyer refused the initial subscription cost of a magazine, then you give them a better deal at a lower price, they will have difficulty saying no.

• **Offer Samples of the Products** – samples are always free, and if you believe in the product, you will be able to offer free samples to your customers. When you receive a free sample, you will realize how useful the item is and give in to buy the product.

• **Offer a trial period** – if you have ever signed up for a service online, you must have been pulled in by the opportunity of a free trial. These trials usually take a few days or even weeks, with the aim of the seller being to make you buy the product at the end of it all. The trial period allows you to use the product and understand its benefits before making a purchase.

Give an Item that is Beneficial to the Recipient

When you force an item on someone, usually they feel manipulated, but if you give them something that they need, they will feel much obligated to return the favor in one way or the other. With this said, you need to be very careful so that your efforts at reciprocating don't look like a ploy.

Offer Something of Value

The more valuable the item is, the more indebted the recipient will be when you request their help. The longer the recipient will use the offer, the more attached to it they become, and the higher the chances that they will give something back.

Maintain the Feeling

Reciprocity might not work when you give out the item just once; instead, make sure you maintain the feeling of indebtedness to make sure you achieve your goal. Continue to add value to the person before, during, and after the transaction.

The Concept of Scarcity

This principle states that an object becomes more attractive when there aren't very many of them available for you. The scarcity can be imagined or real. For instance, when something is trending, and it is not easy to find, then it is precious.

How Important is This Principle

Let's use an example to illustrate this principle. Say that you are sitting down for supper when there is a knock on the door. On opening the door, you find a salesman selling a popular lock that you have been after for some time. When you look at the price, you realize that it is lower than what you would pay at the local dealer.

However, you don't have plans to install the lock that day, but the seller says that this is the last lock-in that offers, and the others are out of stock. You decide to use the money you had saved for something else to install the lock.

What you don't know is that you have been caught in the principle of scarcity, because the seller has first told you that they don't have any more in stock, and this made the lock more valuable to you.

By the seller telling you that you had to make a decision immediately, he made sure you thought that you had the last opportunity to make a decision. The seller also created the false impression that the lock will no longer be available, pushing you to the wall so that you make the decision faster.

You aren't alone in becoming the victim of the scarcity principle. If you have been to any mall, you will agree that the number of special offers is just out of the world. Each day you will come across various offers that tell you of an irresistible offer where you buy two items for the price of one. However, for you to enjoy the discounts, you have to act fast.

Let us look at some of the signs that point out to scarcity in the market:

- **Don't miss out on this offer!** – In your mind, you are sure that the proposal will soon end. A few weeks down the line, and the notice will still be there.

- **Hurry while stocks last!** – You will think that the stocks will run out in a few hours, but a few months down the line, and the notice is still fresh.

- **Don't be left out!** – You will think that many people have bought the offer, only to realize that you are the first one.

- **Save thousands today!** - The seller plays with your mind trying to imply that when you buy the product, you will make savings.

When used the right way, the scarcity principle is an excellent way to take advantage of the fact that if something is scarce, then many people have used it, and this is why it is not available. Additionally, if it is not on the shelves, then other people like the product, and it is good.

The principle takes an everyday item and makes it look attractive; it can also transform something that isn't helpful to seem very desirable. Additionally, it creates a sense of missing out on something great. Due to this, you might end up buying items that you don't need simply because it has been planted in your mind that the thing won't be available anymore.

You can see this during the holidays when kids fight over the latest toys on the market. When the toymakers create the perception that the toys will be scarce, they know that the kids will look at the products to be more appealing.

However, you need to know that just telling people that the item is scarce might not necessarily make the buyer believe it. Instead, the person needs to have proof that it is scarce before they go with what you desire them to do.

The Principle of Authority

An authoritative person is one that has a status that makes people more compliant with a request.

Say you are waiting for a taxi outside a hotel, then a person who is wearing a security uniform comes up to you and instructs you to move to another area of the hotel – the probability is that you will go ahead and move because you know that the security guard has authority in that hotel. By definition, the authority principle states that a person can easily comply with a person in a position of authority – doctors, professors, lawyers, and other experts in the fields.

In this case, the assumption is such that the people who are in authority have greater power and therefore know what they are doing. The authority might come from holding a higher position or having the capacity to influence decisions in a way.

For instance, the student in a school trusts the authority that is held by the teacher. When the teacher says that something is the way it should be, then that is the final decision.

The funniest thing is that you don't need to have a title to create an air of authority. A story is told of a student that entered the first day of class in college, and since he had the confidence, he took the entire class through the session, only for the course to realize he was their fellow student. In this case, we see authority coming in the form of confidence, the air of confidence that the person had made the rest to listen to them.

Chapter 48: Persuasion at Work: How to Create a Better Workplace

Human psychology influences the workplace. As a boss, you have the ability–and somehow duty–to make use of human psychology in the best interests of your workers. To create a happier, safer workforce, to inspire employees to help each other achieve their goals and be successful.

- **I can't make you read the files of Coalmine** – What I can do is to provide you with a high-level understanding of the seven principles of persuasion that I believe can change your job from personal experience.

- Read more to find out how you can manipulate your employees to their own benefit using the power of persuasion and the intranet of your company.

- **Conviction at work** – If someone does something nice for us, a powerful inner motivation tells us that we need to do something nice for them in exchange.

- **Engagement and coherence** – Once we have committed ourselves to something, we believe that we have to remain consistent with it.

- **Social Facts** – We are strongly influenced by our peers' thoughts and opinions.

- **Liking** – If we like anyone, they will tell us more.

- **Authority** – We tend to obey figures of authority. Scarcity-scarcity resources increase competition, and competition increases desires. (And a uniform or title is enough to find a figure of authority!)

- **Unity** – We prefer to divide ourselves into groups of common characteristics mentally (and then physically and emotionally). If someone is in this group with us, we think that they are "one of us," and we are more inclined to help and encourage them.

- **Stir Motivation** – for employees with reciprocity, a sense of duty is strong. When someone does something nice for us, a deep inner voice tells us that in exchange, we have to do something positive for them. Even the most sincere acts of kindness feel like debts to us until we give them back.

An example is the idea of Benjamin Franklin to ask enemies for favors.

This is a quick summary:

Franklin had a tense link with a man in Philadelphia who had a political sweep. He knew that he would have to improve the relationship if he succeeded in Philadelphia. So he sent the man a letter asking whether he might borrow one of his rare files. The man agreed to lease the manuscript to Franklin. And the guy was much friendlier to him from that point on.

Psychologists have written all kinds of theories about this story. Others claim that this induced cognitive dissonance, which occurs when our actions and beliefs are mutually contradictory. If persuasive enough, we often feel driven to reduce ambiguity by modifying our values, attitudes, and behaviors in line with our behavior. In this case, it makes sense.

Many claim that the idea of loyalty and coherence is at stake. When the man committed himself to lend Franklin his manuscript, psychology hit in again, and the man felt compelled to have his acts.

Reciprocity is often and regularly compensated by the workers.

1. Reward your behavior without letting your staff know that you are about to do so. Surprise them with a certificate of the gift. Nomine them for a draw. Call your positive actions at your following meeting with your employees.

This will trigger that sense of reciprocity by doing something nice for an employee. And how to reciprocate a reward better than to reward the first-class behavior?

2. Employees in the right direction with the idea of commitment and integrity. We have a profound need to remain consistent with that commitment when we pledge to something, particularly publicly, like verbalizing to somebody else or posting on social media. This is the core of the commitment and coherence theory.

It's powerful because, in so many ways, it shows up. This is why posting on Facebook to initiate a diet makes your diet more possible. This is why only small changes will change our way of thinking and how we want the world to see us.

That is why we ignore evidence that contradicts that decision once we have decided something. You could never have swayed Hillary Clinton as a supporter of Donald Trump before the presidential election in 2016–and vice versa. That is why — this principle. Interestingly, the commitment must be an internal choice to work. You can't command anyone to commit. And what is important is the greater the commitment it takes to commit to something. This is why brotherhood hazing works so well–the stronger the commitment is to be made to join the brotherhood, the more dedicated he is to that brotherhood. As I stated in the last segment, Benjamin Franklin, when he asked to take a manuscript, activated the concept of dedication and coherence. When the man committed himself to lend his manuscript, this psychological theory began, and the man changed his attitude to remain compliant with his behavior.

Here are a couple of ideas: Firstly, to motivate the workers to use the intranet, sign a pledge. At your following team meeting, distribute paper slots with something like:' I'm [filling your name here] going to use the intranet for whatever I can. I'm going to ask for assistance if I don't know how to use the intranet for something.' This may seem like a primary school move, but it works. I saw it work. The workers are now dedicated and will be much more compliant with it.

Secondly, set up volunteer groups to support the social responsibility efforts of your business. If the workers get together to volunteer or raise money for charitable activities, it brings them together. That's an enormous advantage right there. But there are more advantages than you could realize. It changes the way your employees see themselves in the context of their work roles. A social or environmental impact program helps the workers identify themselves as activists. Since this activity is supported and led by your company or organization, you see your company or organization as supporting people.

Thirdly, allow the workers to use phrases. It could sound really woo-woo to you, but it works again. Have the workers write affirmations related to work. Scott Adams, the popular cartoonist and Dilbert Comic Strip creator, discusses this better than anyone else in this interview.

3. Lead workers toward loyalty through social data. Human beings are affected by our peers. Our colleagues, families, and peers ' views affect us so much more than even the strongest publicity campaign.

This is why case studies and testimonials are so strong in the sales process. We don't know that this app will save you 10 hours a week. But if Jim, your partner for tennis, tells you that, then that's another matter. He would not lie to you. He would not lie to you. He has no interest in whether you buy the gadget or not. The theory of social proof is even stronger when an element of ambiguity occurs. In an emergency, we look at the people around us for guidance about what to do. If no one else is afraid, you say that everything is all right... even if it isn't. Once you have taken a CPR lesson, you will see how this works exactly. Your CPR teacher will advise you to point to a certain person and call 911 before you start CPR. Why do you point to a particular person? Because if you don't, if you just scream,' Someone call 911!' everyone stands by and looks at one another, waiting to see if they have something to do. It can be simplified by "assigning" tasks to individuals in an emergency.

And wonder if you're in the grocers and at the register, you see a long line. You suit and line up the crowd. Then you get closer to the ledger and see that TWO lines actually existed. One or two people chose not to stand on one side but to the center, and everybody behind them followed.

4. Walk the talk for the best results.

Help individuals to identify with the like theory. If we like others, we are more likely to be persuaded of them. Simple and straightforward. There are many ways that this principle takes place in our lives. If somebody praises us, we have a positive psychological response. This is why the good cop / bad cop formula fits so well.

They also tend to associate physical appeal with someone or something positive. The popularity of car ads featuring models draped over the hood of the car is an example. The model is good, so the car needs to be desirable. Where I see this at work is with the fun idea of similarity. Simply put, we like people who are like us.

Knowing this, it's easy to see how it can help your employees get to know each other and get acquainted with others within the company (including management) once workers feel that they are more like one another with friends, colleagues, and peers. And they usually work together well. This is a strong case for your workers to build their intranet profiles

5. Using authority to strengthen the integrity of workers, they strive to comply with figures of authority. This idea is so innate in us that you may not even know that it's psychology at work. Why would you not follow your boss, after all? Or a policeman?

What if the employer or policeman did something illegal? Will you follow them still? The authority theory—and all proof—say yes, so what's an authority doing? Coalmine says that a uniform or title is often everything that is necessary. Human beings blindly follow someone in uniform or with an impressive title (and yes, a suit and tie counts!). We also see the concept of marketing authority. If a person or company offers valuable information, it builds authority, and people follow the suggestions of that person or company more likely. Speak to your ideal household cleaner for all purposes. Now go to the website of the company. They may have hundreds of tools to clean your house, to keep germs in check, or to make unique use of their commodity. You probably think they're the cleanliness authority at home, right? So when they launch a new product, you believe it cleans toilets better and faster than anything else on the market.

This also converts the Intranet into an authority. Employees know that they can get information if they catch the wind of something changing in the business. This helps employers to tackle transition pro-actively before workers begin questions—avoiding a decline in workplace morality.

6. Enhance intranet use (and empower people to help themselves). With Scarcity You might not accept that scarcity has anything to do with the involvement of workers and the use of the Intranet, but stay with me. This triggers frenzies like what you see during Shark Week on the Discovery Channel. Low supply on the market leads to high demand. Do you recall about 15 years ago when ephedrine was considered dangerous and taken off the market? People sold bottles of ephedrine supplements in insane amounts. I'm sure the prohibition era speakeasies cost an alcohol arm and leg as well.

When children are raised, scarcity plays with independence. The more you try to restrict the independence of a child, the more independent they become. (You cannot take it back once freedom is given—so watch out, children's parents and teens!) Scarcity is a powerful psychological force. We want what we can't do—and we're ready to spend time to get it.

At work, you can use this idea to get your workers to use the Intranet. So workers are motivated and more involved by using the Intranet to answer their own questions and find their own tools.

Chapter 49: How to Analyze and Manipulate People

As explored, there are many stimuli that trigger human responses and lead to decision-making, and researchers have developed extensive methods to measure these outcomes, whether using biometrics, surveys, or focus groups. However, these research methods may not be at your disposal on a daily basis. Below are methods techniques you can use in everyday interactions to analyze the cognitive and behavioral processes of individuals around you.

Observe Body Language

Research found that body language accounts for 55% of how we communicate, while words only account for 7%. The tone of voice represents the rest. People can tend to be over-analytical when reading human behavior, and it may seem counterintuitive, but in order to be objective in analyzing people, observe naturally and try not to over-analyze.

Appearance

One of the first things that speak the loudest is the appearance of an individual. Take notice of a person's dressing. Is he or she dressed sharply in a suit, traditional clothing, or casual style? Does he or she look particularly conscious about the choice of clothing or hairstyle? The way a person dresses can determine his or her level of self-esteem.

Posture

When reading people's posture, observe if they hold their head high or slouch. Do they walk indecisively or walk with a confident chest? How do they esteem themselves? Posture also reveals confidence levels or a person's physical pain points.

Movements

People generally lean towards things they like and away from things they do not. Crossed arms and legs suggest self-protection, anger, or defensiveness. When people cross their legs, their toes point to the person they are most comfortable with or away from those they are not. When hands are placed in pockets, laps, or behind the back, it is an indication that the person is hiding something.

Facial Expressions

Aforementioned, emotions may not be visible unless expressed. Frown lines indicate over-thinking or worry, while crow's feet evidence joyfulness. Tension, anger, or bitterness can be seen on pursed lips or clenched jaws.

How to Analyze People Effectively and Efficiently

So, you want to learn how to analyze people effectively and efficiently. Well, you came to the right place! I will teach you everything you need to know about reading others. I will even teach you how to understand yourself. We need to talk about a few things before we get into the meat of the matter, however. There are so many different methods to analyze others, and it can be hard to pick it all apart. Where did this practice come from? Why is it important to understand how to analyze others? As it turns out, the art of analyzing others has existed since— well; we had the intelligence to do it. Human beings are, by nature, herd animals. We are highly in tune with others, and our lives are driven by societal expectations. It can be easy to get caught up in our instincts, though, and to forget that we need to tackle things logistically. This is where learning how to actively analyze others comes in. Understand your boss's motives and learn how to nail down what they want from you without even hearing them say it. Here are some jobs which actively employ analyzing others:

• Politicians

• Lawyers

- Criminal investigators

- Military officials

- Psych professionals

- Forensic experts

As you can see, it truly is a universal tool. Many different people have to analyze others daily in their day-to-day lives.

I hope that these are the skills you want to learn. They are invaluable, and it is my pleasure to help you improve your life, one impression at a time.

There are, of course, incredible benefits to consuming the knowledge I am offering to you today. First off, you will find that you can communicate your needs to other people far more effectively. Being able to tell how they are reacting and changing your approach accordingly is more than helpful. Communication is the most important skill that we can hone, quite frankly. It helps ease tension, earn the confidence of others, and put us in a positive light. Emotional intelligence goes hand in hand with communication as well.

This is another skill that will be furthered when paired with the power to analyze others. Your emotional intelligence greatly relies on your ability to understand others. The goal is always to meet people where they are: understanding what they need and being able to tell how they need to be handled. Whether you lead a team, need to help your children through their struggles, or are feeling the tension in your love life, I am here to help.

Strong relationships are the glue of society and, more importantly, of families. We need to know how to handle our spouses, children, and anybody else directly related to us. Strained relationships lead to strained relations, and none of us want to be caught up in a family feud. Learning how people tick and how to handle tough situations is the key. You will also learn how to watch for red flags with your children. Knowing how to read their body language and pick up on their verbal cues do wonders for seeing warning signs well in advance.

If you are a parent, this will be a key manuscript in taking your parenting to the following level.

As for another skill, leadership, you will soon be at the front of the crowd. You will find that people not only listen to you but that they actively want to listen to you. Becoming a strong leader means being able to tell who a person is just by carefully observing them. True leaders understand the absolute power that body language holds. After all, it is the oldest form of communication of them all.

Many leaders in the business world, as well as in other areas, actively take lessons and classes on analyzing others. This is a skill that can be applied in almost every situation you can think of. It builds your confidence knowing that when you take the lead, others follow suit.

I am pretty sure you are beginning to get the idea of what analyzing others can do for you. The benefits are boundless, and there are new ones at every corner. You cannot imagine how much life will change!

I would like to get you started with a few rules. As you can imagine, there is a baseline to start when it comes to analyzing others. You can remember some steps to help you begin, which are not hard and fast but excellent for helping you to understand the process. Practice makes perfect, so make sure you pay close attention to this list.

These rules are as follows:

1. **Understand What Their Baseline Is**: Everybody is just a tad bit different from the rest. It is almost like how parents can tell their twins apart, but nobody else can. Learning how to analyze others means you can tell them apart on a much different level. Understand that you can only tell their "baseline" after knowing them for a while.

You can watch for signs that they are nervous. Perhaps ask probing questions you know will elicit the emotion you want to pin down. If they tend to become physically restless under duress, you know what sort of body language to watch for.

This is the first rule for many reasons. Most importantly, it reminds us that we need to see the whole person. Cold reading is great.

2. **Notice the Changes**: Take into account the entire picture of the person. This builds off of the first rule. Understand that any gesture can mean something, but you need to put several clues together to really solve the mystery that is a person.

This will also be built by noticing what signs of nervousness you may be looking for. We are using nervousness for these examples, but it goes for any emotion. Anger, unease, discomfort—they are all negative emotions you can begin to pinpoint.

3. **Watch For Warning Signs**: When certain behaviors are brought into the light and therefore meaning in your eyes, you can start to piece it together. If you have noticed that they shift their eyes around when nervous, and their eyes tighten up when they are angry, you will know when you are treading on dangerous territory.

There are several different clusters of behaviors that can be seen across the board. As mentioned, humans are pack animals in nature. This means that we have learned how to communicate with each other, whether we like it or not. Certain tip-offs are pretty well-known. However, a lot more will be missed to the untrained eye. That is why you are reading this!

4. **Compare Behavior Changes**: The following rule in this line-up is to always make sure you watch how they behave with others as well. It is a popular belief that you do not watch the person who is speaking—you watch the reaction of the person you want to impress. Making sure you are taking note of your boss's body language while listening to co-workers, for example. Notice the changes between them talking to you and them talking to others. This will help cue you into their true emotions about you as well as how they feel about others. Are their arms crossing when they talk to their friends? Is their body still turned towards you even while engaged in conversation elsewhere?

5. **Watch Yourself**: One of the most powerful things you can do is be aware of your body language. We do not just need to understand others, but also ourselves. We influence others with our facial expressions without even knowing what it looks like. That is not what you want to be doing. To control a situation or a conversation, or even influence it, you need to practice expressions.

The best way to do this is to do it in the mirror.

6. **Listen To Others Talk**: Identify the strongest person in the room. You will notice them right away, most likely. Sometimes, however, it takes a little time. Look for open body language being used purposefully but elegantly. A big smile, a voice that commands attention and self-confidence to always say, "I am the boss in this situation." They do not need the approval of others, and they often hold the most sway in the situation.

The same idea as watching the boss when others are talking, even if somebody is technically the boss, that does not mean they are completely in control. A confident, strong person will make an impression and quickly become somebody whose opinion the "head honcho" deeply trusts. Knowing which strings to pull will push you further and further toward getting what you want out of a situation.

7. **Watch Them Move**: Looking at body language while they talk to you, especially sitting or standing still, is one thing. You also need to watch their general state of being while moving around. You can tell quite a bit about a person just by the way they walk and how they move. Confident people tend to stand tall, with their shoulders back and chest pushed a little out. They walk with purpose, as though they always have somewhere important to be.

On the other hand, somebody who is unsure of themselves embodies the exact opposite traits. They try to make themselves look small, perhaps hunching over a little, keeping their head low.

8. **Listen For Speech Patterns**: Another rule is to listen closely to how they talk and what they are saying, both about the topic at hand and about themselves. How a person speaks tells you so much about them, both literally and figuratively! When you can identify how they speak when they are being truthful and genuine, you can figure out when they are being the opposite.

Chapter 50: Secrets of Persuasive People, How to Stop and Spot Manipulation

Manipulation is about control and gain. They need to control a person and the situation in order to get whatever it is they are after. While each set of circumstances are different, there are still some very common tactics that manipulators use, think of them as a general blueprint. They can be altered a bit based on certain situations, but they are all generally the same. The ways in which people can be manipulated are also different; for instance, the way someone manipulates someone in a romantic relationship is not going to be the same in friendship and so on. The good news is that the basic principles are similar enough that if you learn to spot one manipulative situation, it can make it easier to spot more in the future.

No matter what type of situation, manipulators still have similar tactics that they will use simply because they work. They will change them a bit depending on their specific wants and the situation at hand, but manipulative behavior is not the norm, so it can still be spotted if you know what you're looking for. Even if they think they are breaking the mold, a manipulator is doing what countless manipulators have done before them. This doesn't make their behavior any better or acceptable, but it does make them somewhat predictable. If you are the victim of manipulation, you might be able to see it for what it is, but others do, and this is important because when you want to cut a manipulator out of your life, those are the people you can depend on.

Common Forms of Manipulation

• **One of the most used forms of manipulation is someone making you think they are better or above you**. They might treat you as if you are a child or throw condescending looks or tones your way when you interact with them. Sometimes it can even go as far as to simply tell you that that they know better and their way is the best and only way. However, it happens, the message is clear, they're the 'superior,' and you are the 'inferior.' This is emotionally exhausting and beats down a person's self-esteem making it less likely that the manipulator will be challenged because at a point, you just stop speaking up because it never worked to begin with.

- **Making jokes at your expense is another common tactic used by manipulators**. This is especially awful because it is not done in private. It is used as a method of putting someone down and making them feel small, and in order to do this, they need a group of people laughing. Sadly, this method has only grown in popularity because of the use of social media, where it is abundant. The jokes can range from physical attributes to how a person dresses, but either way, you are meant to be the butt of the joke and laughed at. When the manipulator is confronted, they usually come back with things like, "I was only kidding, you're too sensitive," making it seem like you are the problem.

- **Sometimes all it takes is a look to manipulate someone**. This might seem childish, but a facial expression has just as much power as words. Manipulators master the art of the death glare, the condescending head tilt, and eye rolling, and shaking their head. Any facial expression or gesture that indicates to you, without words to back down. Even though this seems like something that you wouldn't fall victim to, it can and does happen. As a matter of fact, this type of manipulation can mean stop, you're wrong, you're ridiculous, and many other things that lower your self-esteem, and to make it worse, all of it with no words spoken.

- **Another common tactic is to simply ignore someone**, for instance, saying hello to everyone in the room except you; this can be demeaning and hurtful, not to mention also just embarrassing. Part of this is also acting bored, disinterested, and inconvenienced even when you are simply talking about everyday things. Going right along with this, they will often not answer any questions, phone calls, emails, text messages and always seem unavailable. Many manipulators do this because they know it makes someone feel inferior, and they hope the person will go out of their way to understand what they did wrong and make up for it when in reality they did nothing wrong, and the manipulator is just using them for control and to gain something from the situation.

- **Guilt tripping is another common way for manipulators to get what they want**, this comes out in the language they use, which typically involves things such as, "I thought we were friends, I thought I could count on you, I can't believe how selfish you're being," and so on. This is a powerful way to exert control over the other person because they will wonder if what are saying is true, and they will want to do everything in their power to fix it since they thought they were friends, and they will want to fix the friendship. That is when the demands come in from the manipulator, thus giving them what they wanted at the expense of the other person's feelings.

- **Some manipulative people choose to be deliberately difficult, making others cater to their whim in order to make them feel better.** The more giving and agreeable you are to them, the more difficult they will be escalating the situation and blowing it out of proportion so they can have more control of the situation and wait until the other person goes out of their way to fix the situation.

- **Overly complimenting people and telling them what they want to hear is also a great way for manipulators to get what they want**, they are often called sweet talkers, and they mean nothing they say. They know people like to be complimented, and they use this to their advantage. They will tell you what you want to hear. However, it does not end there. They do this because they know it is one of the best ways to make friends, build trust, and then lower the other person's defenses, which is when the true manipulation can begin. They make it seem like all the praise they have been giving is worthy of something in return, and that is when they name their price. This tactic is also even more deplorable because the closer you are to someone, the easier it is for someone to manipulate you because there has been a friendship or relationship that involves trust that has already been cultivated.

The basic rules remain the same, but with different elements added to it to match the different types of circumstances. Even if they think they are masterminds and you are beneath them, the truth is, a manipulative person is not.

They have just learned to use their behavior to get what they want to the point of not caring about others. They are not invisible; you can see them for what they are when you know what to look for.

There are also ways to determine whether or not you are in a manipulative friendship as well. Since manipulators use different relationships as a way to manipulate others, friendships are definitely not safe from these people either.

Chapter 51: Power is Influence: Strength is Persuasion

Leadership is the willingness of the strongest to pursue you, while power is the ability to keep a long time following you. In addition, influence refers to the ability to influence positive or negative acts, attitudes, and/or opinions of other people. In other words, power is strength, and belief is strength!

If a leader is dominated by another person, he or she cannot convince his or her team to complete the assigned tasks. Nevertheless, affect, and dedication require a base of trust. By confidence, employees tend to take the values, philosophy, and purpose of the company less seriously and permanently. Since the ability to positively influence increases over time, years of experience have been needed to learn to be an effective leader. Studies have shown that all people can influence other people, and each person can lead one or more people to one level...

One thing a leader needs to remember is that he doesn't know how strong he is. Therefore, leaders need to keep a watchful eye on how many people will do for them, nor do leaders realize how much their team members will do when the leader leads them. The power sectors are structured to convince a leader to maximize his / her influence: the power expert, aligned in several areas with the leading expert. The leader has gained more expertise, competence, and reputation than anyone else in the party.

Power of Reward

Power correlated with the reward of the chief. Those benefits apply to jobs including promotions, bonuses, holidays, special prizes, and so on.

Coercive Power

Power associated with a boss who penalizes employees for failing to perform the tasks. The staff are also afraid and fear the consequences. They are usually so frightened of such a leader that it affects their performance. This power triggers the anger and resistance of the worker. Reverent influence–The power associated with a leader has an effect on an individual who specifically attracts a leader. The leader or the powerful person does whatever he does because he is brought to the authority of a leader.

Legitimate Power

Power, which is related to a leader because he is in a leading position. This is known as spatial power. Gender power–a power that is linked to the leader, whose gender status gives power. Sometimes the opposite sex confers control so that all sexes are portrayed equally. Power attitude-The boss, who is constructive and flexible, can manage the team members. He has a lot of experience in conflict resolution and is a peace-builder. On the other hand, he will influence the person who became the leader as all the people within the party have the best attitude or personality. This leader is generally the most violent, strong, and speaker of the party. Leadership is sometimes voted because the group members do not want to be disciplined.

Missing Desire

Power linked to a leader because no one else wants to direct. The head is responsible for the fact that nobody else is responsible for the activities and responsibilities. This chief normally does most of the job.

Charisma or Personal Power

A power connected to the leader through his charismatic personality. These leaders are beautiful, funny, and interesting. We are chosen for the leader because others think their job is creative and exciting.

The Character or Force of Ethics

Power associated with a person leading the organization, as he or she is the most trusted person within the organization. Sometimes this individual does all the work himself.

Capacity to connect with a leader, because many people are relevant, because he or she knows many people who can support and make a financial contribution to the organization.

The various forms of force should be known to an effective leader. This information is a self-assessment to allow the leader to test the power sources are being used by his organization(s). Leaders can also use this knowledge to determine and define the various power forms currently used by their employees. Understanding this knowledge will help a leader make important decisions. Persuasion Your influence and power depend on your ability to persuade. The quality of one's education, employment, professional, and personal experience influences the ability to convince another person. The character and personality traits of an individual are very critical for persuading others. When a leader has to convince an employee, how a leader interacts is important. In other words, the abilities, expertise, and actions of the leader are dictated by the strength of the leader whose influence enabled an employee to perform the tasks.

Both leaders must develop their ability to persuade forces. Improving your persuasive skills will improve your confidence and increase your power. In order to improve your argument, please review the list and highlight the ways in which young people are improved:

- Technology skills

- Life skills

- Marketing and Media skills

- Advertising knowledge

- Technical skills and skills

- Screen...
- Compromise and honesty
- Content and products of quality
- Trust and development of new relationships over time.
- Awareness of work and obligations.

Leaders

- Should be able to...
- Show experience of inspiring people
- Size-based presentations
- Case Print Professional
- Sync and mission statements
- Show facts-content is important
- Provide proof of your status
- Know the dynamics of the team memory

An effective leader is required in each case to decide which energy sources and persuasive techniques should be used and which should not be used to properly develop the organization.

Members who master the meanwhile persuade their employees optimistic that workers perform tasks without difficulty until they comprehend the company's goals and have a good relationship with the members. Know that when you improve your leadership abilities, you need to concentrate on your strength and persuasion skills. In other words, an effective leader should effectively work in all three areas to better and faster performance in one of these areas.

Chapter 52: Subliminal Persuasion

Subliminal persuasion is the technique of convincing your target, or your group of targets, to do something without them knowing. There isn't going to be any outward suggesting of the idea, and often the victim isn't going to realize that you were trying to influence them at all. It is one of the types of persuasion that manipulators and others can use, and it uses words, along with some gestures, to get ahold of different people. So, you may find things like smiling, use of the head, eye expression, and more being used, both in a positive and a negative manner. It is a powerful technique, but often a difficult technique, that not only uses words but uses the meaning behind the words, and body language, to ensure that the victim does what the manipulator wants.

In the modern world, the techniques that are used for subliminal persuasion are going to be powerful weapons that can really help you get ahead. They can help you to manipulate others or even gain an advantage in a market where there is a lot of competition, and you need to stay ahead of the game. According to some experts in the field of marketing and persuasion, many people are resulting in subliminal advertising because it is more effective. As they say, "Persuasion that looks like persuasion isn't persuasive anymore."

Even a manipulator can use this information to help take control of the victim. If the persuasion that they use is too obvious, then the victim is just going to walk away. You see a lot of examples of persuasion in your daily lives that it is easy to recognize the more obvious signs and stay away from them if you don't want to purchase something or do something.

If a manipulator comes at their victim with a big sales pitch, lots of bright flashing lights, and other obvious techniques of persuasion, then they will get nowhere. The victim is smart enough to recognize these signs, and they will get away from the manipulator, and this is where subliminal persuasion can come in.

Every time that the manipulator communicates with their victim, they are going to be very careful about the nonverbal signs that they are sending out as well. The manipulator is going to try and send out extra messages and extra persuasion through the body language and the nonverbal cues that he/she is sending out as well.

Since subliminal persuasion is going to deal with the feelings that the victim has, there is going to be some kind of subconscious element in this kind of persuasion. As a manipulator or another kind of person who needs to use persuasion, you will provide the victim's mind with some feelings of enthusiasm and comfort about doing a given task. Those thoughts and emotions are going to be sent out to the subconscious mind, but then you have to take to the logical mind too. You can then talk to this part of the mind by discussing the things that are rational about the choice.

Some subliminal factors are going to influence whether the manipulator is going to be believable. For instance, the way that the manipulator does dress is going to be a factor. The manipulator is going to make sure that the victim sees him/her at his/her very best. The manipulator will dress nicely, make sure that his/her appearance is kept up, and always look like he/she is doing well. Even when the manipulators are trying to play the victim and say that they are hurt or dealing with a big illness, your manipulator will still dress nice.

You are programmed to be more likely to help out someone with a nice appearance, someone who is well-groomed, compared to someone who is not. If the manipulator wants to exploit this factor, then they are going to take some extra precautions with their appearance.

There can also be a level of subliminal persuasion that is used in the language of the manipulator as they ask for a favor. There is a lot of truth in the idea of "it's not what you say, but how you say it." The manipulator isn't going to say anything that is too out there, because this is something that may raise some flags with their victim. But the way they use their words will make a difference and usually gets them what they want.

The way that the manipulator will use their inflections and intonations will also have a large bearing on the meaning of what you say. If you see a sentence like "I can't promise you that price," you may assume that it has just one meaning, and that is it. But depending on the way that the manipulator, or salesperson, uses it, there may be a few different meanings. Take a look at some of the examples below:

- **I can't promise YOU that price**. This one is going to infer that the manipulator isn't willing to get you that price, but maybe they will promise that price to someone else.

- **I can't promise you that price**. This one can infer that one person can't do it, but maybe there is someone else who can offer that price.

- **I CANNOT promise you that price**. This one is going to infer that there is just no way that the person is going to get that price.

- **I can't PROMISE you that price**. This one is going to infer that there isn't a guarantee but that the manipulator might be able to do them a "favor" and get that price.

- **I can't promise you THAT price**. This one infers that the manipulator is going to see what they can do. They may not be able to offer exactly that, but they could still get you something good.

- **I can't promise you that PRICE**. This one is going to infer that they will still be able to promise you something, even if the price point doesn't fall in the desired spot.

The importance of these statements is a great way to utilize the ideas of subliminal persuasion. And there can be so many different meanings based on the words that the manipulator, or any other person, decides to emphasize. And it is sometimes such a subtle process that you can hear the sentence and infer the meaning without even realizing what is going on.

Think about the intonation that you can use when you say a specific sentence, and then imagine the power that goes behind those words based on what a manipulator would be able to use with them as well. In fact, there are about three choices that come with intonation and the way that it can change up the meaning of the whole sentence. As you go through and say something, the three ways to finish up that sentence would include:

• An intonation that goes up

• A downward, which would mean that the intonation is a deeper voice

• A voice intonation that does not change at all

Subliminal Persuasion Advertising

One aspect of subliminal persuasion that you need to take a look at with this topic referred to as subliminal advertising. This type of advertising aims to use your subconscious minds against you to profit from another company. The business is going to sneak different emotions, feelings, and thoughts into the things that you consume, in the hopes that you are going to want to purchase more of that same products. In some countries, the idea of subliminal advertising has been banned because it has been recognized how dangerous this kind of manipulation tactic can be against the consumer.

However, it is pretty common that an advertiser can get into the head of the consumer, and most of these advertisers are really good at doing it. They sometimes even pay to have potential consumers what the advertisement to monitor how the brain functions while watching that commercial. This helps the advertisers to get a better idea of how the brain is going to work while watching the advertisement, and then they can make adjustments to really make it stronger.

The advertisers are going to monitor several things. For example, they may decide to track eye movement to see what part of the commercial is drawing the attention of the crowd more. The advertising company can then use this information to sell a product and to be as effective with subliminal persuasion as possible. This shows just how powerful advertising can be, and how it has broken into your brains, understanding how to sell you something better than your understanding of capitalism, and what it means to be a consumer.

Think about a chocolate commercial for an example. The advertisement could just show a picture of a peanut butter cup. You see the logo, just for a second, but then there is nothing else on the screen that tells you to purchase that treat. However, this is enough to tell you about the candy bar, and the idea gets stuck in your head. This can make it more likely that you will purchase that same treatment when you head to the store next time.

Of course, you don't always give in to what we see in advertisements, even with subliminal persuasion. You see thousands of advertisements during the week, and of course, you are not going out and purchasing thousands of items. But it is effective. Think about the reason that you do purchase some of the things that you own. Think about the reasons that you have a tone of stuff around the house that you never use. All of this could be due to the process of subliminal advertising and persuasion.

Chapter 53: The Basics of Deception

Deception is going to refer to the idea that we do an act, sometimes big and sometimes small, and it can be kind or even cruel, but the act is going to cause the target, or another group of people, to believe something that is a lie. Even those who consider themselves pretty honest are going to be willing to practice this form of deception on occasion, and it is believed that people will lie a few times a day.

Now, there are different forms of deception out there. There can be a big lie about where you were when you were supposed to be home or who you spent time with. But for most of us, the lies are going to be little and are done to help us avoid a conflict, and maybe even to make sure that the other person is not going to be hurt in the process. For example, it may not be true, but we will tell someone that the outfit looks nice on them. This helps us to spare the feelings of the other person and to make sure that the person telling a lie is able to avoid being uncomfortable.

There is also going to be a lie that people tell themselves, ranging from healthy maintenance of self-esteem to serious delusions that are beyond the control of the person. While lying to yourself is going to be seen as harmful, it is sometimes useful because it can help you to reach a goal that you want, especially when it is hard to accomplish, and you wouldn't be able to do it otherwise.

Now, we can imagine that no one really likes to be deceived, whether the deception is big or small. For example, when a public figure is caught up in one of the lies that they are doing, it is going to be a big scandal. And if the target realizes and started to believe that the manipulator had been deceiving them, they are going to feel upset, mad, and probably want nothing to do with the manipulator again. They will feel like they couldn't trust the manipulator again, and the target will start to question whether the manipulator was actually ever telling them the truth.

But while many people are going to hold them to a higher standard and try to make sure they are distanced from those who are comfortable with lots of falsehoods, the truth here is that everyone is going to lie for a variety of reasons. Of course, for most of us, we are going to try and be a bit better with our lies and only focus on ones that are going to help the target and us in the process. We may say that the outfit looks nice because we know it is important to the other person, and we don't want to hurt their feelings, for example. This may have been an altruistic meaning, but it is still a lie and thus an example of deception as well.

There are a lot of different reasons that we are going to lie and deceive others. Sometimes, the reasons are noble and good; other times, they are going not to be that good, and they are more for our own benefit. Sometimes, the reasons are seen as ethical, sometimes as unethical, and sometimes they are a mixture of things in between. But no matter the reason that we are lying and trying to deceive someone, it is still seen as something that is not good and can make the target of our deception mad and upset.

Manipulators are going to love using the methods of deception to get what they want. If they are able to hide information that is important to the target, the target is going to be more likely to believe the manipulator and do what the manipulator wants. The manipulator learns how to hide the right facts so that they can really work to get the target to act in a certain manner.

For example, if the manipulator is trying to get the target to help them with a project at work, they can use a few forms of deception. They could talk about how the project was just sprung on them, and they have to get it done, or they will lose their jobs. Maybe their job isn't on the line in this scenario. Or maybe it is, but the project was assigned a month ago, not just a few days ago, and they just decided to procrastinate getting it done and now want the target to help. Either way, information was either lied about or hidden so that the target would feel bad and be more likely to help the manipulator out.

In order to get what they want, the manipulator is going to lie about pretty much everything under the sun if it helps them to get what they want out of the target. This may seem low and as though not really an ethical thing to do, but it can be an effective way to get the target to behave and take a certain action that you want. The target is going to make a decision based on the information that the manipulator gave, and they trust the manipulator, so they didn't think anything about it at all. In the process, the manipulator is going to be able to get what they want, they will then be able to deny what the target is saying about the lie, and the target is often going to be harmed in the process.

Chapter 54: Brainwashing

Brainwashing is the collective approach used for influencing or changing other people's beliefs, attitudes, and behavior toward something. Be that as it may, brainwashing could actually be characterized as a social issue in a severe form since it functions at changing the perspective of a subject without the subject agreeing to it.

To carry out a successful brainwashing, the subject has to be totally isolated and dependent since it has an invasive effect on the subject. This explains why most cases of brainwashing happen in prison camps or totalistic cults. The agent or brainwasher needs to gain complete control of the subject. He or she must be in absolute command of their subject's sleeping patterns and eating habits whilst satisfying the other vital needs of the subject, and none of these happen without the knowledge of the brainwasher. While the procedure takes place, the agent seeks ways to break down the subject's entire identity, so it doesn't work right anymore. From the moment that identity is broken, the brainwasher strives to exchange it with the desired attitudes, beliefs, and behaviors.

The idea of brainwashing is not generally agreed upon by everybody, if it works or not is still a certainty, as many people have different opinions about it. Some psychologists believe that if the right conditions are in place, brainwashing a subject is possible. However, the entire task is never as severe as portrayed in the media. Several definitions of brainwashing exist, which makes it really tough to know the consequences of brainwashing on a victim. Most definitions require the presence of some form of threat to the physical body of the victim for it to be called brainwashing. In line with this definition, most practices carried out by extremist cults would not be regarded as real brainwashing since physical abuse was absent.

The remaining definitions of brainwashing make use of control and coercion with no physical force, while aiming at getting the subject to change his/her beliefs. Whichever definition it is, pundits agree that even with all the conditions in place, the results of brainwashing lasts for just a brief moment. Experts also agree that the former identity of the victim is never erased totally with the experience; instead, it is sent into hiding and re-surfaces when the new identity is no longer forced upon the victim again.

Robert Jay Lifton presented fascinating opinions on brainwashing in the 1950s after observing prisoners of the Korean and Chinese War camps. During his studies, he concluded that his subjects (prisoners) went through several stages in brainwashing. These stages start with an attack on the victim's self-concept and conclude with a supposed change in the prisoner's beliefs. Lifton defined 10 steps for the brainwashing process in the prisoners he studied. These steps are:

- Attack the subject's identity;

- Force guilt on the subject;

- Force self-betrayal on the subject;

- Reach a breaking point;

- Offer the subject leniency if they change;

- Compulsory confession;

- Point all the guilt in the intended direction;

- Liberate the subject from supposed guilt;

- Move into harmony;

- A last confession before a rebirth.

These steps must be carried out in a completely isolated area. What this means is that all the regular social references the victim is used to coming in contact with are not available. Furthermore, mind clouding schemes like starvation and sleep deprivation will be utilized in order to speed up the procedure. Even though this may not be what's obtainable in all cases of brainwashing, there' is often the presence of some kind of bodily harm. This makes it difficult for the subject to think critically and independently like they usually do.

Different Techniques of Brainwashing

As we now understand, brainwashing doesn't occur overnight but is usually a series of actions taken simultaneously over a period of time, which eventually results in a changed personality. Perception and behavior change, sometimes to such an extent that the victim becomes unrecognizable to their friends or peers.

The techniques used and the speed with which the personality changes depends on many things, but most of all on whether the target is being subjected to brainwashing against their will (in which case they'll naturally resist as much as they can) or whether they don't know they're being brainwashed (e.g., in cults) and believe all the ideas being impressed upon them are their own and that they themselves are making the decisions. This could be deemed successful brainwashing, as the victim is unaware of what's occurring.

Most common overt and covert brainwashing techniques:

Repetition and Nagging

It's hard not to start believing something or at least begin doubting one's self if someone is constantly repeating the same thing over and over every day, for months or even years.

Isolation

It is easier to control someone if they have no access to sources of information that conflict with the brainwashing material. If the target talks to someone about the ideas being imposed upon them and other people understand what's happening, they may scupper the chances for a successful brainwash. This tactic is often witnessed in abusive relationships, where one partner doesn't want the other to communicate with friends or family in case their motives are uncovered.

Blind Obedience

This prevents the victim from thinking for themselves.

Responsibility

One central brainwashing technique is to make someone feel responsible for their faults and the things that go wrong in their life. If they make mistakes, do something poorly, or if things don't go according to plan, making them feel responsible leaves them feeling negative emotions such as guilt and shame, which lowers their defenses and opens them up for manipulation.

Guilt and Fear

These are used extensively as part of an overall emotional manipulation plan. When a huge guilt complex is imposed, we start believing we're deserving of any resulting punishment.

Self-Brainwashing Techniques

Identify a Negative Thought Pattern

Identify a negative thought or belief that's been holding you back. How long have you felt this way? Can you connect the programming to any early life experiences? Are you aware of how this belief has affected your life? What do you think your life would have been like if it weren't for this negative thought pattern? Do you believe you are what others tell you? What skills or abilities do you wish you had?

Acknowledging the Damage

Be aware of any negative emotional, mental, or physical harm this thought pattern has done to you, and then make the decision to do something about it. Negative programming can be reversed, but it takes time, so be prepared to work on this issue for a long time if need be.

The Power of Suggestion

Much of our negative thinking comes from suggestions we take in from others. Think of how many times someone has spoken to you negatively, said you were fat, stupid, or unintelligent? Eventually, when these suggestions are heard repeatedly they tend to become our reality.

We can reverse such damage by purposefully taking our suggestions onto a more positive path by consciously choosing positive beliefs. Whatever flaws you believe you have, they can often be reversed. One such way is to constantly tell yourself what you'd like to become by verbally affirming (or thinking) how successful, healthy, or confident you are. Eventually, with commitment, these suggestions can come true as our actions and behaviors gradually begin to follow the constant positive reinforcement we're feeding ourselves.

Repetition

Repetition is successfully used in self-brainwashing. Consistently reinforce positive thoughts about yourself or your self-image by repeating confidence-boosting words and affirmations throughout the day. If it helps, use sticky notes on your desk, inside your car, on the fridge, and other places where you'll often see them. Or, try chanting short phrases such as, 'I am smart,' 'I am successful,' 'People like me' or whatever you're trying to change.

Chapter 55: How to Defend Yourself from Persuasion and Manipulation

We are indeed human at the end of the day. It is because of this very reason that we get to dwell a lot on the opinion of others in everything that we do.

We always desire and adore getting validation from others so that we can subconsciously decide whether or not we shall be depressed. In this age of the millennial, the norm has become to just brag about their wealth on social media. A lot of these bragging are often than not the truth.

This ultimately leads to one having a loose relationship with reality. Self-deception of this type can dig deep into the human spicy, that a victim of these may one day wake up and realize that their perfect world is only existent within their maids.

Depression will closely follow suit. The first step to attempting to defend yourself from persuasion and manipulation is confronting the situation and taking the stance of breaking off any illusions you may have. You will not be able to proceed normally with your life. You have to be wary of the fact that you are in control of your own choices.

Then make the conscious choice of seeing things for what they are. That deal, which seems too good to be true, could actually be just that... too good to be true. The other thing you should follow is to definitely trust your instincts.

There are times that a lie has been told to you in the most skilled way imaginable that you will end up believing. But you can feel an imbalance on some instinctive level between what should be, what is, and then what is being projected onto you. There may be no physical signs to show that hey, something is wrong, but you feel something is wrong.

The next important thing when you ask questions is to listen to the responses. This may sound somewhat unbelievable because you'll listen to the answers. The truth is that our self-disappointment can make us choose the answers we receive. We tell ourselves that we listen, but we only pay attention to the answers we want to hear rather than to the answers we receive.

You may have broken the illusions around you, but some of you are still clinging to the comfort of those illusions. The pain of confronting the situation would prevent you from listening to the real answers to your questions.

Actual listening requires a certain sense of detachment, but this time around not from reality. You have to get rid of your emotions. Your detachment from our emotions would lead you to the next step, which would logically process the new information.

It can complicate situations more than they already are to act irrationally. It makes your exit strategy so much difficult to let all the emotions simmer and spring to the surface. When you face the truth, the irrational part of you may want you to let it all go hell. Your rightly justified anger can inspire you to take steps to calm your emotions in the short term.

But you may come to regret these actions in the long term. I'm not saying that you should deny your emotions; I'm not saying that you do not act on these emotions, first deal with the situations and later deal with your emotions.

Act Quickly

It's great that you have come to terms with the reality of things. But defense against these dark manipulative tactics entails so much more. While attempting to defend you from the claws of these manipulators is often intense and exhilarating at first. This intensity of these emotions may cause one to slowly slide into denial. The more you delay in taking any action is usually what accelerates the onset of this denial, and when it happens, there are high chances that you might relapse and end up getting trapped in the same web.

This can be avoided by taking action immediately you realize that someone is trying to manipulate you. This can present itself in the simplest of ways, like when informing a close friend of some reality of the particular situation may be all that's needed, so set in motion a series of events that will eventually lead to your freedom.

You should know that the fabric of illusion is made from a tougher material than glass after making the choice to act. The illusion could work its way back into your heart with your emotions in high gear by using fragments of your emotions to fix it.

When a liar is caught in a lie, he or she may attempt to recruit others to enforce that lie when they feel that they are no longer holding you.

A deceptive partner with whom you have recently broken things off would, at this point try to use the other mutual relationships in your life to change your mind.

If you want to get out of this unscathed, you will need both your logic and instincts. Although the truth of the situation is that when you discover that you've been lied to consistently, you become emotionally scarred, so the issue of leaving the situation unscathed becomes silent.

Priority should be given, however, to take the route that allows you to leave this toxic situation without harming yourself further. You're all over the place emotionally.

Rage, anger, hurt, and deception is the iceberg's tip. But logically, you need to think. Keep your head above the water and warn yourself.

Get Help Fast

When you're trapped by other people's manipulations, confusion is one of the emotions you'd experience. This helps cloud your rational thinking and leaves you feeling helpless. You might even question the reality of what you are facing at this point. It would lead to denial if you continue to entertain these doubts. You're probably going to want to conclude you've got the whole situation wrong, that you misunderstood some things and came to the wrong conclusion.

Such thinking would drive back to the manipulator's arms. Resist the urge to give in by receiving a second opinion. People go to another doctor in a health crisis to get a second opinion. This is to remove any iota of doubt about the first diagnosis that you may have and to affirm the best treatment course for you.

Similarly, getting another person's opinion can help you discern the truth of the situation and what might be your next steps. Just remember, it's better to go to someone who has proved countless times they're interested in your best.

The next step is to confront the perpetrator if you have the help you need. For this, I suggest you choose the scene or location. Choose a place you know that gives you the upper hand. On your part, that would require some careful planning.

If the perpetrator exists in the cyber world, especially if the person swindled you of your money, you would have to involve the police and the relevant authorities.

Do some of your own investigations so as to ascertain the truth. After you face the perpetrator and take the necessary steps to get out of the situation, you must start the healing process quickly.

The scale and gravity to which you were hurt, manipulated, or abused do not matter. You must be able to walk past it and wait until you can "heal" your wounds, rather than sitting on your couch and reliving the past.

Time would give you enough distance from your experience, but if you learned something from this book, it would be almost never healing for emotional scars. If you don't do anything about it, an unhealthy scab could form over the wound, which would make you as vulnerable if not more than you had experienced. Speak to a counselor, attend therapy, and take an active part in facilitating the healing process, whatever you choose to do.

It won't happen overnight, but you are sure that you get closer to improving every day and every step you take in therapy.

Trust Your Instincts

While your brain interprets signals based on facts, logic, and sometimes experience, your heart works in the opposite direction by screening information through an emotional filter. The only thing that picks up vibrations is your gut instinct, which neither the heart nor the brain can pick on.

And if you can groom to the point where you recognize your inner voice and are trained to react to it, you will lower your chances of being seduced by people trying to work on you with their manipulative will.

To begin with, it's hard to recognize this voice. And that's because we allowed voices of doubt, self-discrimination as well as the critics ' loud voices within and without drowning out our authentic voice over the course of our lives.

Your survival depends on this voice or instinct. So, trust that when it kicks in, your brain neurons can still process things in your immediate vicinity.

Some people call it intuition, and some refer to it as instinct, especially when it comes to relationships, they are undoubtedly the same thing. You must accept that it may not always make logical sense to start trusting your instincts.

If you've ever been in the middle of doing something and experienced the feeling of being watched all of a sudden, then you know what I mean. You don't have eyes at the back of your head, there's no one else with you in the room, but you get the tiny shiver running down your spine and the "sudden knowledge" you're watching. That's what I'm talking about.

The first step to connect with your instinct is to decode your mind with the voices you've let in. With meditation, you can do this. Forget the chatter of, "he said, she said." Concentrate on your center. You are the voice you know. Next, be careful about your thoughts. Don't just throw away the eclectic monologs in your head. Rather go with the thoughts flow.

Why do you think of a certain person in some way? How do you feel so deeply about this person, even if you only knew each other for a few days? What's that nagging feeling about this other person that you have? You get more tuned to your intuition as you explore your thoughts and understand when your instincts kick and how to react to it.

You may need to learn to take a step back to pause and think if you are the kind of person who prefers to make spur decisions at the moment.

This moment in which you pause gives you the opportunity to really reflect on your decisions and evaluate them. The next part is a hard part, and it couldn't be followed by many people. Unfortunately, you can't skip or navigate around this step.

This part has to do with trust. You need to be open to the idea of trusting yourself and trusting others to be able to trust your instinct. Your failure to trust others would just make you paranoid, and it's not your instincts that kick when you're paranoid.

It's the fear of you. Fear tends to turn every molehill into a hill. You must let go of your fear, embrace confidence, and let that lead in your new relationships.

Don't enter a relationship that expects to be played. Be open when you approach them, whether it's a business relationship, a romantic relationship, or even a regular acquaintance. You can get the right feedback about them from your intuition.

Do not step into this thinking, too, that your gut will tell you to run in the opposite direction when you meet suspect people.

Chapter 56: Dark Persuasion and Covert Manipulation

Now it's time to know some other aspects of them, which are Dark persuasion and covert manipulation. As in the above paragraphs, you have clearly understood what persuasion is. The difference between dark persuasion and persuasion is of intentions. A persuader always tries to convince through particular techniques or motivation without having any sort of understanding about the person whom they are trying to convince. He is only concerned about doing good for people and thinking of their benefit along with their own. He does everything with a good intention without too many facts and figures of the person whom they are trying to convince.

On the other hand, dark persuader also thinks and analyzes a bigger picture. They very well understand that what are the tactics they need to use to succeed and how far do they need to take it. They only think that they are doing something right but are unconcerned with the morality of manipulation he does. They always try to achieve whatever they want through any means, whichever feel can be more effective.

Persuasion is never without moral implications, but in dark persuasion the moral implications are just not the determining factor. There are many other factors that are more important than being morally correct. The smartest thing about a dark persuader is that in their circle they would be the most selfish person but would show and seem that they are least selfish. They would get exactly what they get, without the other person knowing or even realizing. The other thing that a dark persuader does knows about the weakness of others. This helps them in extracting words, presents, and gifts which they can take or give according to their advantage and situation. For example, if an employer knows that he has illegal immigrants working in his company, he can always lower his wages as per his choice as they know that they cannot work anywhere else in the country.

Dark persuasion can vary from small to very large scale, such as a kid asking his elder brother for all the ice cream he has to a leader trying to ask for help in war to defeat another country. So, to determine dark persuasion it is always vital to understand the different personalities and their circumstances.

Covert manipulation is even worse than manipulation, in this, the manipulator tries to use the emotional vulnerability to their benefit. They would strive to their best so that they can know about your goals, strengths, weaknesses, fear, family, etc. So that they can use all of these factors to make you feel low and weak. It is said to be underhanded methods of control. It operates under your level of conscious awareness. The bad part of it is that the victim is not even aware that they are being manipulated, that is the reason it becomes prime for you to know about the manipulation games that these people use.

Covert manipulation is very dangerous as it is so subtle and underhanded that it takes a long time before you can make out that you were being manipulated. According to research, it was also found that there are few manipulators with such sharp skills that they are called puppet masters, you would unknowingly become their puppets, so it is important for you to know their signs so that you can take the actions accordingly. They would make you feel that you are doing according to your own wish, but the truth is that you do that only what they ask you to do.

Sometimes you might feel that something is wrong, but you would not be able to analyze that someone is trying to manipulate you. In covert manipulation the first thing which is prime is that you should ask yourself if you are being manipulated? As covert manipulation is adverse and has a negative effect on us, so it would be easier for you to understand that you are being manipulated.

It is significant for you to understand a few characteristics of a covert manipulator, so it becomes really easy for you to spot them if they are around you:

1) Lying

They would lie straight in your eyes, and you would not even get to know that they are lying. They would tell you twisted truth or half-truth, which you might or might not get to know later. If you ever have any doubts about the other person about the truth, you should always double-check the information so that it does not hamper your relationship or work.

2) Backhanded Compliments

This is something they are best at. Covert manipulators are great at giving backhanded compliments. They would give compliments as you did it in a great way, although you are so weak and low in confidence, still, you handled it well. You cooked so well, although you do not cook for me often. These compliments make you feel even more embarrassed and awkward, where you do not even know how to react. In such cases, the best thing is to ignore or giving them the taste of their own medicine by replying in the same way.

3) Mirroring

The coincidences would be extravagant. They would agree to all your points, likes, dislikes, taste, color, etc. just to impress you or to be with you. When they want to take benefit from you, they would agree to all your things and choices. Once they get what they wanted everything would change. You would feel that the person has fully switched. So, you should always beware of the person who agrees to whatever you say without keeping their point of you, it straight away means that they are trying to be manipulative.

4) Rationalization

This is something many people would do to cover their lies or fault. They would cook new stories to cover their flaws, such as the reason why you did not tell that you had a girlfriend before me, the reason they would give you would be like I did not want to lose you by telling this or I did not know how you would react after listening to this, etc.

Thu they would have answers for all the lies, so make sure that you know and follow your gut feel to analyze if he is saying right or just faking it.

5) Hurried Intimacy

This is a very alarming sign of a covert manipulator. They would very quickly tell you about their goals, achievements, passion, and past and what ask you the same things. Once you open up with them, they would use this information to control and manipulate you. Therefore, you should always be wise enough to understand when to share the information and how much information to share. They would be very quick in proposing for marriage and talking about the future, but you need to be careful before telling your weaknesses.

6) Playing the Victim

This is another thing they do to gain your sympathy. Just to gain your love and attention they would lie to you to any extent. They might say that their childhood was very bad as the parents were not good, etc. Just to get more love and care from you. They might make any stories for your love and care, so always know the past first before you get so much involved.

7) Silent Treatment

Leaving room or house for a couple of hours would not engage in any activity, etc. They also hide behaviors or start avoiding you so that you realize it is your mistake or you start the conversation. They keep the concerns unspoken within them, which is a dangerous sign too.

8) Belittling

They do react weird such as rolling the eyes, scoffing, mocking, teasing, etc. They do not even respect other's point of view or abilities, and they always want another person to feel low and always try to demean them. You should always maintain a distance from such covert people who are jealous of your success and feel bad seeing you rise.

9) Word Play

A covert manipulator very well knows what you want to hear and would please your ears by saying that. They know how to put a convincing statement, paint the picture well, and also to induce an emotional reaction in front of you. Not only this, they are great at talking double meaning things, they would mean something else but say it in a different context. For example, please marry me, I will change your life. This can be in any aspect, positive or negative. So be precise and clear while talking to a covert manipulator.

10) Finance Controller

Covert manipulator not only restrict by playing with your emotions that are also good at controlling and gaming with your finances too. For example, accessing your account but denying access to their account, taking things on loan in joint names without even asking you, running up debts, borrowing and not paying, etc. These are very tricky things that you should be careful about and take a step in time before they make your account nil.

These were the few characteristics of a covert manipulator, which you should be diligent about so that nobody can take advantage of you or humiliate you.

Chapter 57: How to Turn a NO into a YES

Have you ever rented a car and been adamant that you didn't want insurance but somehow walked out with it anyway? Have you wondered how they got you to believe that you needed something that you didn't want in the first place? There is a sort of power and control within the resounding no. The rental agent already knows that you are going to walk in telling them what you want and don't want. Most people do not want the extra insurance because they have their own insurance and feel like paying extra for more insurance isn't worth it, especially when you probably aren't going to need it. The resounding "no" is so common that it is something salespeople don't even pay attention to anymore.

It is an instant reaction that is driven by the fear of getting swindled into doing something that you do not want. So, you walk in already with your mind made up.

However, the rental agent found a way to get you to buy the product still. Think about it, before they even work on your contract, they go outside and walk you around the cars.

During this time, they ask you questions about your trip, what you need it for, and then they start telling you about the amenities of the car – that they carry car seats, and they sell you the coverage based on what appeals to you through the conversation you had. You felt like you had a great conversation with the salesperson, but in reality, they were using the time to prey on you because they know what you will need on this trip you are taking and how what they have to offer will alleviate your stress and/or solve your problem.

When changing your audiences' answer from no to yes, it is about understanding how they make decisions, what appeals to them - by testing the waters – how they remember things, and how they look into the future. Most of the time, people remember important dramatic experiences that turn out badly.

The rental agent might ask you if you have car insurance, and you tell them that you have what the law requires because you own your car.

This is when they realize that they want to protect their car, but they also want to make you think that they are protecting you from having to pay tons of money out of your pocket.

So, they will tell you that they have rental coverage that covers the car bumper to bumper. It is only $11-$14 a day depending on the car size, and there is no deductible. If anything happens to the car, it will be covered, and you will just walk away without paying a dime. This might sound appealing to the customer, but they still feel like they don't need it. So, they tell the rental agent no again.

This is when the agent moves to a story to sway the customer. The agent tells the customer they understand how they feel. Telling them that they buy the coverage doesn't help. They need to tell them a story that they will remember, a dramatic one, which will sway them to their side. The agent brings up an encounter with a previous customer who felt the same way as the current one.

The customer was adamant about not getting the coverage that covered the car and rented the car without it.

Another car ended up hitting them in the parking lot, and they walked back in asking if they could get the coverage. The rental agent had to end the rental contract and not give them the coverage because it is illegal to sell it after the rental agreement has been made and after an accident. The customer ended up paying for the damages out of their pocket, as well as the life of the rental in the shop, which means they had to pay the amount of the rental up to five days. All because they didn't want to pay an extra $30. Due to this story, the current customer ended up purchasing the coverage that covered the car.

When the agent was telling the story to the new customer, all they remembered was the outcome of the crash in the parking lot. They didn't remember anything else about the story, just that they didn't want to go through what the previous customer went through.

Covert Persuasion can be used in different situations, especially when you are trying to win and bring them over to your side. In customer service, you want them to talk about your competitor and discuss their past experiences because if they were satisfied with that experience, they wouldn't be talking to you. One of the things that you have to do is make sure that you don't scare them away so that they do not want to purchase from you.

Have them tell you a story of a great purchase experience they had.

This helps you from not scaring them off because you are having them remember a fun experience. For instance, if you are a stockbroker and the potential customer is someone who has lost money in the stock market, you will understand why they don't want to risk money again. But isn't that the risk with the stock market? You're not going to make money every time.

The broker has to be careful in this situation, and they cannot guarantee the potential customer or investor that they will not lose money again. That will be a lie, and that will break their trust right there. The broker has to point out that it is a possibility that they would lose money again. However, it is more likely that they will get typical returns with their investment.

Persuasion research is very clear, especially with covert persuasion. The speaker must show the audience both possible outcomes for them to be successful. If the speaker doesn't indicate that the investor might lose money in the stock market, they will continue to be afraid of it and choose not to invest with your brokerage firm.

When you show them that losing money is a possibility, you also show them what else could happen within reason. If you make it sound too good to be true, the possible investor will feel like they are being manipulated, and they will still choose not to go with your firm's offer. By keeping it realistic, there is a high chance that they will succumb to your persuasions. Be clear with your message delivery. If the possible investor lost the first half of the game, they need to come in strong during the second half. Never let what happened in the past determine what they could possibly achieve in the future.

The whole idea of persuading people is to take away their fear of saying yes, which is normal. People tend to have a fear of the unknown and how their life will change. If you are trying to help someone quit smoking, the person will resist at first because the fear of deterring from their normal routine is too much for them. To help them overcome this fear, you will have to substitute their current fear with one that is far worse. Basically, you are scaring them beyond their worst fears. For instance, the speaker tells the person that if they continue to keep smoking every day that it is going to cause you to die. Can you imagine your kids and grandkids standing over your casket?

They will remember you the way you looked in that casket. The idea of their family looking over their dead body scares them, especially when it is something that they could have prevented. This is when the speaker makes the fear less painful by helping them cut down. Tell them to start small by cutting down to half a pack a day this month, and then only one every day next month, and by the next month, you don't need them anymore. Wouldn't it be great to show your family that you don't need to smoke? Wouldn't it be great to show them how healthy you are?

The speaker used fear to persuade the person to stop smoking and then gave them a set of instructions that will help them with the new decision that they made. The person was able to see how changing their life and going with what you wanted wasn't hard if they worked at it.

They weren't going to be worse off because of the decision, but better.

So, once the speaker can change or is persuaded to do what you want them to do, they should be happy that they listened to you and took your advice – whether it be to change their attitude or behavior or purchase what they are selling.

This is not always the case, though.

There is a principle known as option attachment. Someone has a choice to purchase one of two puppies. Either puppy would be a good pet for her, but each one is different. They ponder which puppy they could see themselves keeping, and no matter which one they choose, even though they are not aware of it, they worry that the other puppy will be the better of the two because the person did not choose them. Wouldn't they feel good about the choice they made? You would think that they would be happy, relieved, or even comfortable with their decision. Yet, they are miserable. They start to question the decision that they made. When someone is left thinking about their options too long, they tend to think that whatever they choose, they are losing something by not choosing the other thing. The initial problem is the choice they are left with. The person feels a sense of disappointment and loss when they realize that they have to let the other option go. Persuasion research indicates that it doesn't matter if the person has personally experienced both options set in front of them or just imagining one.

Whatever option they choose, the other one becomes more attractive because they cannot have it.

The second factor of option attachment is the feeling of loss. The person felt attached to the other option when they were deliberating.

Chapter 58: Traps of Persuasion

Persuasiveness is an effective aptitude everybody ought to learn. It is helpful in incalculable circumstances. For both your business and your personal life, being inspiring and influential to others will be the foundation for accomplishing objectives and being successful.

Learning about the traps of persuasion will give you new awareness for when they appear in the sales messaging you read. The greatest advantage? Your cash stays in your pocket. It literally pays for you to understand exactly how sales representatives and marketers offer you items that you don't really require. The following are some persuasive techniques that work on a subconscious level.

Outlining Impacts Thought

Let's say you're thirsty, and someone hands you a glass of water not-quite full. "The glass is half full." An optimist would "outline" the reality of your glass of water in that way. Outlining is used as an approach to modify how we classify, connect, and attach meaning to every aspect of our lives.

The headline "FBI Operators Surround Cult Leader's Compound" creates a mental picture strikingly different from another version of the headline for the same story: "FBI Specialists Raid Small Christian Gathering of Women and Children." Both headlines may convey what happened, however, the selected words affect the readers' mental and emotional responses, and therefore direct the impact the target events have on the article's readers. Outlining is employed by apt government representatives. For example, representatives on both sides of the abortion debate refer to their positions as "pro-choice" or "pro-life." This is intentional, as "pro" has a more positive association to build arguments on. Outlining an event, product, or service this way unobtrusively utilizes emotional words strategically to persuade individuals to see or accept your perspective.

Creating a convincing message is as easy as selecting words that summon strategic pictures in the minds of your audience. Indeed, even with neutral words surrounding it, a solitary stimulating word can be powerful.

Reflecting as Persuasive Strategy

Reflecting, often called "the chameleon effect," is the act of replicating the movements and non-verbal communication of the individual you want to persuade. By mirroring the actions of the individual listening, you create an appearance of empathy.

Hand and arm motions, inclining forward or reclining away, or different head and shoulder movements are types of non-verbal communication you can reflect on. We, as a whole, do this without much thought, and now that you're becoming aware of that, you'll notice not only yourself, but others doing it as well.

It is important to be graceful, thoughtful about it, and allow just a couple of seconds to pass between their movements and you reflecting them.

Highlight Scarcity of a Product or Service

The concept of scarcity is often employed by marketers to make products, services, or associated events and deals appear to be all the more engaging on the grounds that there will be restricted accessibility. The belief is that there is a huge amount of interest for it if availability is scarce. For example, an ad for a new product might say: Get one now! They're selling out quickly!

Again, it literally pays to know that this is a persuasion strategy that you will see everywhere. Consider this concept the next time you settle on your buying choice. This principle triggers a feeling of urgency in most individuals, so it is best used when applied in your marketing and sales copy.

Reciprocity Helps Make a Future Commitment

When somebody helps us out, we feel responsible for providing a proportional payback. All in all, the next time you need someone to accomplish something beneficial for you, consider doing something unexpectedly pleasant for them first.

At work, you could pass a colleague a lead. At home, you could offer to loan some landscaping tools to a neighbor.

The details, where or when you do it, won't make a difference; the key is to supplement the relationship without being sought out first. Lead with value and give it freely, without overtly expecting anything in return, and their response will come.

Timing Can Bolster Your Good Fortune

Individuals will be more pleasant and accommodating when they're mentally exhausted. Before you approach somebody for something they may not otherwise participate in, consider holding back until they've recently accomplished something mentally challenging. Consider making your offer toward the end of the work day, for example, when you can get a colleague or collaborator on the way out of the office. Whatever you may ask, a reasonable reaction could be, "I'll deal with it tomorrow."

Enhance Compliance to Acquire a Needed Result

To avoid cognitive dissonance, we all try to be true to how we've acted in the past. A reliable technique business people use is to shake your hand as they are consulting with you. We have been taught that a handshake equals a "sealed deal," and by doing this before the arrangement is really sealed, the business person has taken a step to persuade you into believing the deal is already done.

One approach to employing this yourself is influencing individuals to act before their minds are made up. Let's say that you are roaming downtown with a companion, and you decide you want to go see a movie at the local theater; yet, your companion is undecided. Compliance can come into play if you begin strolling toward the theater while they are still thinking about it. Your companion will probably consent to go once they realize you are strolling in the theater's direction.

Attempt Fluid Discourse

In the natural flow of our speech, interjections and reluctant expressions act as fillers when we need a moment to think or select the "right" word, for example, "um" or "I mean," and obviously the newly pervasive "like." These fillers have the unintended impact of making us appear to be unsure and doubtful and, in this way, less convincing. When you're certain about your message, others will be more effectively persuaded. If you have trouble finding the right words at the right time, practice some free-flow association every day in front of the mirror for 60 seconds.

You can add it to your morning ritual, or you can do it while having a shower, like I usually do. Basically, your goal in these 60 seconds is to jump from one topic to another very quickly by associating words; do your best to avoid "um," "like," or other fillers. Example:

The water on my back right now is so hot; it reminds me of the hot weather in California. I love Cali; I like the food there. Mexican food is so spicy and hot, like Mexican women. I remember Marcella, that one Mexican girl I met last time I was there; she was probably the only blonde girl from Mexico. She was blonde like a Swedish model. I've never been to Sweden, but I've heard it's cold out there...

And so on, until you get to 60 seconds without pauses or interjections. Once you reach that point after some practice, you can aim for 120 seconds. Once you've done that, the next step is to practice this game with other people. You don't need to go on for a full two minutes straight, but while you're talking to someone, you can go on a tangent for 20 seconds and practice the free-flow association skill. You'll practice and improve tremendously, while they'll be wondering, "This guy is interesting. I really want to know what he's going to say next..."

Group Affinity Can Affect Decisions

We have a much higher tendency to imitate or be persuaded by somebody we like or by somebody we see as an influential leader.

A compelling approach to make this work for you, bolstering your good fortune, is to be viewed as a leader by your target audience—regardless of whether you officially have the title. It helps to be enchanting and sure, so individuals will have more confidence in your message. Keep improving yourself, and you'll soon become more magnetic than everyone else. If you're interacting with an individual who doesn't consider you to be a powerful person (for example, a rival at work or your irritating in-laws), you can, in any case, exploit group affinity. For example, if you praise a leader that individual respects, that praise then activates the positive associations in that individual's brain about that admired leader, which creates a mental space where they can relate those qualities with you.

Create a Photo Opportunity with Man's Best Friend

Give your target audience the idea that you're trustworthy, and motivate them to be loyal to you by taking a photo of yourself with a pooch (it doesn't need to be your own puppy). This can make you appear kind and cooperative, but keep these kinds of photo-ops to a minimum; setting up an excessive number of pictures looks amateurish. On a side note, it pays to know your audience; if you know they share a lot of cat pictures, maybe try a picture or two with a feline friend, too.

Offer a Drink

This might seem too easy, but giving the individual you want to persuade a warm drink to hold while you're conversing with them can be persuasive in itself. The warm vibe you've offered their hands (and their body) can intuitively make them see you as candidly warm, affable, and inviting. Offering a chilly drink can do the opposite! As a rule, individuals tend to feel "frosty" and seek out warm beverages when they're feeling stressed or overwhelmed, so take care of that need keeping in mind the end goal to make them more open.

Start with a Simple "Yes" Question

Start the discussion with an inquiry that creates a "Yes" reaction. "Nice weather we're having, isn't it?" or "You're searching for a great price on a car, right?"

When you get somebody saying yes, it's anything but difficult to motivate them to proceed, up to and including "Yes, I'll get it." You can counter this in your daily life by giving cautious answers to even the simplest questions.

Gently Break the Contact Boundary

You could be sealing a deal or asking somebody out for coffee, and touching them (in a modest and suitable way) can enhance your odds of hearing "Yes," because you have intuitively triggered the human yearning to connect.

In a professional setting, it is normally best to "touch" verbally by giving consolation or acclaim, as a physical touch could be seen as lewd behavior.

In sentimental circumstances, any delicate touch from a lady will more often than not be taken well. Men will need to proceed here with extreme caution—keeping in mind the end goal is to abstain from making a lady feel uncomfortable.

Chapter 59: How Persuaders Sell You Anything

We are all consumers. We shop in shops and supermarkets looking for clothes, beauty and body care products, perfumes, shoes, accessories, food, drinks, computers, smartphones, books, appliances, furniture, and the list could potentially go on forever.

We search for the products that best suit our needs, and we believe (and justify) that our choices are always dictated by our rationality, our critical and judgmental capacity, and our experience, which guide us in that magnum sea of Brands and alternatives so similar to each other, where only our careful evaluation can make the difference. But this is not always true.

Let's imagine this situation: there are two shops, one in front of the other, perfectly identical, selling the same products (clothes for example) displayed in the same way, both have the same attractive colors and have the same prices.

We enter the first one, we are not greeted at the entrance by the salesman, and we look at the goods on display and pick up an item of clothing. The clerk approaches us saying, "if I can be of any help to you, I'm here." We thank him, and after a short while, we leave the store. I'm sure that this scenario is part of the everyday life of all of us.

We enter the second one, we immediately receive a warm greeting from the salesman who welcomes us with a large smile, we return the greeting out of politeness and also in this case we look at the goods. Dropping our attention on a particular item of clothing, the salesman approaches us and tells us "I'm sure that those trousers would look great on her, if she has 60 seconds I would like her to try it on, just for today the clothes trial is free". We laugh at the witty joke, 60 seconds is nothing after all, and we try on the garment and most likely at the end we buy it, together with who knows how many other products the salesman will have managed to offer us in a captivating way.

The shops are identical and sell the same products, but from the first, we went out after a short time, while from the second we went out with envelopes in our hands. We are convinced that this purchase was exactly what we were looking for, what we needed. Or, simply, following our instinct, we bought it because that dress enhanced our body and we are sure we could show it off on some special occasion making a good impression.

The point is that the persuasive ability of a third party convinced us of all this: he put us at ease, made us feel important, convinced us how much better we'd look in that dress. So he persuaded us to do something that a few minutes earlier, in the first store, we didn't do.

Robert B. Cialdini, a well-known American psychologist and marketing professor at Arizona State University, in his book "The weapons of persuasion - how and why you end up saying yes," describes another very interesting anecdote about how certain elements in marketing can make a difference.

She tells of a woman who had opened an Indian costume jewelry store in Arizona and despite the tourist season is at its peak, she couldn't sell a certain lot of turquoise, even using all the appropriate gimmicks such as placing it in the window or in plain sight at the entrance to the store.

She lost hope and left a note to the store manager saying that the next day she would have to put the turquoises at half price. Having misinterpreted the ticket, the manager understood that she should increase the price of the turquoise by twice the original price. You can imagine what happened. The lot ended that same evening. This happened because consumers, mostly tourists who didn't know much about Indian and turquoise costume jewelry, put in place a fixed scheme of automatic action, a stereotype, which is part of everyone: expensive = good. And so, rightly searching for "good" items, they ended up buying turquoise at twice the price of the original list price.

Before going any further, it is necessary to define the concept of persuasion. "Persuading means influencing the mind of the interlocutor with arguments, reasons, suggestions, in order to change the attitude towards an object, a person, a political or philosophical-religious idea, etc., sometimes, in the current language, we use the term convince as if it were a synonym for persuading. In fact, convincing means overcoming logical and rational obstacles, with means that have the semblance of logic and rationality, to overcome resistance and doubts with the logical force of arguments.

Persuading, on the contrary, appeals to mechanisms that are also emotional and passionate, using the same arts that we see at work in seduction".

Nowadays companies, marketing directors, and advertising agencies use a whole series of tricks and psychological strategies designed to leverage our deepest fears, dreams, and desires: all in order to persuade consumers to buy their brands and products.

Conclusion

Thank you for making it to the end. Persuasion is something intended to get one to do or think something. Another significance for persuasion is that the act of influencing somebody to do something or to change your own thoughts. As an instance, very good salespeople use persuasion to get people to purchase things, as kids use persuasion to get permission to do particular things.

Persuasion at work involves compelling other people to follow a plan of action, to agree with a dedication, or to buy a service or product. Employers especially appreciate persuasive abilities in their employees since they can impact numerous characteristics of the office, leading to increased productivity.

Persuasive skills are needed when one should influence stakeholders. These stakeholders may include clients, co-workers, present or prospective supervisors, business partners, subordinates, donors, financing resources, judges, juries, consumers, voters, and potential workers. Persuasion, like conclusion or charisma, is a "soft skill" for most individuals -- one which is frequently an innate character trait.

A lot of people need the capability to convince in several scenarios which are vulnerable to them and can be tough to conquer only with the certainty of one of those parties to another ruling, as many matters and issues cannot tolerate half answers, irrespective of social existence and the talks and debates on various issues, the areas of company demand great ability in the practice of persuasion acquired by lots of the employees throughout the accumulation of expertise, but youthful newcomers to the labor market have to be conscious of the most crucial way of persuasion was shown to work and educated in self-development lectures concerning the planet M, and one or more of those methods may be utilized in most discussions that need persuading a person in your opinion.

The technique is chosen based on the essence of the topic and the person who you would like to convince. On the other hand, the craft of persuasion can surely be enhanced (like concrete hard skills) together with the ideal training. For a long time, people have been using persuasion, and sometimes in a less subtle manner: torture. This can be either physical or psychological torture. Hardwired to keep us away from destruction is the human mind, which is why we have our sense of touch that keeps us from burning ourselves even though it hurts. That's why we are programmed sub-consciously to 'give-in' to things.

Such persuasion methods help us to open the unconscious window and use psychological tactics to plant a thought or idea. These are usually barely visible hidden, which gives them the power they possess. The CIA used hypnosis, large corporate companies used subliminal advertising, scammers used manipulation, and small businesses used tactics for short but powerful salespersons. This is known to the public as brainwashing and psychological regulation and is often viewed as mystical because of its strong existence. Yet rest assured, these strategies do exist, such strategies are used to convince us to do something we might not normally even consider. Therefore, there is no doubt that the best form of persuasion is regulation of the mind, and that it's easier to do than you think. All these combined techniques allow the mind, plant an idea of someone to be controlled and studied as a parasite grows into life.

If you want to make sales and profits, you have to learn how to persuade someone to buy something from you. Today, however, several tips give us the wrong information and flood us with fluff. Therefore, I will give you a simple but successful persuasive strategy to increase sales and profits.

One of the easy ways to convince someone to buy from you is to use a concept called "economic power." Studies have shown that the behavior of others influences most of our behaviors. Parents, celebrities, and social people are rapidly observed and emulated as they study other people's attitudes and behavior to bring us into life and decision-making. I hope you have learned something.

CPSIA information can be obtained
at www.ICGtesting.com
Printed in the USA
LVHW051110040121
675400LV00002B/137